Adjustment and Financing in the Developing World

The Role of the International Monetary Fund

edited by

TONY KILLICK

Published by the

INTERNATIONAL MONETARY FUND

in association with the

OVERSEAS DEVELOPMENT INSTITUTE, *London*

Washington, D.C. 1982

Papers of a seminar jointly sponsored by the
International Monetary Fund and the
Overseas Development Institute, held at
Addington Palace, near Croydon, England,
October 16–18, 1981.

International Standard Book Numbers:

ISBN 0-939934-18-3 (cloth)
ISBN 0-939934-19-1 (paper)

Library of Congress Card Number: 82-9213

Library of Congress Classification Numbers:

HG3890.A38   1982   332.1'52

Price: US$12.00 or £6.75 (cloth)
US$8.00 or £4.50 (paper)

International Monetary Fund
Washington, D.C. 20431, U.S.A.

Overseas Development Institute
10-11 Percy Street, London W1P OJB, England

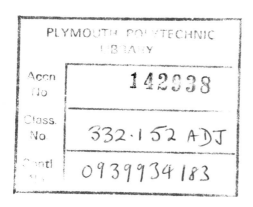
Foreword

The last decade has been a particularly difficult one for many developing countries. They have experienced a slowdown in the growth of export markets, deteriorating terms of trade, higher interest costs, and, in some cases, impaired access to international capital markets. The tightening of the balance of payments constraint has intensified the problems these countries face in maintaining satisfactory growth rates or even current living standards. The worsening environment has, at the same time, posed new challenges for the International Monetary Fund in its efforts to help developing countries address their balance of payments problems.

In attempting to meet this challenge, the Fund has adapted its policies and practices in a number of ways. It has introduced facilities that provide financial assistance in larger amounts, in support of longer-term programs, and with extended repayment periods. In the past two years, the number of Fund-supported adjustment programs in the developing world and the demands on its resources have reached record levels. Even as the tempo of its activities has risen, there has emerged a growing need to explain them to a wider community of scholars, journalists, and others interested in the work of the Fund. In 1981, we began experimenting with a program of seminars aimed at promoting understanding of what the Fund has done and is doing to help members solve their balance of payments problems. The seminars are also designed to improve the Fund's perception of the way it is viewed in academic, business, and other circles and its knowledge of the ideas the latter may have for enhancing the effectiveness of the Fund's role.

The papers included in this book originated in the first of these seminars, arranged jointly by the Fund and the Overseas Development Institute, London, and held in October 1981. A wide range of views was represented at the seminar, and participants included senior academics from the United Kingdom and developing countries, bankers and officials, as well as senior members of the Fund staff. All attended in a personal capacity, and the emphasis was on informality and frankness. If the seminar did not resolve the problems that were discussed, it did serve to draw out their complexities and to strengthen lines of communication among the participants.

This book marks the first occasion on which the Fund has published a wide variety of views about its role and activities in the developing world. The views are not, of course, necessarily shared by the Fund, but should contribute to a better understanding of the problems addressed.

J. DE LAROSIÈRE
Managing Director
International Monetary Fund

April 1982

Acknowledgment

A special tribute is due to Mr. Azizali F. Mohammed, Director of the External Relations Department of the International Monetary Fund, who originated the concept of a seminar jointly sponsored by the Fund and the Overseas Development Institute. He was active in each stage of the planning and preparation, and he played a prime role in bringing the project to fruition. The seminar and this volume were made possible largely through his initiatives, encouragement, and counsel. It was a pleasure to work with Mr. Mohammed and his colleagues at both the personal and professional levels.

I should also like to place on record my indebtedness to Mrs. Margaret Cornell, the Meetings Officer of the Overseas Development Institute, for her most valuable contribution to the planning and organization of the seminar on which this volume is based; and also to Margaret Beringer and Ramila Mistry, who did much of the typing in ODI. Equally fervent thanks are due to the Editorial Division of the IMF External Relations Department, and particularly to Mrs. Ella H. Wright, who put the manuscript into publishable form and saw it through all stages of production.

TONY KILLICK
Editor

Seminar Papers

Seminar Participants

Authors and Discussants

GEORGE C. ABBOTT*   Senior Lecturer, Department of International Economic Studies, University of Glasgow.

GRAHAM BIRD   Senior Lecturer, University of Surrey, and Research Associate, Overseas Development Institute.

GRAEME S. DORRANCE*   Professor of Economics, London School of Economics.

ALEJANDRO FOXLEY*   President of CIEPLAN, Santiago, Chile.

MANUEL GUITIÁN   Senior Advisor, Exchange and Trade Relations Department, International Monetary Fund.

TONY KILLICK   Research Officer, Overseas Development Institute.

GEOFFREY MAYNARD*   Vice-President and Director of Economics, Europe and Middle East Division, Chase Manhattan Bank, London.

AZIZALI F. MOHAMMED*   Director, External Relations Department, International Monetary Fund.

BAHRAM NOWZAD   Assistant Director, External Finance Division, Exchange and Trade Relations Department, International Monetary Fund.

RICHARD O'BRIEN   Senior Economist, Amex Bank, London.

DANIEL M. SCHYDLOWSKY   Professor of Economics, Center for Latin American Development Studies, Boston University.

---

*Discussant.

MARY SUTTON	Research Officer, Overseas Development Institute.
BRIAN TEW	Midland Bank Professor of Money and Banking, University of Nottingham.
ROSEMARY THORP*	Fellow of St. Antony's College, Oxford.
JOHN WILLIAMSON*	Senior Fellow, Institute for International Economics, Carnegie Endowment for International Peace, Washington.

Other Participants

ANTHONY BOTTRILL	Assistant Secretary, Her Majesty's Treasury, United Kingdom.
E. A. BRETT	Lecturer, University of Sussex.
MARGARET CORNELL	Meetings Organizer, Overseas Development Institute.
RONALD GILCHRIST	Advisor, Bank of England.
REGINALD GREEN	Professorial Fellow, Institute of Development Studies, Sussex University.
HELLMUT HARTMANN	Chief Information Officer, External Relations Department, International Monetary Fund.
PENDARALL KENT	Advisor, Bank of England.
DAVID LLEWELLYN	Professor of Money and Banking, Loughborough University.
RUPERT PENNANT-REA	Economics Editor, *The Economist*, London.
STANLEY PLEASE	Senior Advisor to the Senior Vice-President, Operations, World Bank.
ROSEMARY RIGHTER	Diplomatic and Development Correspondent, *Sunday Times*, London.
JENNIFER SHARPLEY	Research Fellow, Chr. Michelsen Institute, Bergen.
ANTHONY P. THIRLWALL	Professor of Applied Economics, University of Kent.

---

*Discussant.

Contents

An Overview

Tony Killick and Mary Sutton[1]

The accelerated inflation and large payments imbalances that have plagued the world economy in recent years have created new challenges for economic policy. Institutions such as the International Monetary Fund have found themselves operating in a global environment markedly different from that for which they were originally designed, and developing countries have found their aspirations threatened by large increases in their payments deficits. There have been wide disagreements about the most suitable policy responses by developing countries to these problems and about the appropriateness of the stabilization programs favored by the Fund. During the 1970s the growth in international commercial bank lending to some developing countries served a purpose in recycling the surpluses of the members of the Organization of Petroleum Exporting Countries (OPEC)—but at the cost of a growing external debt, and there are signs that debt problems may intensify during the next few years.

The seven papers in this report are revised versions of papers that were originally presented at a seminar jointly arranged by the

[1]The authors are Research Officers of the Overseas Development Institute, London. They are particularly grateful for the many helpful comments by the seminar participants on an earlier draft of the final section of this overview. They would like to stress that any remaining mistakes of fact or judgment are entirely their responsibility.

Fund and the Overseas Development Institute in Croydon, England, in October 1981. This overview sets out to do three things. The first section presents a brief factual background for the content of the report as a whole, organized around key tables presenting various dimensions of the global disequilibria. The second section summarizes the papers presented at the seminar and published here, while the final section examines some of the issues arising from the seminar discussions. This latter, however, presents only the interpretation of the authors; no attempt is made to provide a systematic record of the proceedings nor can it be said that the interpretation of the arguments represents conclusions agreed to by the participants. It is safe to assume that all participants have their own ideas about what is concluded here—and these undoubtedly range over a wide spectrum.

GLOBAL DISEQUILIBRIA AND THE NON-OIL DEVELOPING COUNTRIES

The general nature of the global disequilibria that first emerged after 1973 is well known. The intent of this section is therefore only to present some of the most recent information on this topic (mostly based on the Fund's *World Economic Outlook, 1981)* and to draw attention to the special situation of the non-oil developing countries. Very briefly, the following appear to be the salient points.

1. The second oil shock of 1979–80 recreated large global payments disequilibria (Table 1).[2] The oil exporting group of countries has been running massive current account surpluses, and a large proportion of the counterpart deficits appears in the payments accounts of the non-oil developing countries. The nominal value of the deficits of the latter has been growing and is expected to continue to grow in 1981–85. In absolute terms, most of these deficits have been incurred by the major exporters of manufactures and "other net oil importers" (largely middle-income exporters of primary products).

---

[2]Following Fund classifications, several of the tables include under the heading of "non-oil developing countries" a subgroup described as "net oil exporters." This refers to countries—*other than the major oil exporters*—whose oil exports exceeded their oil imports in most years of the 1970s. Examples include Egypt, Malaysia, and Mexico (see IMF, 1981 a, p. 108).

Table 1
WORLD PAYMENTS BALANCES ON CURRENT ACCOUNT[1]
(billion U.S. dollars)

	1977	1978	1979	1980[2]	1981[3]	1985[4]
Western industrial countries	−5	31	−8	−44	−29	65
Oil exporting developing countries	31	3	68	112	96	50
Other developing countries[5]	−29	−38	−58	−82	−97	−140
Net oil exporters	*−7*	*−8*	*−8*	*−11*	*−15*	*−33*
Major exporters of manufactures	*−8*	*−10*	*−22*	*−32*	*−38.5*	*−49*
Low-income countries	*−2*	*−7*	*−11*	*−16*	*−15.5*	*−19*
Other net oil importers	*−11*	*−13*	*−17*	*−24*	*−27.5*	*−39*
Centrally planned economies and other countries not elsewhere specified	−7	−4	−1	−1	−3⎫	25
Balancing item	10	8	−1	15	33⎭	

Sources: Various tables from IMF, *World Economic Outlook*, IMF Occasional Paper No. 4 (July 1981); and IMF, *Annual Report of the Executive Board for the Financial Year Ended April 30, 1981.*

[1]Excluding official transfers.
[2]Provisional figures.
[3]Forecasts.
[4]From "Scenario A," as described in Chapter II of the *World Economic Outlook*, 1981.
[5]Excluding the People's Republic of China.

2. As can also be seen in Table 1, the surpluses of the oil exporting developing countries as a group are expected to diminish by 1985 but to remain large, and most of the counterpart improvement in the rest of the world is expected to be concentrated in the Western industrial countries. Forecasts by the Organization for Economic Cooperation and Development (OECD) to 1982 show the same general result (OECD, 1981, Table 30). In billions of U.S. dollars, the current deficits of the subgroup "low-income countries" are of second-order magnitude, suggesting that these deficits could be financed without major international reforms if political decisions were made to do so.

3. But data for balances on current account may be misleading because of the importance of capital movements, with large net inflows to non-oil developing countries, and because some countries are experiencing such a compression of imports that current balances tend to understate their payments problem. The grouping by "oil exporting developing countries" also disguises the fact that only a few of these countries actually have large surpluses; more than 90 per cent of the current account surplus of the oil exporting developing countries in 1980 was accounted for by Kuwait, Iraq, Libya, Qatar, Saudi Arabia, and the United Arab Emirates (IMF, 1981 a, p. 44).

4. Large increases in import prices for the non-oil developing countries in 1979–80 played a key role in the balance of payments situation described above and resulted in a serious deterioration in the commodity terms of trade (Table 2). Taking all non-oil developing countries together, the terms-of-trade index was 11 per cent lower in 1980 than in 1977; among the subgroups, the "low-income countries" were particularly affected, with a 27 per cent fall in their terms of trade. The expansion of export volumes slowed down, partly because of the recession in the industrial world, which also weakened world commodity prices. There was also a sharp deceleration in import volumes, especially during

Table 2
PRICE AND VOLUME TRENDS IN MERCHANDISE TRADE OF THE NON-OIL DEVELOPING COUNTRIES
(percentage change over previous year)

	1977	1978	1979	1980	1981[1]
Import volumes					
Major exporters of manufactures	4.3	− 7.9	12.0	3.6	− 3.8
Low-income countries[2]	9.6	15.2	2.3	4.0	−0.8
Other net oil importers	10.1	3.3	5.2	2.8	2.5
Overall percentage change	6.7	7.3	8.6	3.4	2.7
Export volumes					
Major exporters of manufactures	10.3	12.3	9.5	8.6	6.9
Low-income countries[2]	−3.2	7.4	3.4	3.9	3.0
Other net oil importers	−2.0	87	5.9	5.7	3.7
Overall percentage change	4.4	10.7	7.8	7.3	5.2
Import prices					
Major exporters of manufactures	8.2	10.7	18.6	23.1	6.3
Low-income countries[2]	5.4	9.7	19.4	21.0	6.1
Other net oil importers	7.6	9.9	18.8	22.2	6.3
Overall percentage change	7.4	10.3	18.2	20.8	6.1
Export Prices					
Major exporters of manufactures	10.4	6.7	15.9	17.0	2.6
Low-income countries[2]	22.8	−0.5	11.7	8.9	0.8
Other net oil importers	14.2	4.2	15.6	15.2	2.8
Overall percentage change	14.2	4.1	17.6	17.1	3.5
Terms of trade					
Major exporters of manufactures	2.0	−3.6	−2.3	−4.9	−3.5
Low-income countries[2]	16.5	−9.3	−6.4	−9.9	−5.0
Other net oil importers	6.1	−5.2	−2.7	−5.7	−3.3
Overall percentage change	6.3	−5.6	−0.5	−3.1	−2.5

Source: IMF, *World Economic Outlook*, 1981, Table 11.
[1]Forecasts.
[2]Excluding the People's Republic of China.

Table 3
CONTRIBUTION OF OIL AND OTHER ITEMS TO DEFICITS OF NON-OIL DEVELOPING COUNTRIES
(billion U.S. dollars)

	1973	1978	1980
Oil trade balance	−5.2	−26.0	−66.5
Non-oil trade balance	−4.0	−1.4	7.3
Net services and private transfers	0.3	−2.1	−10.6
Gross investment income	−8.1	−20.8	−38.5
Balance on current account	−8.9	−29.5	−69.8

Source: IMF, World Economic Outlook, 1981, Table 13.

1980, and this is expected to continue in 1981. Here, too, the forecasts are in line with OECD expectations (OECD, 1981, p. 125).

5. Obviously related to the developments in import prices, Table 3 shows that virtually all the deterioration in the current account of the non-oil developing countries in 1973–80 could be attributed to a drastic deterioration in the balance of oil trade. Over the same period, non-oil developing countries were able to improve their non-oil trade balance, although this was partly achieved by cutting back on import volumes, causing a worsening in the balance on services and private transfers. Much of the deterioration in the services account was due to the rising cost of interest payments on externally owned debt.

6. The data summarized in Tables 2 and 3 provide strong prima facie evidence for the proposition that the balance of payments situation of the non-oil developing countries can only be understood in the global context and that their payments problems are essentially international, or exogenous, in character.

7. Viewed in relation to gross domestic product (GDP) and to exports and imports, the deficits of the non-oil developing countries in 1980 and since then are enormously larger than those of the industrial countries (Table 4), although this is much less evident when the deficits are simply expressed in U.S. dollars (column 1). In relation to GDP, the problem is particularly acute for the "other net oil importers," whose deficit is equivalent to 6.5 per cent of GDP; in relation to trade values, the deficit is particularly serious for the low-income countries. A comparison of the ratios of trade values to exports and imports for the low-income countries shows that these countries are already heavily dependent on cap-

Table 4

CURRENT ACCOUNT DEFICITS IN RELATION TO GROSS DOMESTIC PRODUCT, EXPORTS, AND IMPORTS, 1980[1]

	Absolute Size of Deficit (billion U.S. dollars)	Deficit as Percentage of		
		GDP	Exports (per cent)	Imports
Industrial countries	−44	0.7	3.6	3.4
Non-oil developing countries	−80	4.8	20.5	22.4
Net oil exporters	−11	3.8	14.5	18.9
Net oil importers				
Major exporters of				
manufactures	−32	4.3	16.2	18.0
Low-income countries	−14	4.7	62.3	37.3
Other net oil importers	−24	6.5	25.7	26.7

Source: IMF, *World Economic Outlook*, 1981, Tables 18 and 31 for non-oil developing countries. Data for industrial countries were computed from various Fund and World Bank sources.

[1]Weighted averages.

ital inflows to finance current imports. Table 4 provides a useful first approach to an understanding of the magnitude of the adjustment problems of the low-income countries. It also reinforces the point made above—that the dollar size of the deficits of the low-income countries is small in relation to total world payments (and thus could be financed without a great deal of international effort) but that it is very large relative to the trade and output of these economies.

8. Although the absolute size of the external debt of the non-oil developing countries has greatly increased, its rise has been more moderate in relation to export values (Table 5). Nevertheless, there was a fairly sharp deterioration in the debt and debt service ratios in 1977–80—particularly in the interest-payments ratio, which is the most onerous because it cannot normally be rolled over by new borrowing. Among the subgroups "low-income countries" and "other net oil importers," this ratio nearly doubled during the three years in question and a further increase is anticipated by 1985.

9. The ratios of gross external reserves to imports of goods and services, also presented in Table 5, show a considerably sharper deterioration, again expected to continue until 1985. However, these ratios are biased downward because the gold element in reserve holdings has been valued at SDR 35 an ounce. The deteri-

Table 5
NON-OIL DEVELOPING COUNTRIES: TRENDS AND PROJECTIONS OF EXTERNAL DEBT BURDEN[1]
(per cent)

	1972	1977	1980	1985[2]
Net oil exporters				
Ratio of gross external reserves to				
imports of goods and services[3]	26.7	23.8	19.8	117.0
Ratio of external debt to exports of				
goods and services[4]	130.8	156.3	105.9	104.8
Debt service ratio[5]	25.3	25.8	23.7	26.3
Interest payments ratio	6.9	8.6	10.5	8.7
Amortization ratio	18.4	17.1	13.1	17.6
Net oil importers				
Major exporters of manufactures				
Ratio of gross external reserves to				
imports of goods and services[3]	40.2	25.1	15.6	11.9
Ratio of external debt to exports				
of goods and services[4]	96.0	79.0	73.0	80.4
Debt service ratio[5]	17.7	13.2	18.5	21.1
Interest payments ratio	5.8	4.2	7.3	6.8
Amortization ratio	11.9	9.0	11.2	14.3
Low-income countries[6]				
Ratio of gross external reserves to				
imports of goods and services[3]	23.7	20.8	12.8	7.2
Ratio of external debt to exports				
of goods and services[4]	144.7	191.7	211.0	246.0
Debt service ratio[5]	10.1	9.9	20.7	21.6
Interest payments ratio	3.2	3.8	6.3	8.7
Amortization ratio	6.9	6.1	14.4[7]	12.8
Other net oil importers				
Ratio of external reserves to				
imports of goods and services[3]	30.2	23.9	21.4	14.4
Ratio of external debt to exports				
of goods and services[4]	89.6	82.2	95.3	128.4
Debt service ratio[5]	12.3	11.6	17.1	25.2
Interest payments ratio	3.7	3.8	7.1	9.5
Amortization ratio	8.7	7.7	10.0	15.6

Source: IMF, *World Economic Outlook*, 1981, Table 32.
[1]For the classification of countries in the groups shown here, see *World Economic Outlook*, 1981.
[2]"Scenario A," as described in Chapter II of *World Economic Outlook*, 1981.
[3]Total reserves (with gold valued at SDR 35 an ounce).
[4]Includes medium-term and long-term debt, with and without public guarantee.
[5]Payments (interest, amortization, or both) as percentages of exports of goods and services.
[6]Excluding India and the People's Republic of China.
[7]Amortization ratio is abnormally high because of debt rescheduling in a number of countries.

oration has been sharpest for the major exporters of manufactures and low-income countries; by 1985, their ratios are expected to be between a fourth and a third of 1972 levels. When
reserves are measured *net* of liabilities, the deterioration is even
more drastic, as indicated by the following Bank of England estimates of net external financial assets of the non-oil developing
countries (Stanyer and Whitley, 1981, Table F):

(billion U.S. dollars at year-end)

1973	− 54	1977	−123
1974	− 72	1978	−141
1975	−100	1979	−172
1976	−114	1980	−229

10. The deterioration in the debt ratios mentioned in paragraph 8 was related to changes in the composition of the debt and
to changes in the terms of borrowing. Data on the structure of
external debt of non-oil developing countries in Table 6 show a
relative decline in debt to official creditors (aid, export credit
agencies, etc.) and a rise in the proportion of debt to private
financial institutions. However, Table 6 also shows very large
differences between the country subgroups. "Low-income
countries" have experienced only modest changes in the composition of their debt, whereas the position of the "other net oil
importers" has changed most radically. The low-income countries
remain largely dependent on aid and other official inflows; the

Table 6
COMPOSITION OF EXTERNAL DEBT OF NON-OIL DEVELOPING COUNTRIES
(percentage of total at year-end)

	Official Creditors			Private Financial Institutions			Other Private Creditors		
	1973	1977	1980	1973	1977	1980	1973	1977	1980
All non-oil developing countries	50.4	45.1	42.1	35.5	45.0	48.9	14.2	9.7	9.0
Net oil exporters	*39.6*	*35.0*	*34.2*	*41.7*	*54.2*	*57.1*	*18.7*	*10.8*	*8.7*
Net oil importers									
Major exporters of manufactures	*27.4*	*25.4*	*22.7*	*54.4*	*62.7*	*64.2*	*18.2*	*11.9*	*13.1*
Low-income countries	*88.0*	*86.7*	*84.3*	*6.2*	*8.1*	*12.0*	*5.8*	*5.2*	*3.7*
Other net oil importers	*88.6*	*54.7*	*51.2*	*5.4*	*35.7*	*42.4*	*6.1*	*9.6*	*6.4*

Source: IMF, *World Economic Outlook*, 1981, Table 29.

other subgroups, especially the "major exporters of manufactures," borrow large proportions from private financial institutions, chiefly because of their superior access to commercial bank
sources. Since credits from private sources have an average maturity of less than 9 years, against nearly 24 years for official creditors, the relative growth in the former types of borrowing has led
to a shortening in the average debt maturity of developing countries, from 18.0 years in 1973 to 14.6 years in 1979 (Nowzad,
Williams, *et al*, 1981, Table 7).

Table 7
TRENDS IN INTEREST RATES PAID BY DEVELOPING COUNTRIES FOR EUROMARKET CREDITS
(per cent)

	Average Interest Rate	Increase in Export Prices[1]	Real Cost of Credit
1976	8.0	5.7	2.3
1977	8.1	7.5	0.6
1978	10.7	12.0	−1.3
1979	13.0	12.9	0.1
1980[2]	14.5	12.7	1.8

Sources: Column 1: World Bank, *World Development Report, 1980*, Table 3.5; Column 2: IMF, *World Economic Outlook*, 1981, Table 11.
[1]Three-year moving average.
[2]Authors' estimate.

11. Average interest rates have also risen, partly because of
the changes in debt structure and partly because of rising nominal
interest rates (Nowzad, Williams, *et al*, 1981). The first column
of Table 7 shows trends in the rates paid by developing countries
for Euromarket credits, recording a near doubling of rates in
1976–80. The coincidence of the second oil shock and high nominal
interest rates in 1979–80 has resulted in larger transfers of income to the OPEC surplus countries than would have occurred
under the rates prevailing in 1974–75. On the other hand, when
adjusted for a trend value of export prices to obtain an estimate of
the real resource cost of debt servicing (columns 2 and 3), the cost
was still modest. It had, however, risen by over 3 percentage
points in 1978–80.

12. Data on the purchasing power value to non-oil developing
countries of development aid flows (Table 8) show these to have
grown only slowly in 1970–72 through 1980. In fact, the implied

Table 8
TRENDS IN AID FLOWS

	1970–72	1975	1980
Net official development assistance *(billion U.S. dollars at current prices)*			
DAC countries[1]	7.2	13.8	26.7
OPEC countries[2]	0.4	5.5	7.0
CMEA countries[3]	1.1	1.4	1.8
Total	8.7	20.7	35.5
Total deflated by import price index of imports of the non-oil developing countries *(1970–72 = 100)*	8.7	9.7	10.4
Total as percentage of current account deficit of the non-oil developing countries *(at current prices)*	91.6	39.1	44.4
DAC total as percentage of gross national product *(at current prices)*	0.34[4]	0.36	0.37

Sources: Various publications of the OECD (DAC) and the Fund.

[1]Development Assistance Committee members of the Organization for Economic Cooperation and Development.
[2]Members of the Organization of Petroleum Exporting Countries.
[3]Members of the Council for Mutual Economic Assistance.
[4]1970 figure.

annual growth rate is only 2.0 per cent, which is below population growth. Aid went down sharply as a proportion of the current account deficits of non-oil developing countries between 1970–72 and 1975 but then staged a modest recovery in 1980. Although low-income countries are particularly dependent on aid, the largest share still goes to middle-income countries. In 1979, low-income countries (excluding the People's Republic of China), whose populations made up 55 per cent of the total population of developing countries, received only 37 per cent of total OECD and OPEC aid and only 32 per cent of bilateral aid (World Bank, 1981 a, p. 56). Even within the low-income countries, there are numerous inequalities of access to aid.

13. Despite a downturn in 1980 and predictions of further difficulties in 1981 and beyond, there has been a recovery in bank lending to non-oil developing countries, as indicated by the following data on Eurocurrency bank credits:[3]

(billion U.S. dollars)

| 1978 | 26.67 | 1980 | 24.01 |
| 1979 | 35.23 | 1981 | 32.86 |

[3]From Morgan Guaranty and Trust Company of New York, *World Financial Markets* (September 1981), p. 16. The figure for the year 1981 is estimated on the basis of January–September data.

However, some qualifications are in order: (a) the purchasing power of the projected 1981 lending is well below 1978–79 values; (b) non-oil developing countries are also large depositors in the Euromarket, so that net flows to non-oil developing countries are much smaller; [4] (c) access to the Euromarket is highly skewed and is determined by criteria that coincide roughly with the level of development, so that the low-income countries are actually net depositors (Killick, 1981).

14. In 1974–80 net Fund credits financed only a little over 4 per cent of the total current account deficits of non-oil developing countries, but the volume of Fund credits rose sharply in 1980–81. That there has been a resurgence in utilization of Fund resources is indicated by the following data on credit tranches and extended facility commitments to developing countries, although not all of the money has been disbursed:[5]

(billion SDRs)

| 1978 | 1.8 | 1980 | 7.0 |
| 1979 | 2.2 | 1981 | 12.4 |

This enlarged utilization has had the effect of bringing more of the Fund's current lending into the high-conditionality classes, so that while two thirds of the Fund's lending in 1973–74 was on low-conditionality terms, three fourths of its current new lending commitments involve high conditionality, or "rigorous adjustment policies" (IMF, 1981 a, p. 18). The coverage in this seminar report of the nature of the Fund's conditionality is thus timely.

15. Data on the growth of per capita GDP indicate, for all non-oil developing countries as a group, that the rate of expansion has slowed by about a third since the first oil shock, compared with the preceding seven years (Table 9). This constitutes prima facie evidence for the proposition that many non-oil developing countries are now constrained by a lack of foreign exchange, evidence of which is reinforced in Table 9 by the predictions of a superior growth record of the net oil exporters for 1980–81. Sustained over a long period, import compression would undoubtedly have adverse effects on economic performance; and undoubtedly a continuing neglect of effective measures to strengthen or finance

---

[4]The Bank for International Settlements (BIS, 1981, Table 5) shows gross borrowings of the non-oil developing countries as of March 1981 at $74.8 billion and gross deposits at $45.3 billion.

[5]From *IMF Survey*, October 26, 1981, p. 340. The figure for the year 1981 is estimated on the basis of January–September data.

Table 9
GROWTH OF PER CAPITA GROSS DOMESTIC PRODUCT IN NON-OIL DEVELOPING COUNTRIES[1]
(per cent at constant prices)

	1967–74 Average	1974–80 Average	1979	1980[2]	1981[3]	Assumed Population Growth
All non-oil developing countries	3.5	2.4	2.6	2.1	2.7	2.3
Net oil exporters	3.5	2.6	4.4	4.0	4.1	2.7
Net oil importers						
Major exporters of manufactures	5.8	2.8	4.3	2.5	2.4	2.2
Low-income countries	1.0	1.4	−2.1	0.8	2.6	2.3
Other net oil importers	3.1	2.3	1.9	1.2	1.9	2.2

Sources: IMF, *World Economic Outlook*, 1981, Table 2, adjusted with population growth data from the World Bank, *World Development Report*, 1981.
[1]Excluding the People's Republic of China.
[2]Estimates.
[3]Forecasts.

the balance of payments would have adverse effects. There are considerable differences between the various subgroups, however, with income growth in the subgroups "low-income countries" and "other net oil importers" being the most precarious.

16. Inflation rates have accelerated markedly in non-oil developing countries during 1979 and 1980 (Table 10), and the absolute gap between them and industrial countries has widened considerably. This acceleration may be explained partly in terms of a diversion of excess demand away from import volumes (which have been compressed) and into the domestic price level. However, there are considerable differences in the records of the various subgroups, and the figures are distorted by the records of a few cases of hyperinflation. Nevertheless, if inflation continues to accelerate, or even to remain at the rather high general levels of 1980, it too will probably tend to have an adverse effect on investment and growth.

17. As is the case in almost all the tables, it is crucially important to differentiate between various subgroups in the "non-oil developing countries" category because their circumstances and prospects differ radically. In terms of the relative severity of their current account deficits, their access to international finance, their net reserve position, and their rate of economic

Table 10
INFLATION RATES FOR CONSUMER PRICES[1]
(per cent)[2]

	1958–65	1965–72	1972–80	1978	1979	1980
Industrial countries	2.1	4.2	9.0	7.2	9.2	11.9
All non-oil developing countries	13.6	10.6	24.5	23.7	28.9	37.7
Net oil exporters	...	...	16.5	17.7	17.7	24.7
Net oil importers						
Major exporters of manufactures	...	...	33.1	37.3	44.6	56.0
Low-income countries	...	...	12.5	6.7	11.5	15.9
Other net oil importers	...	...	23.9	19.3	24.2	32.6

Sources: IMF, World Economic Outlook, 1981, Table 3, and International Financial Statistics.
[1]Excluding the People's Republic of China.
[2]Weighted averages.

growth, the position of the low-income countries emerges as particularly vulnerable, especially because of their dependence on the policy decisions of a small number of other governments for development assistance and other resource transfers.

SUMMARIES OF THE SEMINAR PAPERS

Below are summaries of the papers presented at the seminar and published in this report. The summaries appear in the order in which the papers were presented.

TONY KILLICK AND MARY SUTTON

Disequilibria, Financing, and Adjustment in Developing Countries

The paper by Tony Killick and Mary Sutton sketches the background against which the other, more specialized, papers are written. It begins by outlining the conventional belief as to how payments disequilibria might be overcome. This states that financing without adjustment is not a sustainable strategy since it involves amassing an external debt that ultimately erodes creditworthiness. Equally, adjustment without financing is not feasible, as structural adaptation cannot be accomplished instantly. The optimal approach, therefore, appears to be a judicious blend of the two, with financing allowing the inevitable costs of adjustment to be minimized.

The paper suggests, however, that the conflicting objectives of various groups of countries greatly reduce the scope for achieving this balance. The objective of the major surplus countries, chiefly the members of OPEC, is to create a portfolio of fairly liquid assets that will at least maintain the real value of their resources. The deficit countries, primarily non-oil developing countries, do not offer investment opportunities that would satisfy either the rate of return or liquidity requirements of the potential investors. Nor would stabilization necessarily be the prime objective of the non-oil developing countries even if financing is available. The observed tendency for deficit countries to use available financing as a substitute for corrective measures reflects in part the fear that adjustment programs impede, rather than promote, development. Furthermore, the preoccupation of the OECD members with reducing domestic inflation has effectively shifted part of the deficits that are the counterparts of the OPEC surpluses to the non-oil developing countries, thereby increasing the requirements for financing and adjustment. Thus, the objectives of the three groups—OPEC members, non-oil developing countries, and OECD members—tend to militate against achievement of the standard solution.

The paper also questions whether adjustment is, in any case, feasible. A large part of the deficits of non-oil developing countries are essentially counterparts of the OPEC surpluses, and these surpluses are likely to persist. Unless the essentially international nature of the problem is recognized, there is a danger that the strategies of individual deficit countries will amount to "competitive adjustment" as each tries to shift its share of the collective deficit to other non-oil developing countries.

However, a policy of inaction is undesirable, since a planned response to the changed world environment is likely to be a lower-cost solution than a solution that would ultimately be imposed in the absence of financing. The paper, therefore, goes on to consider, on the basis of some Latin American experiences, alternative responses to disequilibria. It identifies three "stylized types" of response, distinguished by the relative weights attached to reduction in aggregate demand and structural adaptation. The combination of these two elements reflects the time horizon within which adjustment is to be achieved and the analysis of the domestic causes of the problem, as well as the priorities of the government in question. The first, the so-called conventional type, generally addresses payments problems, seen as essentially short-term, by using exchange rate adjustments and the traditional demand management techniques of fiscal and monetary policy. The remaining two types, the so-called new orthodox and structuralist/populist types, are based on the view that structural adaptation is the key to sustained stability, but they draw very different policy inferences from this. The new orthodox type is often part of a total economic strategy designed to restructure the economy along laissez-faire lines. To this end demand management, relying heavily on the use of monetary rather than fiscal instruments, is supplemented by financial, trade, and exchange rate reforms. The structuralist/populist tradition largely seeks to avoid using the traditional demand management instruments, relying instead on exchange controls.

The paper discusses some of the difficulties encountered in practice with each of these broad approaches. It argues that the structuralist tradition does not contain within it a coherent approach to short-term economic management and that, in the absence of a viable alternative set of policies, the arguments about least-cost methods of short-term adjustment concern the range of options within orthodoxy. It stresses, however, that the scope for imaginative policy design and implementation narrows as the payments imbalance becomes critical and that the only viable policy option becomes crisis management by means of generalized demand restraint. On the politics of stabilization programs, the paper suggests that the tendency for programs to be abandoned may be attributable to the fact that they are often perceived as resulting in larger net political costs than the problems to which they are addressed. It is pointed out, however, that if the popularity of governments is positively correlated with the performance of the economy, persistent economic disequilibria will also undermine a government's legitimacy and successful stabilization will increase it.

Bringing together the global and national scenarios, the paper concludes that the standard solution is basically correct but that present-day global conditions have shifted the desirable balance between financing and adjustment markedly toward the former. It argues that conventional programs—the type with which the Fund has been associated—have erred in trying to achieve too much too quickly. It contends that, given the long-term nature of the adjustment task and its implications for the structure of production and demand, stabilization programs must be seen as inputs into the development effort and be integrated into countries' development strategies.

MANUEL GUITIAN

Economic Management and International Monetary Fund Conditionality

Manuel Guitián's paper begins by examining the rationale for the principle of conditionality and the resulting fiscal, monetary, external debt, and exchange rate policy implications. The purpose of conditionality is to ensure that an adjustment need is answered by a commensurate adjustment effort so that a viable payments position is attained within a reasonable period of time. Typically, the imbalances creating the adjustment need result from expansion of aggregate demand, coincident with a relatively stable aggregate supply function. The aggregate demand expansion is often fueled by excessive public sector expenditure, and corrective action, therefore, normally includes measures to restrain government spending or to raise revenue. These measures will have a direct impact on the public sector borrowing requirement and the need for domestic bank financing. This link that exists between monetary flows, public sector spending, and aggregate demand makes monetary policy a key element of demand management and stabilization policies. However, in most open economies, the total money supply is not within the control of the authorities; consequently, monetary policy is formulated in terms of domestic credit expansion. When the exchange rate is fixed, domestic credit policy is necessary to make compatible the public's demand for money and the authorities' demand for international reserves, while when the exchange rate is flexible, it is necessary to satisfy the public's demand for money and the authorities' exchange rate and price stability objectives.

Over the longer term, economic policy is concerned not only with the overall balance of payments but also with its composition. Domestic credit policy alone need not produce a satisfactory balance of payments outcome in terms of both level and composition, particularly if it is formulated without reference to potential foreign borrowing. Domestic credit policy is, therefore, complemented by foreign borrowing guidelines in order to ensure that the total available flow of financial resources is compatible with the objectives sought for the balance of payments, economic growth, and inflation. In contrast to domestic credit flows, which help to shift resources among sectors, foreign borrowing adds to the economy's total available resources. In some cases, this allows for a higher growth rate than would have been possible in its absence and thereby lessens the constraint of domestic demand management measures on the longer-run evolution of the economy. On exchange rate adjustments, Guitián argues that the correction of the imbalances is likely to require less restrictive domestic policies when devaluation is among the measures because the expenditure-reducing effect of the exchange rate change, *ceteris paribus*, lowers the adjustment burden that would have to be ensured by demand management measures. Furthermore, he points out that scope for avoiding a devaluation diminishes as the size of the imbalance is allowed to grow because, given downward rigidity in domestic prices and costs, exclusive reliance on demand management measures would entail allowing domestic employment and output to bear the brunt of the adjustment.

Turning to recent developments in conditionality practices, Guitián outlines the considerations that led the Fund to extend the time frame of its lending arrangements and to enlarge the scale of its assistance. For many Fund members, payments imbalances associated with increases in world energy prices were superimposed on difficulties of a long-standing nature. They were not likely to be transitory, and being essentially structural, they were not amenable to correction over a short period of time. The lengthening of the adjustment period had implications for the choice of policy objectives and instruments. For example, the fact that, during many stabilization programs, growth rates in the short run had fallen below their previous trend prompted examination of whether too much emphasis had been placed on demand management and whether there was a need to supplement overall demand management with measures directly aimed at improving the allocation of resources and stimulating the growth of productivity and aggregate supply.

The experience with inflation control—indicating that the measures taken have tended to stop inflation from rising but have had mixed success in reducing it—raised the issue of the appropriate way of setting an inflation target. Guitián argues that programs should aim at significant, but feasible, reductions in the rate of inflation, even when these may appear ambitious, with a view to influencing expectations. With regard to the balance of payments, as the adjustment period is lengthened it ceases to be a matter of indifference how the targeted improvement is achieved in terms of the mix of current and capital account outcomes. A viable payments position over the medium term to long term requires a sustainable balance of payments structure. The current account, therefore, becomes a policy objective in itself. Similarly, lengthening the adjustment period has implications for the choice of policy instruments. It has a bearing, for example, on the appropriate mix of measures designed to control aggregate demand and the measures to stimulate domestic supply. Whether an adjustment in aggregate demand is brought about through a curtailment of consumption or of investment becomes relevant, given the importance of investment to the future performance of the economy.

Finally, turning to methods of assessing and interpreting results of adjustment programs, Guitián suggests three possible standards: (1) positive—what the position is now, relative to what it was, (2) normative—what it is, compared with program targets (that is, with what it should be), and (3) conjectural—what it would have been in the absence of a program. With reference to the first standard, he argues that the general experience has been that—in relation to balance of payments, growth, and inflation objectives—the degree of disequilibrium after the introduction of the policies has been reduced, with the relatively more favorable outcomes being those for the balance of payments. Judged against the normative standard, the experience is also relatively more favorable for the balance of payments objective than for the inflation and growth targets. However, Guitián argues that the relatively better balance of payments outcome should not be interpreted as a policy bias because, in contrast to inflation and growth, a perceived improvement in the balance of payments need not reflect a policy improvement as it could also be the result of a financing constraint imposed by the lack of foreign exchange. In his view, each of the standards can be useful, depending on the nature and purpose of the assessment, but the conjectural standard, which from many standpoints is the most controversial, is also the most appropriate.

DANIEL M. SCHYDLOWSKY

Alternative Approaches to
Short-Term Economic Management
in Developing Countries

The thesis of Daniel Schydlowsky's paper is that, applied to developing countries, generalized devaluation and demand restraint are blunt instruments. They fail to elicit potential supply-side responses that could bear fruit in the short run and could contribute to containing the costs of stabilization. The principal features of developing economies that inhibit the operation of the traditional prescriptions vis-à-vis the balance of payments are (1) low price elasticities of export supply and import demand, and (2) excessively large non-traded goods sectors. The price elasticity of export supply is low typically because the aggregate supply curve for products that could be exported is S-shaped. It has a fairly inelastic portion corresponding to activities such as mining and industrial agriculture, an intermediate segment for food production, and a very elastic segment for industry. These differing supply elasticities reflect the varying cost structures of the activities—structures that differ for a variety of reasons, including differences caused by economic policies that discriminate between them. While its supply curve is relatively elastic, the industrial sector depends, more than any other sector, on imported inputs. For this reason, devaluation tends to increase the profitability of industrial production much less than that of primary production. Since the elasticity of mining and industrial agriculture with respect to the exchange rate tends to be low, the aggregate elasticity of exports with respect to devaluation is also low. The elasticity of demand for imports with respect to the exchange rate may be lower than the price elasticity of demand, if the import components of goods offered on the domestic market are similar or if domestic factor remunerations are very responsive to changes in the exchange rate, so that devaluation does not significantly change relative prices. The nontraded goods sector typically comprises both nontradable goods and tradable nontraded goods, rendered thus by policies that, as part of an import substituting industrialization strategy, impose duties on imports and offer a low exchange rate for exports.

The objective of the alternative stabilization strategy suggested by Schydlowsky is to operate on the elastic upper section of the supply curve of exports and to transform tradable nontraded goods into traded goods. The mechanism for accomplishing this aim is a differential devaluation. Such a policy would, by setting the rate for each product at a level at least comparable to the total exchange rate affecting industrial costs, raise the revenue from the export of industrial goods in terms of local currency. This would bring the structure of exchange rates on the sales side into line with the implicit structure created by trade restrictions and other policies on the cost side. Thus, Schydlowsky says, "the cost differences that cause the export supply curve to be S-shaped would be offset and the kink in the export supply curve would disappear ..." (p. 119). The same mechanism would transform tradable nontraded goods into traded goods by raising the export point. Such a policy, in addition to offsetting existing implicit multiple exchange rate structures on the cost side, would complement import restriction and export promotion, provide an outlet for excess capacity typically built up over the years of an import substituting industrialization policy, and allow existing idle capital and labor to be employed as the economy overcame its balance of payments problem. Schydlowsky explores three possible ways of implementing such a policy: compensatory export bounties, compensated devaluation, and domestic tax and price measures.

The same mechanism could, Schydlowsky argues, contribute to a more cost-effective price stabilization strategy. By assuming that output cannot be expanded in the short run and by proceeding as if inflation always results from generalized excess demand, traditional prescriptions close off viable policy options. In Schydlowsky's view, there is scope for expanding output within the time frame in which aggregate demand reductions can be achieved. Many developing countries have unused capacity in their industrial sectors that can be used to contain price increases. Schydlowsky identifies four types of inflation (demand-pull, cost-push, exchange rate, and spiral) and argues that there is a role for differentiated devaluation in combating each type. In the case of low-grade inflation (up to 20–25 per cent), it is possible to try to drown excess demand in increased supply by means of a differentiated devaluation that provokes export-led capacity utilization in the tradable nontraded goods sector. In the case of cost-push inflation, the objective of weakening the link between wage increases and cost increases would be facilitated by economies of scale attendant on fuller utilization of installed capacity and increased efficiency as a result of higher and more stable volumes of production. Similarly, differential devaluation is an appropriate policy for forestalling exchange rate inflation by bringing into production the excess capacity in the tradable non-traded goods sector to earn foreign exchange and alleviate the scarcity threatening to generate inflation. In the context of virulent spiral inflation, differentiated devaluation—allied to an incomes policy and an active crawling exchange rate—could change the context in which the economic agents are operating from a zero-sum to a positive-sum game by holding out the prospect of expanded real incomes.

RICHARD O'BRIEN

Roles of the Euromarket and the International Monetary Fund in Financing Developing Countries

Written from the perspective of the commercial banks, Richard O'Brien's paper discusses the current level of international bank lending to developing countries, the relative roles of the banks and the Fund, and the issues of unequal access to private credit markets and of the efficiency of recycling methods. O'Brien notes that bank lending to developing countries in the form of syndicated credits, having fallen dramatically in 1980, began to recover in 1981, with Arab banks playing a more active role and showing a greater willingness to lend to non-oil developing countries. At the same time, the number of countries seeking to reschedule existing debt is increasing and a larger proportion of new financing is to refinance maturing debt. On the question of how much more the private banks could lend to developing countries, he points out that (1) the entry of Arab banks, (2) the possibility of greater lending by banks that have been less active in lending to developing countries to date, and (3) the fact that the exposures of most of the major national banking groups are still less than those of the American banks make further growth quite possible. On the other hand, given that a higher risk perception of developing country debt now prevails, the non-U.S. banks may be reluctant to increase lending to the level reached by the U.S. banks.

Concerning the relative roles of the Fund and the banks, O'Brien argues that while both are contributing to financing payments deficits, their roles and responsibilities are distinct and should remain so. The banks are lending to developing countries in the pursuit of profit while the Fund is increasingly playing a "policeman's role" for the international financial system and is acting as a lender of last resort to countries in financial difficulty. Having summarized the standard criticisms leveled at the banks and the Fund with regard to their speed of action, procyclical or countercyclical lending, conditionality, and country distribution of credit, O'Brien suggests that both the banks and the Fund are now at a critical point. The banks have increased their lending, and exposures are higher than they were in the early 1970s. The Fund has increased its financing capabilities and has eased its loan conditions. In O'Brien's view, Fund reforms have now gone far enough. If the lending policies of the Fund become too liberal, its dual role will be undermined, with the Fund becoming "merely a source of finance with which indirectly to rescue banks from difficult country positions" (p. 147).

On the question of unequal access to financing, O'Brien discusses the prime determinant of any country's access—its creditworthiness—and reviews some of the criteria employed in assessing credit risk. He argues that the unequal distribution of lending is the natural consequence of the proper application of credit assessment techniques. While he sees a limited case for attempting to widen access to private capital markets, he argues that countries that cannot service commercial debt nor prove themselves creditworthy should not be encouraged to build such debts. Financing the deficits of the poorest countries is a problem for governments rather than for the private banks. While the incidence of rescheduling indicates some of the weaknesses in the system, O'Brien contends that, on the whole, bank financing has proved an efficient method of recycling funds.

BAHRAM NOWZAD

Some Issues and Questions
Regarding Debt of
Developing Countries

In his paper, Bahram Nowzad notes the increasing importance of the debt issue as the number of countries experiencing debt ser-

vicing difficulties grows. He suggests that the origins of these difficulties are to be found in overly ambitious government expenditure
programs, investment of borrowed resources in projects with inadequate rates of return, mismanagement of debt, and general balance
of payments problems. The problems are dealt with by imposing
restrictions, compressing domestic expenditure and imports, accu-
mulating arrears, or seeking debt rescheduling. The incidence of
requests for rescheduling of debt service obligations is increasing.
For example, during 1981 eight Fund member countries sought multilateral debt renegotiations, compared with three each year during
the period 1976–80.

Nowzad describes the growth in total debt and debt servicing
obligations over the decade of the 1970s and the change in the
structure of debt, reflecting increased borrowing at commercial
rates on the private capital markets. He notes that the growth rate
of the medium-term and long-term obligations of non-oil developing
countries slowed in 1980, largely because of a slower expansion rate
of outstanding debt to private creditors. However, he points out
that, as was the case in 1974–75, this initial response reflects a
reliance by non-oil developing countries on their reserves and on
short-term credit to finance their current account deficits. Since
this strategy cannot be sustained over the longer term, he antici-
pates a faster growth of medium-term and long-term debt in the
future. The doubts expressed by some bankers about the ability of
private financial institutions to channel sufficient funds to deficit
countries proved unfounded in 1981, and it is widely accepted that
developing countries as a group can absorb further external debt.
However, Nowzad emphasizes that some non-oil developing countries that have enjoyed access to the international capital markets
may not continue to do so. Creditors are becoming increasingly
dubious about the ability of some countries to bear additional foreign debt or even to continue to service existing obligations.

Much of the debt contracted by developing countries on the private capital markets in recent years has, through the mechanism of
floating rates, borne the full impact of high and variable interest
rates. Interest payments increased by a third in 1980, and this
increase accounted for three fifths of the 25 per cent increase in debt
service payments. The present historically high interest rates on
international capital markets are the result of rapid inflation and
stringent monetary policies in industrial countries. Variable inter-

est rate loans incorporate an inflation premium to compensate the creditor for deterioration in the real value of loans. The impact of this on the debtor is that the real loan is fully repaid at a faster rate than was originally expected, with the result that in the short term a country would require larger gross borrowing to maintain the same transfer of net resources. Thus, debtors are exposed to uncertainties as to the speed at which their debt will be amortized. Variable interest rates also complicate investment decisions and analysis of the future sustainability of external debt. Nowzad discusses three types of indexation (financial, maturity, and price) that have been suggested as possible solutions to the problems associated with variable interest rate loans. He concludes that each falls short of the objective of significantly reducing debt service uncertainties and that only policy measures that reduce both the level and variability of inflation and interest rates can achieve this aim.

Nowzad argues that the size and persistence of payments imbalances facing non-oil developing countries necessitate that financing be reinforced by adjustment. The Fund is in a better position to assist with both aspects than it was in 1974–75, as it has increased the amount of resources a member may draw and has adopted a more supply-oriented policy approach. He also discusses whether— in view of the degree to which lending has been concentrated in a small number of countries and the implications of the switch from official to private creditors for maturities and interest rates—the institutional arrangements employed for recycling funds during the 1970s are in need of modification. He speculates as to whether the middle-income developing countries can be weaned away from official development assistance so that it can be directed toward countries that do not have access to the international capital markets. He points out that the Fund expects to lend its resources more heavily to the low-income countries and other net oil importers among the non-oil developing countries in the coming years.

BRIAN TEW

*The Position and Prospects
of the International Monetary
System in Historical Context*

Crucial decisions affecting the operation and development of the international monetary system are taken, *de facto*, by the industrial countries. In his paper Brian Tew examines the implications for developing countries of some of the courses of action followed by the Group of Ten members acting individually or collectively. During the 1960s and 1970s, the impact on the developing countries was mixed. On the one hand, the Group of Ten has contributed to the maintenance of open world trade and payments systems. Members of the Group of Ten have been disinclined to introduce restrictions for balance of payments reasons or as a remedy for general unemployment. On the other hand, their abandonment of pegged exchange rates in the early 1970s constituted, from the viewpoint of developing countries, a deterioration in the monetary environment. The floating of the major currencies introduced uncertainties about real export earnings and real import costs. For some developing countries that prefer to peg their currencies rather than to float them, it became more difficult to decide to what currency they should peg. It also made it more difficult to decide in what form to hold reserves. Differing views within the Group of Ten on whether the members should float their currencies individually or jointly, whether the float should be clean or managed, and to what extent domestic fiscal and monetary policy should be used to moderate exchange rate movements increased the unpredictability of their official actions. This has been further accentuated, in Tew's opinion, by their conversion to "practical monetarism." This has entailed policies of "benign neglect" or adoption of monetary targets. The former, favored at times by both the United States and the United Kingdom, has produced disharmony in the Group of Ten as a whole, making its behavior even more uncoordinated and unpredictable. The use of monetary targets has contributed to the increased volatility of exchange rates and interest rates.

Tew argues that the actions of the Group of Ten have contributed significantly to the problems facing the non-oil developing countries. The impact of the recession in the industrial countries has been aggravated by the adoption in those countries of deflationary fiscal and monetary policies. These policies, such as floating exchange rates and targeting on monetary aggregates, were adopted primarily in response to anxiety about the pace of inflation. However, Tew contends that the Group of Ten countries have also tended to tighten their fiscal and monetary policies in response to any weakening of their currencies without being as ready to relax them in response to a strengthening of their currencies. This asymmetrical policy response has imparted a deflationary bias to the adjustment process. It has enabled the Group of Ten to reduce its share in the counterpart deficits of the OPEC surpluses and to impose a disproportionate share on the non-oil developing countries.

With respect to the role of the Fund, Tew discusses how it has responded to the payments problems of the non-oil developing countries. He notes the extent to which the Fund's borrowing activity is constrained by its Articles of Agreement and considers that there may be a case for amending the Articles to take into account the changed role of the Fund. He also discusses the role of the Group of Twenty-Four developing countries as a counterbalance to the Group of Ten. He outlines three proposals of the Group of Twenty-Four— related to the issuance of special drawing rights (SDRs), the revaluation of monetary gold, and conditions for drawing on the Fund—all designed to effect a transfer of real resources to the developing countries. He argues, however, that no major alteration of the international monetary system is in prospect.

GRAHAM BIRD

Developing Country
Interests in Proposals for
International Monetary Reform

Finally, Graham Bird's paper examines a number of proposals for international monetary reform from the point of view of their likely impact on developing countries. He discusses Fund conditionality, an international commodity-backed reserve currency, and a "Southern" currency, but the paper's prime concern is with proposals relating to the SDR link, the substitution account, and gold. In discussing these proposals, Bird stresses that some developing countries are likely to respond differently to particular versions of them. The heterogeneity of the developing countries makes it difficult to decide what proposals would be in their collective interest or against it.

With reference to the long-standing debate on the link, Bird explores the interplay of efficiency and equity considerations, as well as the costs and benefits, from the developing country viewpoint, of the introduction of a market-equivalent interest rate on special drawing rights (SDRs). The objective of the proposed link is to provide additional aid to developing countries by reallocating to them some or all of the seigniorage associated with the creation of international reserves. In the past an "informal link" has operated, insofar as the initial flow of real resources arising from the present SDR scheme has been toward developing countries. The majority of developing countries have been net users and have therefore benefited from the relatively low interest rate for SDRs. The introduction of a commercial rate has reduced the value of SDRs to developing country users. On the other hand, if the new rate succeeds in promoting acceptance of the SDR as the principal reserve asset, it will enhance the effectiveness of the proposed formal link. However, Bird argues that, even in the context of the present scheme, the introduction of a market-equivalent rate has not eliminated the benefits of SDRs to developing countries. A major advantage of SDRs is that they are a form of unconditional credit to which developing countries have security of access. He examines five versions of the proposed link and emphasizes that, while the developing countries are agreed in preferring an organic and untied version, beyond that the interests of individual developing countries would be expected to diverge with respect to particular proposals. Bird also discusses the proposal that SDRs should be commodity-backed. He contends that the arguments advanced in favor of such an arrangement—that it would contribute to reducing primary product price instability and world inflation and that it would facilitate the growth of world output and employment—are spurious. Developing countries would be better advised, in his view, to seek modifications in the present SDR system than to pursue such a proposal.

Turning to the substitution account, Bird notes that the reservations expressed by the developing countries have not related to the principle of substitution but to the form of the proposed substitution account. He assesses the validity of developing country reservations about the effect of the substitution account on the SDR, international adjustment, exchange rate stability, and global liquidity management, as well as on the developing countries as holders of reserves. He notes that the introduction of a commercial interest rate on SDRs has removed what was perhaps the greatest deterrent to developing country support for the substitution account—that is, the fear that a competitive rate of interest on assets issued by the account would raise the rate on SDRs and thereby raise the charges for the use of Fund resources in general. He concludes that it is not in the interest of developing countries to resist all efforts to introduce a substitution account. Such a device, by ensuring that there is some structural connection between reserve growth and SDR creation, would contribute to making the SDR the principal reserve asset, assist in bringing the quantity of international reserves under greater control, and reduce instabilities generated by central bank changes in the composition of their reserves. Since these developments would be of benefit to them, the developing countries should, in Bird's view, concentrate on devising ways in which an SDR system based on competitive interest rates might be used or adapted to direct additional financial flows to developing countries.

With regard to gold, Bird describes how the revaluation of reserve gold to its market price and the dramatic rise in that price during the 1970s frustrated demonetization and created a wealth effect that primarily benefited gold-producing and gold-holding countries. Based on the premise that the distribution of the gains from these developments has been inequitable, a number of proposals have been made that are designed to redirect any further such resource transfers toward the developing countries. Bird dismisses such suggestions as a gold substitution account and a tax on the windfall profits of gold holders on the grounds of unacceptability to industrial countries. He ascribes greater significance to proposals for using the remaining stock of gold held by the Fund to provide finance for developing countries, and he discusses the relative merits of various approaches.

COMMENTARY

Clearly, many issues are raised by the papers presented at the seminar and summarized here, and this number was considerably increased during the seminar discussions. What follows is a commentary on some of these. Much of what follows is derived directly from notes on the discussion, but this is not intended to be a systematic record of the proceedings nor does it represent a consensus of those who participated. It is rather the authors' interpretation of what seemed to be some of the key issues. On the grounds that the proceedings were intended to be informal and also that frequent references to the participants by name would be tedious to the reader, this is a general commentary. The authors owe an intellectual debt to all who participated in the discussion and whose views have influenced the commentary that follows.

What actually is the problem?

Global disequilibrium sounds like "A Bad Thing," something for serious-minded people to worry about. But what actually is the problem and how precisely does it impinge on human welfare? To some extent, this amounts to prosaic questions about the interpretation of balance of payments accounts. Tables 1, 3, and 4 above, for instance, report data on the current account deficits of non-oil developing countries. Do these offer a measurement of the problem? The most obvious reason why the answer to this question is negative is that non-oil developing countries have long been importers of capital and can depend on being able to finance a current deficit of some magnitude. Does the problem thus consist of that part of current deficits which cannot be financed by normal capital inflows? There are difficulties with this, too.

First, it is wrong to think of the capital account as responding passively to finance any given current account deficit. To some extent, countries have to adjust their current deficit to whatever inflow of capital is thought feasible or desirable. This, presumably, accounts for a large part of the import compression reported in the first section of this overview. To this extent, then, the current deficit understates the size of the problem.

A second difficulty is that the size of the current deficit is strongly influenced by economic policies within non-oil developing countries. Excessive demand expansion, or policies that frustrate the efficiency and growth of output of tradable goods (including the maintenance of overvalued currencies) all result in enlarged current deficits. But these are endogenously caused weaknesses, and when economists talk of the problem of global disequilibrium, they desire rather to focus on deficits whose sources are exogenous to those experiencing them. In such cases, the current account deficit exaggerates the problem.

Perhaps one way to solve this difficulty is to return to the concept of a balance of payments equilibrium and to view the problem as constituted by those forces that prevent the achievement of equilibrium. For example, it may well be that an important aspect of a country's payments situation is that it can only keep its import bill within manageable bounds by maintaining unwanted deflationary policies at home. Since it would not be desirable to describe such a country as having achieved a payments equilibrium, the problem then crystalizes as the deflation imposed on the domestic economy.

But while there are objective tests of the presence of deflation, judgments are likely to differ about the extent of any deflationary impact and about what would constitute a "reasonable" domestic macroeconomic balance. Indeed, differing views about what constitutes a viable balance between aggregate demand and supply underlie many of the disagreements between the Fund and its member governments.

The size and nature of the problem must also be related to the view taken of trends in the external indebtedness and international reserves of deficit countries. Whether external indebtedness should be regarded with concern is an issue taken up later, and such debt is likely to be strongly influenced by the future course of world interest rates. To the extent that the growth in debt and the terms on which it is obtained threaten future debt servicing capacity and creditworthiness, the financing of current deficits may be viewed as part of the problem. As Guitián suggests, such considerations favor placing weight on the current account as an important payments indicator.

An alternative line of approach would be to judge the problem according to some yardstick of economic efficiency. Here it might be useful to distinguish loosely between positive and normative ways of viewing efficiency or between those chiefly concerned with allocative efficiency and those whose primary emphasis is on reducing international income disparities.

A *positivist* might regard current global payments disequilibria as a problem because they reduce the efficiency of global resource use. In a world of many market imperfections, there is no assurance that the scale and geography of capital flows resulting from the present pattern of surpluses and deficits is such as to equalize marginal rates of return to investments. The well-known asymmetry of adjustment between deficit and surplus countries, which John Maynard Keynes foresaw at the Bretton Woods Conference in 1944 and for which no remedy has been found, rather creates a presumption that the resulting pattern of resource use and economic growth will be suboptimal, with deficit countries being forced into the pursuit of measures more deflationary than would be the case if there were a fuller equivalence of adjustment. A positivist might also be concerned with the potential instability of present international monetary arrangements, but let us return later to consider whether there is a real threat of a serious breakdown in the international monetary system.

By contrast, those of the *normative* school (to which the authors belong) would argue that the worst aspect of present-day disequilibria is that they tend to increase the global concentration of income and to affect most seriously the poorest nations. It is rather obvious that trends in world oil prices since 1973 have resulted in massive transfers of income from oil importing to oil exporting nations and that this transfer mechanism was reinforced by the emergence of positive real interest rates (just as it was ameliorated by the previously negative rates). To be sure, most of the oil exporting countries are, or were, relatively poor, whereas the major oil importers are the countries of the industrial West. Against this, the assertion of OPEC power has had the effect of superimposing a new form of income concentration on a world that was already marked by considerable skewness. The redistribution that has occurred could scarcely be regarded as socially optimal, and the suspicion is that in the longer term today's poorest countries will be the most seriously affected.

The data presented in Table 9 provide some support for this view, as do the generally gloomy views of the World Bank and others about the medium-term and long-term prospects of the oil-importing countries of Africa.[6] A world pattern of deficits, surpluses, and financial flows that threatens the living standards and future aspirations of many of the world's poorest countries can itself be regarded as a form of economic inefficiency, but only if the premise is accepted that it is desirable to reduce international inequalities. Some, of course, would not accept such a premise, and others would point out that, in welfare terms, the most significant type of inequality is interpersonal, not international. Many citizens of oil exporting countries have benefited little from the improvement in their countries' commodity terms of trade since 1973, just as there is no assurance that greater financial flows to low-income deficit countries will actually benefit the poor. Apart from this, there are also dangers in using broad categories like "non-oil developing countries." The range of country characteristics, circumstances, experiences, and interests makes it essential to differentiate various subgroups of non-oil countries, as Bird's paper emphasizes, but even when that is done, there are still likely to be large variations between the members of subgroups such as "low-

---

[6]See World Bank (1981 b, Table 9.1, and *passim*).

income countries" or "other net oil importers" as presented earlier in the tables.

It would clearly be a mistake to insist on a sharp distinction between the positive and normative schools. Most economists are, in fact, concerned both with allocative efficiency and some notion of distributional justice. But the two lines of approach do lead to somewhat different policy recommendations about adjustment strategies and possible international monetary reforms. Such differences are reflected, for example, in alternative views of the desirable role of the Fund, to be discussed later. There were also echoes of these two approaches in the considerable discussions during the seminar about the desirable balance between adjustment and financing (including the terms on which the financing is made available), with the stronger pleas for more or softer financing for non-oil developing countries tending to be associated with the normative school. There was, it might be added, a statistically significant tendency for development economists and journalists to fall into the normative category and for bankers and officials to adhere to the positive school, with international economists falling neatly into neither category.

The design of adjustment and conditionality

What actually can be meant by "adjustment" in circumstances of large-scale and persistent global disequilibria? To this large question no clear answer emerged from the seminar, perhaps because it has to be made more specific before it becomes answerable. There would, nevertheless, be fairly broad support for some generalizations, as follows:

1. Viewed collectively, adjustment for non-oil developing countries cannot be other than a most difficult and gradual process.

2. There is thus a need for large amounts of funding to finance the deficits during the transitional period, with a mixture of terms suited to the varying circumstances of the deficit countries.

3. There is some danger of "competitive adjustment," analogous to the competitive devaluations of the 1930s, in which individual non-oil developing countries take actions that, if effective, will do little more than shift deficits to other non-oil developing countries, leaving the aggregate deficit largely undiminished.

4. But, as Guitián suggests, inaction by the non-oil developing countries in the face of large and persistent deficits is likely to

bring about extremely high-cost results, with "adjustment" being forced on countries because of a breakdown in creditworthiness, the exhaustion of foreign exchange reserves, and disrupted supplies of imports.

5. Quite apart from the desirability of avoiding such results, effective adjustment programs in non-oil developing countries as a whole can contribute to a reduction in their deficits by increasing exports to the oil surplus countries as well as to the industrial countries and by reducing dependence on energy and other imports. The main effect of such measures would probably be to shift more of the counterpart deficits back to the OECD countries rather than to actually accelerate the reduction of OPEC surpluses.

6. The ability of non-oil developing countries to reduce their collective deficits at minimum cost to their economies is contingent on trends and policies within both the OPEC and OECD groups. The provision of more concessionary finance and the exercise of moderation in the exploitation of its monopoly powers are the two potentially most important OPEC contributions. More concessionary finance and the resumption of faster economic growth are the two potentially most important OECD contributions.

7. The avoidance of excess domestic demand is generally a necessary but often insufficient condition of successful adjustment programs. Improved performance by the productive structure is also likely to be a crucial ingredient, particularly in increasing the supply of tradable goods.

The place of demand management in stabilization programs is, of course, a field on which famous battles have been fought, particularly in debates about the appropriateness of the Fund's conditionality. The lines are well drawn, the armies are deeply entrenched, and the din is occasionally deafening. To some extent, however, the center of the debate has moved on, for the Fund has been explicit in recognizing the importance of structural factors in adjusting to present-day circumstances. At least since the introduction of the extended facility in 1974, the Fund has sought to pay more attention in the design of its programs to supply-side and other structural variables, and the maturity of some of its credits has become longer.

On the other hand, experiences with the extended facility have not been entirely happy. Partly because of the large uncertainties in world economic conditions, difficulties have been experienced in putting together medium-term adjustment programs that are implemented to a reasonable extent. Quarterly credit ceilings remain the hard core—the key performance criteria—of most extended facility programs and in that sense they are not very different from conventional Fund stand-by arrangements.

Underlying these facts is a considerable ambiguity on the part of the Fund's member governments about the role they want the Fund to play. On the one hand, the Executive Board revised the conditionality guidelines to give recognition to the importance of supply considerations in balance of payments adjustment; on the other hand, it has been reluctant to see the introduction of supply variables (microvariables) as performance criteria governing continuing access to Fund credit in other than exceptional circumstances. Developing country governments have frequently criticized the Fund for overconcentration on demand management through the limitation of domestic credit, but they have at the same time resisted any extension of Fund leverage to supply-side policies. They might have been less resistant if supply-side variables had been offered *as an alternative* to demand-side performance criteria, but such a trade-off would not have been countenanced by the representatives of the industrial countries nor, it might be added, is there any enthusiasm for such a trade-off among the Fund staff. Some long-held positions would need to be abandoned before structural adjustment could become the central feature of Fund programs.

These ambivalences would perhaps matter little if the conventional approach could be shown to be cost-effective in contemporary conditions, but the seminar was told of tests that apparently indicated that the establishment of a Fund program has no statistically significant impact on key macroeconomic variables.[7] The Fund's own appraisals—which have the advantage over independent work of being based on a fuller range of information—are somewhat more positive, indicating that Fund programs do generally move

---

[7]Connors (1979) concluded that Fund stand-by arrangements in 1973–77 "did not have much effect" on balance of payments and other key macroeconomic variables. The Overseas Development Institute's project on the Fund and economic management in developing countries has built on Connor's work and obtained similar results, although that work is still proceeding. Another participant also reported work that similarly appeared to indicate that Fund programs have had little impact on countries' macroeconomic performance.

key balance of payments variables in the desired directions. But these appraisals claim only mixed results, both by comparison with the immediate past and with program targets.

While there might be general agreement that, at most, only limited success could be claimed, the interpretation of such a result is by no means simple. The independent tests just cited all utilize the first of the tests mentioned in Guitián's paper, comparing outcomes during program periods with the record of the immediate preprogram years. It was argued at the seminar, however, that the tests just reported have little meaning, since countries normally only seek high-conditionality assistance from the Fund when their balance of payments is deteriorating. Fund programs might have been successful in reducing the extent of a deterioration, but they would be recorded as failing in simple comparisons of preprogram and postprogram outcomes.

It might be retorted that Fund programs set out to do more than to slow down a deterioration, but it should, in any case, be evident that program shortfalls can be attributable to a variety of causes and do not, therefore, imply that all are due to defects within the programs themselves. Thus, the Killick and Sutton paper gives evidence that developing country governments often seem to give low priority to short-term economic management, and the frequency with which governments exceed the ceilings they have agreed with the Fund may partly reflect such attitudes.[8] Again, programs may "fail" because of the supervention of exogenous disturbances that could not reasonably have been foreseen when the program was being prepared (although such contingencies can be accommodated by waivers and modifications of the original programs). But programs can also fail because they are not well conceived or because they place too great a burden on the efficacy of a few fiscal and monetary measures.

There is, in any case, The Dilemma of the Missing Alternative. It is easy to point to the limitation of demand management programs in the presence of large global disequilibria, but the type of adjust-

---

[8]Recent evidence suggests that about two fifths of the programs under stand-by arrangements are canceled prematurely, chiefly as a result of nonobservance of performance criteria, and that the performance criteria written into the original agreements are observed in less than a fourth of all programs. However, many of these deviations are covered by formal modifications or waivers by the Fund and almost all canceled programs are superseded by new programs.

ment that would be enforced by a policy of inaction would almost
certainly lead to even greater losses of output, consumption, and
employment. It is necessary, therefore, to establish that some more
cost-effective alternative is available. The World Bank and others
emphasize the need for structural adjustment and supply-side measures. Does this approach perhaps offer a cost-efficient alternative?

It was in this context that particular interest attached to Schydlowsky's treatment of alternatives to the demand management
approach. He was particularly concerned with formulating an alternative to general devaluations or currency depreciations, which
he saw as resulting in dysfunctional stagflationary and cost-raising
effects and as also tending to be self-defeating as organized labor
and other interest groups reacted to protect their real incomes.
He thus argued eloquently for a "differential devaluation" approach
targeted at the price-elastic segments of the supply curves of nontraditional export industries, raising capacity utilization and bringing goods that formerly were nontraded into the export trade. Such
forms of supply-led stabilization were advocated as minimizing
the costs often associated with conventional programs and as raising creditworthiness, hence permitting a longer period in which
to achieve the necessary results. Under such an approach, a Fund
stand-by arrangement might be geared specifically to supply measures, disaggregated into a few major sectors, with credit ceilings related to the *ex post* response of output—a major change from
the Fund's traditional programs. Doubts and reservations persist,
however.

For one thing, it seems that the differential devaluation approach
would be of less than general applicability. In particular, it appears
most relevant to conditions in the more industrialized developing
countries, which have a major industrial sector with a substantial
export potential. Second, the proposal was directed at only one
facet of conventional stabilization programs—general devaluation—
and hence only offered a partial alternative to the standard approach. Depending on its success in raising capacity utilization, a
differential devaluation would probably need to be supported by
reduced domestic absorption—that is, by rather orthodox fiscal and
monetary demand management measures. Moreover, the argument
for differential devaluation was presented in mainly theoretical
terms, which made it difficult to gauge its probable real world applicability and effectiveness.

Against these reservations may be cited the experiences of Indonesia (1967–70) and Bangladesh (1974–76), which have been claimed by Papanek[9] to be successful examples of expansionary stabilization, even though these countries were mainly exporters of primary products during the years in question. Certainly, these experiences and those of some Latin American countries provide valuable lessons in the potential of supply-led stabilization.[10] Of even greater potential interest is the World Bank's approach to conditionality in its new program of structural adjustment loans (World Bank, 1981 c). To restore creditworthiness and a viable payments situation, the Bank has adopted a relatively strict stance in this respect, requiring borrowing governments to commit themselves to a detailed and often wide-ranging medium-term program of measures largely directed toward increasing the production of tradable goods, which are then subject to fairly close and frequent monitoring by the Bank. This innovation is too recent to permit any conclusions about the results achieved, but the extent of its success will be watched carefully. It will also be interesting to discover whether the Bank's conditionality—which is arguably more demanding than the Fund's—will be better tolerated politically than the demand control programs of the Fund. The first signs are that it will be.

Quite apart from the content of specific supply-side approaches to adjustment, one of the recurring themes of the seminar discussions was the importance of not losing sight of the real wood among the financial trees. The problem was one that concerned levels and structures of production and demand rather than the refinements of financial intermediation. Perhaps the most important single task in attempts of non-oil developing countries to adjust their economies to worsened terms of trade was to sustain investment and to channel it in directions that would strengthen the balance of payments. It was thus crucial that payments financing should contribute to this. One of the underlying propositions of Schydlowsky's paper—and one that was not seriously contested—was that an adequate response on

---

[9]See contributions by Gustav Papanek in Cline and Weintraub (1981), pp. 233, 399–405 at 404.

[10]The structuralist/populist type of programs, as employed, for example, in Argentina and Chile, placed much emphasis on the improvement of capacity utilization and the breaking of supply bottlenecks, but the Killick and Sutton paper suggests that these were not stabilization programs as such.

the supply side might itself be prevented by shortages of imported inputs. In such cases, it would be essential to allocate foreign exchange in ways that would increase the productivity of existing capacity.

An emphasis on the use of financing to facilitate structural adjustment carries some major, if rather obvious, implications for various parties. The lesson for the governments of deficit countries is that they must ensure that payments financing is indeed devoted to productive uses rather than to raising or sustaining consumption standards. Demand management retains a central supporting role in a process of structural adjustment not only in limiting aggregate absorption but also in ensuring an efficient distribution of absorption between investment (broadly conceived) and consumption. The lesson for donor governments is that their aid programs must be designed to provide maximum relief to the recipients' balance of payments—which argues for shifts toward program lending and local-cost financing (including the use of aid to maintain existing infrastructure and supply existing productive capacity)—and that aid projects should be appraised with their contribution to payments adjustment in mind. There is also a lesson for the commercial banks that have been such important sources of financing for some non-oil developing countries. It was suggested that the banks tend to take only a pro forma interest in the actual use of their funds and that they should pay more attention to such uses, especially because the degree of wisdom with which the credits are utilized will have an important bearing on the future creditworthiness of the borrowing countries.

But what should be the thrust of structural adjustment programs? Specifically, what are the rival merits of export-led strategies and of approaches that focus on achieving greater domestic self-sufficiency? Familiar positions were taken in the discussions on this issue. Probably a majority of the participants were inclined to emphasize the potential positive effects of an open-economy approach and to draw attention to the past successes of a number of countries that have chosen this route. Others were skeptical of the extent to which such solutions could be generalized for the non-oil developing countries as a whole, both because of the limited potential for manufactures and other nontraditional exports in many of them and also because of the probability of saturating the market. What proved less controversial, however, was the proposition that the range of options open to non-oil developing countries was itself contingent on the amount and terms of financing available and on policies in the industrial countries. Unimproved flows of financing or high interest rates would not provide sufficient latitude for successful export promotion and import substitution, so that governments would, whether they desired it or not, be forced into deflation, exchange controls, and increased protection. Continuing stagnation in the OECD member countries, or an intensification by them of protective measures directed at nontraditional Third World exports, would push non-oil developing countries in the same direction.

That actions by the OECD countries have had negative effects on non-oil developing countries is one of the themes of Tew's paper. However, his view that they have imparted a deflationary bias to the world economy that, in turn, has had serious consequences for the fortunes of non-oil developing countries, did not go unchallenged. Tew himself described the evidence as somewhat anecdotal, and it was also pointed out that throughout the 1970s non-oil developing countries (and most subgroups within this category) continued to achieve rates of economic growth that were high by the standards of the nineteenth century industrial revolution. Some support was also expressed for the policy stance of a number of the major OECD member governments, on the grounds that their domestic attempts to reduce inflation offer the best hope of resuming the sustained growth in the economies of the West that would also be the most beneficial to non-oil developing countries.

If, indeed, the OECD group continues to give priority to bringing down inflation—and there is every sign that it will do so—then the predictions of the Fund that during the early 1980s the OECD member countries will achieve major improvements on current account while the deficits of the non-oil developing countries will worsen (see Table 1) are likely to prove correct. There would then be a world in which the OPEC group continued to run large surpluses, OECD members would also have substantial surpluses, and the non-oil developing countries would have very large current deficits. This prospect, as well as the present global payments situation, gave rise to some discussion of what would constitute a sensible pattern of surpluses and deficits. If the existence of some OPEC surpluses is taken as inevitable, given the difficulties of the low-absorption OPEC surplus countries in further accelerating their imports, does a situation in which all the counterpart deficits (plus the counterparts of any OECD surpluses) are borne by non-oil developing countries make economic sense?

The participants expressed two points of view on this. One was that developing countries needed to augment their own limited saving capacities by tapping the net savings (i.e., current account surpluses) of the oil exporting and industrial countries. There was therefore nothing alarming about the deficits of the non-oil developing countries as long as the financing was available in the forms and on the terms suited to the needs and capacities of the non-oil developing countries. There were echoes here of the earlier discussion on the concept of payments equilibrium in contemporary circumstances. A contrary argument was also expressed. If the world is looked at through bankers' eyes, the industrial countries are the most creditworthy, with many of the poorer non-oil developing countries being regarded as bad credit risks. The logic of this situation is that OECD member governments should pursue more expansionary policies and finance the resulting payments deficits through the Euromarket on the basis of their superior credit ratings. Such expansionary OECD policies would assist in a revival of world trade and make it easier for non-oil developing countries to overcome their deficits through an increase in exports. There are echoes here, too, of demands for "trade not aid."

Whichever of these two views is accepted, one is led to consider the adequacy of existing international monetary arrangements. In accepting the first argument, it is essential to form a judgment about the ability of international institutions to sustain the stable and dependable financial flows needed to support the deficits of non-oil developing countries. In accepting the second argument, it is important to ensure that the international monetary system could facilitate the global expansion envisaged. These arguments, therefore, lead to a survey of the range of views expressed by the seminar participants on the adequacy of present international monetary arrangements.

The adequacy of the system

In turning to the range of issues discussed, it is desirable to recall the distinction made earlier between positivist and normative concerns—the former concentrating on the allocative efficiency and stability of the international monetary system and the latter focusing on its distributional consequences. With the positivist approach, two issues tended to recur during the seminar: the state of health of the recycling process; and the problem of asymmetrical adjustment.

The Recycling Process. Many participants formed themselves roughly into pessimistic and optimistic camps. The most pessimistic position ran as follows. A large proportion of post-1973 recycling of surplus funds to non-oil developing countries was achieved through the intermediation of private banks, which have been in the intrinsically risky business of borrowing short and lending relatively long. For much of this period, they have had a surplus of OPEC deposits to invest, creating considerable competitive pressures to lend and resulting, perhaps, in less prudent lending than in former times. These factors, plus the standard criteria employed by banks in country risk analysis, led to a heavy concentration of claims in a small number of non-oil developing countries. In some degree, therefore, banks have found themselves in the familiar trap of having to offer fresh financing to the same favored few countries in order to safeguard their past commitments. They have also found themselves vulnerable to the possibility of default by one of the major borrowing countries, perhaps because of a political upheaval, and to the consequential dangers of banking collapses. Bankers must necessarily maintain a confident public front on such matters, but it was suggested that some do privately express concern "after the second martini." Moreover, bank lending has tended to be procyclical—lending to countries when prospects look good and trying to disengage from it when problems begin to emerge. On this view, then, there are serious questions about the stability of international banking, and the consequences of its failure could be enormous.

A less pessimistic position could be added to, or put in place of, the more pessimistic viewpoint, and it is one that finds some expression in Nowzad's paper. Even if there is no serious danger of a major banking failure, there are some doubts about the future willingness of the banks to sustain the pattern of recycling flows that they achieved so successfully in the 1970s. The new pattern of payments financing by the non-oil developing countries has led to a sharp deterioration in the maturities of their external debt and in the interest rates payable—rates which by 1981 had risen to historically very high levels with no assured prospect of much decline in real terms. Fears were expressed that in many non-oil developing countries the rates of return to investments and the export prospects were not sufficient to sustain continued large inflows of nonconcessional finance without undermining creditworthiness. The dangers of declining credit ratings and a consequent reduction in recycling flows to the main borrowing non-oil developing countries were all the greater because of the relative disinterest shown by the banks in the ways in which their credits were utilized by the governments in question.

Other participants (see, for example, O'Brien's paper) were optimistic about the market's ability to finance the deficits. Not only did the Euromarket respond very effectively to the challenges posed by the first oil shock, but predictions that it would be unable to sustain this role in response to the second shock have not been borne out by the lending figures for 1981. An increasingly wide range of banks are moving into recycling of surplus funds, and there is felt to be considerable scope for further expansion. True, an increasing number of countries are seeking debt rescheduling, but the machinery for dealing with such situations is in place and working better than was expected. While new bank commitments resulting from rescheduling are probably regarded by the banks as less attractive than their original claims and pose awkward accounting problems, there is nothing calamitous about rescheduling as such.

While it is true that there is a heavy concentration of bank claims in a small number of non-oil developing countries, in all cases such claims are modest in relation to total bank assets. It was suggested that the banks need to be more watchful over the economic prospects of, say, Italy or Spain than of Argentina or Korea. Moreover, national central banks now recognize the need for greater supervision of international lending, so that there is more effective regulation today than in the mid-1970s. So much is at stake that national monetary authorities would do everything in their power to avoid a major banking collapse. In short, in this view no imminent breakdown is in prospect; international bankers—and their depositors—can still sleep easily.

Readers can make their own choice between pessimism and optimism. Most observers would probably agree that there are potential dangers in the situation, that these call for vigilance, and that strengthened central bank supervision is thus to be welcomed. What was certainly agreed by the seminar participants—and is spelled out explicitly at the end of O'Brien's paper—is that banking flows will do little to meet the payments financing needs of quite a large number of developing countries—generally the poorer ones—

that have low credit ratings and hence limited access to the private market. This point is discussed again below.

Asymmetries and Codes of Conduct. Although it is of probably greater fundamental importance to the efficient operation of world economic arrangements, what has to be said about asymmetries and codes of conduct can be put briefly. That there is an asymmetry of adjustment burdens is a frequently criticized feature of postwar arrangements. A disproportionate share of the burden falls on deficit countries and, because they generally have to respond by measures to restrain domestic demand, this tends to slow down the overall growth of the world economy. The "scarce currency" clause in the Fund's Articles of Agreement (Article VII, Sections 2 and 3) has never been used to bring effective pressure on persistent surplus countries, such as the Federal Republic of Germany and Japan in the 1960s, and international attempts to induce these countries to reduce the global imbalances they were creating proved singularly fruitless.

The pattern in the post-1973 period is somewhat different. The nouveau riche group of OPEC surplus countries have not been open to the criticism of pursuing excessively restrictive policies; they have, in fact, increased their imports enormously but even so have experienced a great deal of inflation. Once again, the deflationary bias has emanated from the ways in which OECD member countries have reacted and the *de facto* effect this has had of shifting more of the deficit burden to the non-oil developing countries.

This is a familiar tale, but what can be done about it? It cannot be claimed that any startling new solutions were presented at the seminar, but there was a call for a new international code of conduct that was impressive in coming from speakers located at widely differing points on the spectrum of opinion. There was a suggestion that the Fund's Articles needed a third amendment to include some new rules and to give the Fund more effective powers of surveillance over the policies of surplus countries. The case was also made for providing more continuous guidance to deficit countries on adjustment policies and for linking the policy conditions for Fund credit to past performance in implementing these guidelines.

Normative Aspects. Here, too, coverage can be brief but perhaps for regrettable reasons. Reference has already been made to the ways in which the international monetary system and the post-1973 pattern of global disequilibria impinge on the international distribution of income and wealth. There has also been recorded in the discussions a general acceptance that the developing countries of Africa and elsewhere are in danger of suffering gravely from the existing world situation. For reasons such as these, many argue that international monetary reform should be seen as a way of redressing the tendencies toward even greater international disparities.

Bird's paper admirably summarizes the pros and cons of the chief proposals on the agenda for using reform as a way of securing resource transfers to the Third World, but these received little systematic attention during the seminar. The discussion of concrete reforms mainly concerned the future role of the Fund, and this is an apt topic on which to conclude because it encapsulates the contrasting attitudes expressed at the seminar.

Role of the Fund. Uncertainty about the part the Fund should play in the contemporary world situation not only underlay many of the deliberations at the seminar, but is also apparent in the attitudes of Fund member governments. Without wanting to place too heavy a weight on the positive/normative distinction, it is possible to interpret some of the differences of view in this way. A positivist is inclined to want the Fund to develop in the direction of a world central bank. It should be able to exert some control over changes in the world supply of money, conduct surveillance over international banking activities, and have influence over national economic policies. It should act as a lender of last resort (although to national governments rather than to banks), and it should be properly firm in the conditionality it attaches to its credits, so that other financial institutions can have some assurance that establishment of a Fund program will restore a country's debt servicing capacity. It should not become a development agency—an instrument for the transfer of resources to developing countries—and the traditional division of responsibilities between it and the World Bank should thus be maintained.

The normative position, on the other hand, points out that there is no way in which the Fund's actions can be distributionally neutral either within or between countries. In one sense, the positivists have already lost in their attempts to keep the monetary role of the Fund sharply separate from the development aid role of the World Bank. Much of the Fund's credit is at concessional interest rates and much of it is tailored specifically to meet the needs of developing countries. The compensatory financing facility, the former Trust Fund, interest subsidy arrangements, and other provisions have all in practice blurred the monetary and aid distinction, even though formal differences remain. So, even more fundamentally, does the Fund's shift toward longer-term credits in support of programs of structural adjustment blur this distinction, even though the Fund's approach to structural adjustment is much less thorough than that of the World Bank. There are important senses in which the Fund is already in the business of concessional resource transfers and development financing, albeit through the medium of balance of payments support. But there has been a reluctance to recognize explicitly the significance of the changes that have occurred, and there is a danger, therefore, of satisfying neither the Group of Ten industrial countries nor the Group of Twenty-Four developing countries. A more open recognition of the situation would, among other things, help the Fund more fully to change the substance of its conditionality (especially the performance criteria) toward supply-side measures and to take the impact of its programs on development aspirations more completely into account than has traditionally been the practice.

The existing uncertainties about how the Fund should fit into the world economy were vividly conveyed by one participant, who had this to say:

> ... we do not yet seem to have made up our minds as to the social role that we are expecting the Fund to perform. It is clear that the Fund does not play the role of *banker*, for bankers lend only to those who they are sure can repay, i.e., those who do not really need the money, whereas we expect the Fund to lend to those who do need money. Richard O'Brien likens the Fund in his paper to a *policeman*, keeping the world safe for banks by punishing the irresponsible. The left sees the Fund as a *teacher*, aiming to inculcate a set of values that will make the young into respectable members of the international bourgeoisie. UNCTAD argues that the Fund should act as a *social worker*, caring for those left stranded by the tide of economic change. The Fund itself seems to regard its role as that of a *doctor*, with the duty of curing the sick. One may get sick because one does something silly, or because of bad luck, but the cure is the same in either event. The cure is a matter of objective fact, not of subjective opinion. And a cure usually requires taking some nasty medicine, and perhaps giving up some bad habits; the doctor's duty is to force these unpleasant actions on the patient. The cure is likely to be less unpleasant if the patient reports in good time.

In the end, however, perhaps the most perceptive description of all was provided by another participant but in a different forum.

Viewing the Fund in a broad context, Pennant-Rea (1981, p. 7) saw it as in search of a role:

> Through no fault of its own, the IMF has lost some of its clearcut functions. Once the ministry responsible for the world's monetary system, it now resembles a ministry without portfolio—frequently assured of its importance, in practice unsure of itself.

Few of the key issues of international monetary reform in a world of massive disequilibria will be satisfactorily resolved until those who control the destinies of the Fund, and the international monetary system as a whole, can make up their minds to give it a portfolio with unambiguous terms of reference. By allowing the relative value of Fund quotas to decline, the Group of Ten industrial countries appear in the past to have signified a reluctance to assign to the Fund a more powerful financial role. As long as the industrial countries do not need to use the Fund's financial resources, it is unlikely that the Fund will be able to exert any real control over conduct of the national economic policies of these countries. As Tew's paper stresses, the preferences of the Group of Ten predominate in major decisions (although the influence and veto powers of the Third World countries are growing, especially those of the OPEC group). The well-publicized advocacy by the U.S. authorities in 1981 of firmer adjustment policies by countries provides only the most recent example of this. Ultimately, international power politics will decide these issues, as it has decided many others in the past. Nevertheless, it is to be hoped that all major country groups will see it as being in their long-term interests to give the Fund an enhanced role in international monetary arrangements.

REFERENCES

Bank for International Settlements (BIS), Monetary and Economic Department, *International Banking Developments* (First Quarter, 1981).

Cline, William R., and Sidney Weintraub, eds., *Economic Stabilization in Developing Countries*, Brookings Institution (Washington, 1981).

Connors, Thomas A., "The Apparent Effects of Recent IMF Stabilization Programs," Federal Reserve System International Finance Discussion Paper No. 136 (Washington, April 1979).

International Monetary Fund (1981 a), *World Economic Outlook: A Survey by the Staff of the International Monetary Fund*, IMF Occasional Paper No. 4 (Washington, July 1981).

—— (1981 b), *Annual Report of the Executive Board for the Financial Year Ended April 30, 1981* (Washington, 1981).

Killick, Tony, "Eurocurrency Market Recycling of OPEC Surpluses to Developing Countries: Fact or Myth?" in *The EEC and the Third World: Survey*, ed. by Christopher Stevens (London, 1981), pp. 92–118. The article is also reproduced in *The Banker*. See "Euromarket Recycling of OPEC Surpluses: Fact or Myth?" *The Banker* (January 1981), pp. 15–23.

Nowzad, Bahram, and Richard C. Williams, *et al, External Indebtedness of Developing Countries*, IMF Occasional Paper No. 3 (Washington, May 1981).

Organization for Economic Cooperation and Development (OECD), *OECD Economic Outlook*, No. 29 (Paris, July 1981).

Pennant-Rea, Rupert, "Ministry Without Portfolio: A Survey of the International Monetary Fund," *Economist*, Vol. 280 (September 26, 1981), pp. 1–36 of special section following page 54.

Stanyer, P.W., and J. A. Whitley, "Financing World Payments Imbalances," *Bank of England Quarterly Bulletin*, Vol. 21 (June 1981), pp. 187–99.

World Bank, *World Development Report, 1980* (Washington, 1980).

_____ (1981 a), *World Development Report, 1981* (Washington, 1981).

_____ (1981 b), *Accelerated Development in Sub-Saharan Africa: An Agenda for Action* (Oxford University Press, 1981).

_____ (1981 c), "Structural Adjustment Program," Background Note for the Press (December 7, 1981).

Disequilibria, Financing, and Adjustment in Developing Countries

TONY KILLICK AND MARY SUTTON[1]

This paper is intended as an introduction to the subject matter of the seminar and as background for the more specialized contributions that follow. It should be read in conjunction with the first part of the overview chapter, which provides factual background material that was originally part of this paper. Salient facts established there include the large nature of present-day payments disequilibria and adjustment problems; the largely exogenous nature of non-oil developing countries' difficulties and their deteriorating external debt and net reserve positions; the decline in growth rates of non-oil developing countries in the 1970s and the probability that foreign exchange shortages will increasingly be the binding constraint in the 1980s; the accelerating inflation in the non-oil developing countries and the widening gap between their inflation rates and those of industrial countries; the importance of disaggregating the non-oil developing countries as a group; and the special vulnerability of low-income countries.

The first section of this paper is concerned with the desirable balance between the financing of payments deficits and their elimination through stabilization programs and with the obstacles to achieving this balance. It suggests that the latter are considerable

---

[1]The authors are Research Officers of the Overseas Development Institute, London, engaged in a research project on the policy of the Fund in regard to economic stabilization in developing countries. The paper draws on materials prepared for the project.

and involve major conflicts of national objectives among various country groupings, but it doubts the practicability of adjustment, however desirable it may be. The second section draws on Latin American experiences to sketch various responses of governments to disequilibria and discusses difficulties associated with alternative policy approaches. While policy responses should be viewed as a continuum, three stylized types are selected to illustrate the range of options—namely, conventional, new orthodox, and structuralist/populist responses. Also discussed is the issue of the politics of stabilization programs. The final section suggests some directions for seeking solutions, in an attempt to compensate for the negative tone of the preceding sections.

SOLUTIONS TO PAYMENTS DISEQUILIBRIA: FINANCING AND ADJUSTMENT

Many non-oil developing countries are experiencing payments difficulties that are likely to persist at least for several years and that threaten their long-term development aspirations. To a substantial extent, the imbalances are due to world forces beyond the control or influence of the deficit countries and are best considered as an international problem, although they may be compounded by domestic failures to come to terms with the hostile world environment of today. In considering possible lines of action, there is first the question of the balance and relationship between the financing of deficits and the adjustment of domestic economies in order to reduce payments deficits.

Complementarity of financing and adjustment

Let us start from what is called the standard position—that what is needed is a judicious blend of financing and adjustment, which should be seen as complementary to each other—but then let us go on to suggest certain complicating factors. This standard position can be summarized in the following propositions.

1. Since the deficits are neither temporary nor self-reversing, financing is not a long-term solution. A policy of financing without adjustment will rather quickly result in a very large external debt, with a heavy burden of debt servicing, and will erode creditworthiness. Adjustment is therefore inescapable, and those coun-

tries that act most effectively are also the most likely to attract capital inflows. Adjustment involves reducing absorption in relation to income in order to accommodate the global changes in the distribution of income resulting from higher real oil prices. It also involves the restructuring of domestic demand and supply so as to promote exports and import substitutes—i.e., tradable goods vis-à-vis nontradable goods. To an even greater extent than ever before, economic management and development policies need to be blended into a single strategy.

2. This type of result cannot be secured quickly, however. Structural adjustment can only be achieved over several years, which is essentially why it must become part of the development effort. Large-scale resource shifts are involved, but these generally have to be achieved by a succession of marginal changes (e.g., investment in any one year is only a small proportion of the preexisting capital stock); and elasticities are larger in the long term than in the short term.

3. Large-scale financing is thus also needed to tide over developing countries in the interim period and to provide a breathing space during which the necessary policies can be executed and have their effects. The costs of adjustment constitute the foremost balance of payments problem—i.e., the costs to short-term living standards and employment, to longer-term development, and perhaps to social and political stability. The virtue of financing is that it helps to minimize these adjustment costs.[2] The task is to marry adjustment and economic development—and to permit enough time for a successful courtship.

National objectives versus international adjustment?

In considering the application of these propositions, a number of complications arise, however. In particular, it is questionable whether the national objectives of the parties involved are consistent with achieving the blend of financing and adjustment just described.

---

[2]If a country has to save, say $10 million in foreign exchange, it can do so through demand management by reducing the demand for imports by this amount. If so, it must reduce demand by a multiple of $10 million, depending on the size of the foreign trade multiplier. Alternatively, if it can borrow the $10 million, it can leave domestic demand and incomes untouched, at least in the short run (cf. Krueger, 1978, p. 240).

Let us consider first the objectives of the major surplus countries, chiefly the "low-absorption" members of the Organization of Petroleum Exporting Countries (OPEC). The overriding objective of these countries is to invest their surpluses in a portfolio of fairly liquid assets that will yield a positive real rate of return or will at least avoid any erosion of real asset values. They have turned especially to the Euromarket to achieve these objectives. In an inflationary world, positive real rates of return mean high nominal interest rates, which in turn may generate debt servicing difficulties for countries willing and able to borrow extensively from the Euromarket. As has often been the case in the past, debt problems tend to lead to payments crises and the dangers of default.[3]

Any large-scale recycling of OPEC surpluses in support of structural adjustment in non-oil developing countries has to surmount the twin obstacles (a) that many of the deficit countries do not offer investment opportunities that would satisfy the rate-of-return objectives of surplus countries and their banking intermediaries (without subsidization of interest rates), and (b) that, in any case, it is difficult to reconcile the long-term nature of investments in structural change with the liquidity objectives of the surplus countries and their banks. What in deficit countries is seen as a recycling problem is seen in surplus countries as an investment decision, and these two perceptions have different implications for allocations. The two might be reconciled by means of development assistance, but while aid from OPEC did accelerate markedly in 1973–75 it has since declined by a third in real terms.[4] Current OPEC aid is only a small fraction (5.6 per cent in 1980) of its aggregate current surplus, and in the past little of this aid has gone to non-Arab countries.

Second, there is the question of objectives within the non-oil developing countries themselves, some of which have been slow to react to the radical implications of the successive oil shocks. Among industrial countries and non-oil developing countries alike, there is

---

[3]Krueger (1978, p. 135 and *passim*) emphasizes the role of debt in payments crises. Similarly, the Fund identifies debt servicing problems as among the most frequently recurring sources of the payments problems of the countries with which it negotiates stand-by credits (cf. Killick, 1981 a, Table 3).

[4]According to a press release of June 15, 1981 by the Organization for Economic Cooperation and Development, the total nominal value of OPEC aid (net disbursements) increased by 27 per cent in 1975–80. In the same period, import prices in the developing countries rose by 86 per cent on average (OECD, 1981, Table 58), implying a 32 per cent fall in the real value of OPEC aid (see Overseas Development Institute, 1980).

a strong case for the proposition that, in the absence of policy conditionality, governments generally use access to financing as a substitute for corrective measures rather than as an input into the adjustment process. The Organization for Economic Cooperation and Development (OECD) has complained of this misuse by its own member states, and the International Bank for Reconstruction and Development (World Bank, 1981 b, Table 6.2) has provided clear evidence of an inverse correlation between access to finance and structural adjustment in non-oil developing countries. Balassa (1981) also found that countries such as the Philippines and Morocco used access to the Euromarket and other sources to postpone necessary domestic measures. Black (in Cline and Weintraub, 1981) has drawn attention to asymmetrical reactions to external forces in the non-oil developing countries' monetary policies. Thus, these countries made little attempt to offset the expansionary effects of the 1972–73 commodity boom by restraint of domestic credit, whereas they did attempt to correct for the contractionary effects of the first oil shock. The Fund (IMF, 1981, p. 48) has reported that in 1979–80 a majority of non-oil developing countries pursued expansionary financial policies despite payments deficits—i.e., policies that the Fund regarded as overexpansionary in many cases.

That governments often appear to attach a low priority to economic stabilization is also strikingly illustrated by the use to which they put the proceeds of the windfall gains resulting from the commodity booms of 1974–78. Studying the cocoa and coffee booms, Davis (1980) found that nearly all the exporting countries obtained increased foreign exchange receipts that were exceptional even by the standards of the volatile markets for those commodities. While formal or informal tax systems in these countries were quite effective in preventing much of the windfall gain from accruing to the producers, virtually all the governments were quick to spend the extra revenue, often on hastily conceived projects that bore little relationship to the needs for structural adjustment, even though the first oil shock had already occurred and it was manifestly clear that the commodity prices could not for long remain at the exceptional heights they had reached in 1976–77. In consequence, there was a rapid expansion in money supply and imports, and by 1978 the reserve position of most of the countries was no better than before the commodity boom. The World Bank (1981 b, p. 74) reached similar conclusions on the basis of a wider range of commodities and, therefore, of exporting countries. They also found a tendency for governments to borrow externally when the commodity boom ended in order to maintain government spending at its new higher levels so that, perversely, the boom often left countries in a weaker payments position at the end than they had been in at the beginning. Covering a wide range of non-oil developing countries—straddling all the major regions of the Third World and a wide variety of country experiences—these studies point to a general tendency for governments to opt for quick spending in preference to longer-term stabilization.

It is precisely for reasons of this kind that the Fund—and now the World Bank, in connection with its structural adjustment program (World Bank, 1981 a)—insists on relatively tight conditionality and "rigorous adjustment policies" (IMF, 1981, p. 18), reflecting a fear that governments will not use the financing to promote payments adjustment unless required to do so by policy conditions. Underlying such a perceived necessity is a conflict of objectives, priorities, and time horizons between the international agencies and the borrowing governments. Many of the latter place only secondary weight on stabilization as such, partly because they fear that in practice stabilization programs impede development rather than promote it—a fear for which there is supporting evidence.[5] Perhaps even more influential is a fear of what the execution of a stabilization program will do to a government's popularity in sociopolitical situations often marked by instability—another fear that may be well founded.

Third, it must be doubted whether the objectives and actions of certain Western industrial nations are consistent with the global achievement of a mutually reinforcing mix of financing and adjustment in the non-oil developing countries. Most OECD member governments are placing the highest priority on reducing domestic inflation, with adverse consequences for the expansion of world trade

[5]Killick (1981 a) cites work by Fund staff members and others showing that the model underlying the Fund's emphasis on credit ceilings has contributed to a neglect of the adverse consequences of its stabilization programs for economic growth. He also suggests that the Fund has found difficulty in translating into practice its intellectual recognition of the changing nature of payments adjustment policies so as to match them better with development efforts.

and for the export prospects of the non-oil developing countries. There is also the apparent view of at least the U.S. and U.K. Governments that proposals for increased flows of financing to developing countries represent global—and inflationary—Keynesianism and that the strengthening of their domestic economies must take precedence over increased development aid, which has been substantially cut in these countries.[6] By means such as these, industrial countries have succeeded in shifting more of the deficits that are the counterpart of OPEC surpluses from themselves to developing countries, thus imparting a deflationary bias to the global economy (see Brian Tew's paper). Such responses by the industrial world will undoubtedly reduce the prospects of both adequate financing and adjustment in developing countries. Emphasis by those governments on the efficiency of private capital markets in recycling surpluses neglects the skewed distribution of access to such markets mentioned earlier, the probable difficulties of sustaining the financial flows in the 1980s (but see Richard O'Brien's paper), and the unsuitability of much of this capital for the financing of long-term structural investments.

It seems, then, that there are not only conflicts between the objectives of the three major country groupings but also that in each case these objectives are not consistent with the execution of the standard position with which this paper began. The kernel of the matter seems to be that a problem essentially international in character is being confronted by objectives and policies concerned more with short-term national (or special interest) gains. But even if the will existed, would the required adjustment be feasible?

Is adjustment feasible?

There is first the logic of double-entry bookkeeping: so long as payments surpluses are earned by one group of countries, then

---

[6]The United Kingdom (1980) argued, in response to the proposals of the Report of the Independent Commission on International Development Issues (Brandt, 1980) that improvements in the U.K. domestic economic situation must take precedence over such considerations as the desirability of increasing aid, which "must bear a share in public spending cuts" (present expenditure intentions would lower the ratio of aid to gross national product from 0.51 per cent in 1979 to between 0.3 per cent and 0.4 per cent in 1983/84). It looked to the private sector to play the major role in recycling surpluses to developing countries and rejected suggestions for loan guarantees and interest subsidies as "an unacceptable extension of the state role into the realm of private banking."

equivalent deficits will be recorded by the rest of the world.[7] Since there is an obvious connection between the large increase in the deficits of non-oil developing countries and the oil shocks of 1974–75 and 1979–80, a large proportion of these deficits should be regarded as the counterpart of the OPEC surpluses (Dell and Lawrence, 1980). Since the non-oil developing countries as a group are not in a position to shift this counterpart deficit to the industrial countries, it follows that while there are OPEC surpluses it is logically impossible for the counterpart deficits to be eliminated. Viewing the non-oil developing countries as a group, to tell them to adjust is to tell them to achieve the impossible, although this is not true of any country taken singly. Focus on individual adjustment programs carries the danger of competitive attempts by some countries to shift "their share" of the collective deficit to other non-oil developing countries by means that may slow their own growth and, if successful, may so worsen the payments positions of the remainder that their economies are also pushed into stagnation. It is tempting to derive from these considerations the policy inference that there is, after all, an economic case for large-scale and long-term financing as an alternative to shorter-term adjustment, although this statement is qualified below.

There are, in any case, doubts about whether the composition and dynamics of world trade are such as to permit the type of adjustment that was set out earlier. On reasonable assumptions about real oil prices, an eventual elimination of global disequilibria requires a much increased absorption of imports by the OPEC surplus countries. Not only are there obvious limits to the speed with which this might be accomplished but also much the larger proportion of the additional imports demanded is likely to be supplied by OECD countries rather than by non-oil developing countries.[8] The main hope of the latter is to take advantage of the increased import capacity of OECD members by selling more to them, but there are obvious difficulties with such a strategy: (1) the relatively low price and

---

[7]This is not exactly true, of course, because of certain timing asymmetries, as well as errors and omissions, but it is true in substance.

[8]For example, in 1973–78 the value of imports into Saudi Arabia increased between ninefold and tenfold. During that period the import share of developing market economies fell from 33.4 per cent to 13.7 per cent and the import share of developed market economies rose from 63.7 per cent to 80.9 per cent (United Nations, 1979, pp. 829–30).

income elasticities of demand for many primary products, and (2) the resistance to larger imports of developing countries' manufactured consumer goods, of which the "new protectionism" (IMF, 1978) is a symptom and which will be reinforced by higher rates of unemployment in some industrial countries. The structural adjustment required within the industrial world to the emerging international division of labor may not move far enough and fast enough to accommodate the structural changes required in developing countries (another variation on the theme of inconsistent objectives). Commenting on the strategy of export-led adjustment and development, which he takes to be favored by the Fund and others, Brett (1979, p. 8) carries this view considerably further:

> This strategy could, in fact, be successfully practiced by a few countries or, more likely, by a few favoured regions within them. But it could not be generalised to the mass of the world's population, precisely because the success of these regions would be based upon their ability to subordinate the markets of the rest to the domination of their more advanced productive capacity.... For the rest it must be more austerity, fewer social services, less favourable employment opportunities, and greater inequalities for as far ahead as anyone can hope to predict.

This analysis perhaps rests on too static a view of the world economy, but the difficulties are compounded by the technical and political obstacles to successful adjustment policies surveyed in the next section. Conventional approaches have severe limitations, but a satisfactory alternative has yet to be demonstrated, and political considerations underscore the difficulties, as will be argued shortly. Moreover, the very difficulties of the non-oil developing countries may make feasible solutions all the harder to find.

On the other hand, a policy of inaction is simply not viable. More effective energy policies could reduce the deficits. Depending on country circumstances, there may also be some scope for reducing other imports without severe consequences for productivity and development.

However, it is suspected that much of this slack was taken up by the first oil shock and subsequent events—a suspicion that helps to explain why growth in the non-oil developing countries slowed to the extent that it did in the second half of the 1970s. Particularly if international financing is not available, governments are tempted, perhaps forced, to suppress their payments problems with exchange controls which, however, lead to worse results (Little *et al*, 1970, p. 330):

Sooner or later, all the countries which experienced balance of payments difficulties ... ran out of inessential imports which could be restricted. They then realised that measures to increase exports *must* be used as otherwise essential imports would have to be cut very severely with disastrous effects on domestic output, consumption and investment. Hence, even those countries using import controls had, in the end, to keep their balance of payments in equilibrium by a combination of devaluation ... deflation and foreign borrowing. The only major difference between them and other countries was that they had to maintain this balance in a situation in which their economic structures had been distorted by the existence of severe import restrictions ... this can only have made the task of reconciling growth with balance of payments equilibrium subsequently more difficult.

And if the economic problems are worsened, so too will be the political dangers.

In the absence of financing, adjustment eventually takes place through import compression. But this is likely to be a particularly high-cost form of adjustment, and it is thus desirable for governments to retain a degree of control over the economic fortunes of their countries by adopting policies consciously designed to accomplish the needed changes. But what, in this case, is the range of stabilization measures open to governments? Drawing primarily on Latin American experiences, let us next survey the ways in which governments have responded to disequilibria.

Alternative Responses to Disequilibria

Objectives and program types

Reverting to the standard position with which this paper began, the rationale for adjustment programs can be simply stated. Existing policies are not sustainable because the balance of payments deficit cannot be financed much longer by running down reserves or by borrowing; the deficit signifies a loss of balance in the economy; corrective measures are necessary in order to restore equilibrium. The progression from a nonviable position to a new sustainable equilibrium will involve some combination of stabilization through reductions in aggregate demand and structural adaptation.

Abstracting from the impact of any policy conditions that may be attached to payments assistance, two factors are likely to weigh particularly heavily in the chosen combination of demand restraint and structural change. Time horizons are of crucial importance, to which the availability of finance will obviously contribute. In principle at least, aggregate demand can be cut quite quickly, whereas structural adjustment requires more time. Clearly, in situations of acute payments crises or where hyperinflation is seriously distorting the allocation of resources, a higher priority is imposed on the stabilization objective, and there is little alternative to quick action. An analysis of the domestic sources of payments difficulties is the second key factor, on the principle that adjustment costs are likely to be minimized if the policy responses are directed at the causes: responses to excess demand with supply-side measures or to supply bottlenecks with monetary curbs are both likely to be high-cost responses. Even in crisis situations, however, equilibrium remains a complex and elusive concept, easier to recognize by its absence than to define precisely.[9] While progress toward equilibrium may be assessed by monitoring performance against targets related to one or two payments indicators and to financial aggregates such as domestic credit, such tests lend an air of precision to the adjustment exercise that tends to obscure the complexity of the objective, that it is pursued in a dynamic context, and that the degree of control over the key variables is highly imperfect. In the more usual cases, where the need for adjustment is recognized but the disequilibrium is of less critical proportions, stabilization remains one goal among several. The objective then is to restore approximate stability with the minimum sacrifice of other government objectives.

Depending, then, on the time factor and the analysis of the domestic causes of the problem, as well as on their predilections and priorities, government responses to disequilibria may be viewed as ranged along a spectrum. It may be useful for present purposes to select a few examples to illustrate the range of choice and the differentiating characteristics.[10] However, since responses to disequilibria represent a continuum and in practice never fall entirely into any "pure" model, the cases presented are inevitably arbitrary and are intended largely for expositional purposes. At one end is what

---

[9]Killick (1981 b, p. 16), for example, suggests the following definition: "Balance of payments equilibrium exists when, in a normal year, the basic balance (or that balance chosen as most appropriate for the country in question) approximates zero in conditions where: there are no major unwanted restrictions on trade and payments; external debts and debt servicing are not regarded as too large; foreign exchange reserves are regarded as adequate; and the equilibrium does not depend on the maintenance of unwantedly deflationary domestic policies."

[10]The following is largely based on materials presented in Sutton (1981).

may be termed a conventional package of policies of the type traditionally associated with the Fund. The key characteristics of this
type are, first, that the objective is seen as essentially a short-term
one, usually the resolution of an immediate payments problem; second, the chief instruments employed are exchange rate adjustments
and the traditional demand management techniques of fiscal and
monetary policy. At the other end of the spectrum are responses
that emphasize the restructuring of the economy as the chief means,
or as a precondition, of sustained stability. And among those who
emphasize structural change, two further quite distinct schools can
be identified.

The first, the so-called new orthodox school, stresses the need to
supplement conventional demand management policies with trade
and financial reforms viewed as essential in order to avoid the continuing recurrence of high inflation and balance of payments problems. These programs are often part of a total economic strategy
designed to move the economy in a laissez-faire direction. The second school—the so-called structuralist/populist response—sees the
removal of structural supply bottlenecks in the economy as a prerequisite for stability. The causes of the disequilibria are diagnosed
as resulting from resource immobility, market segmentation, and
disequilibria between sectoral demands and supplies, which cause
bottlenecks in the supply of foreign exchange, intermediate inputs,
domestic saving, or food production. In these cases, structural and
institutional changes do not supplement conventional demand management policies. They are rather themselves supplemented, at
least in the short run, by measures such as price and import controls
designed to contain the immediate problem while the longer-term
restructuring is achieved.

Conventional stabilization programs seek to restore the economy
to a course from which it has been jolted. The payments disequilibrium is viewed as threatening progress toward other goals, and
stabilization is therefore likely to be accorded high priority, with
the primary emphasis on demand restraint. In the cases of new
orthodox and structuralist/populist responses, structural adjustment is accorded top priority as a prerequisite for sustained
stability.

Next, let us look at some of the implications of the differing
priorities attached to structural adjustment and demand management in the three stylized types of policy response.

Conventional responses

In many respects the capacity to correct a payments imbalance is positively related to the level of development. Conditions such as the immobility of resources or the inelasticity of the foreign trade sector, which are common characteristics of developing countries, may mean that restoring equilibrium will necessitate a relatively larger decline in economic activity in countries that have achieved a lower level of development. Even when the payments problem is the result of excess demand, the traditional correctives of reducing the fiscal deficit and curbing the growth of domestic credit may exact a price in terms of reduced output that appears disproportionate to the gain.

The scope for controlling government deficits and the money supply tends to be more limited in developing countries.[11] Fiscal systems typically lack the built-in stabilizers that help to make fiscal deficits countercyclical in industrial countries. Opportunities for changing the tax base and the tax rates are likely to be restricted, at least in the short run, owing to poverty or limited administrative capacity. The difficulties of raising revenues may force reductions in government expenditure, but it will be easier to cut back on investment projects than on current expenditure, possibly with serious implications for long-term development.

The underdeveloped nature of financial institutions and the openness of developing countries' economies limits the scope for controlling credit and the money supply. The range of instruments available to policymakers is restricted. Of the three components of the monetary base, only central bank credit to the commercial banks is typically used as an active policy instrument, and it tends to be a more potent instrument for expanding, rather than contracting, domestic credit. Of the other components, net foreign assets fluctuate with the balance of payments, while central bank credit to the government is often adjusted passively to the deficit finance requirements of the treasury. The potential instruments of monetary policy are, therefore, open market operations, variations of bank reserve requirements, official regulation of interest rates, and ceilings on bank credit. The usefulness of open market operations is

---

[11]This issue is fully explored in Sharpley (1981), on which the following brief discussion is based.

limited by the underdeveloped nature of the organized capital market, while official interest rates are pegged in most developing countries and are not used as an instrument of monetary control. The range of available policy instruments is therefore reduced to the manipulation of reserve requirements and the less frequently employed direct ceilings on commercial bank credit. The difficulty of controlling monetary aggregates is often further exacerbated by large short-term variations in the money multiplier.

These features of developing countries' economies have prompted misgivings about the appropriateness of conventional stabilization policies in developing countries, and the impact of the 1973–74 and 1979–80 oil price rises on the payments positions of non-oil developing countries has rekindled the debate about the cost-effectiveness of conventional programs. In circumstances where exogenous factors, such as a fall in world demand for exports or a rise in import prices, were significant contributory causes of the disequilibrium, adjustment by means of demand restraint alone would be a high-cost strategy. As suggested by the standard position described earlier, the optimum strategy would be some combination of demand restraint and structural adaptation, with access to financing largely determining the type of combination and the speed of the necessary adjustment.

Both the more limited scope of traditional demand management policy instruments and the importance of exogenous factors as contributory causes of non-oil developing countries' payments imbalances argue for the use of a wider range of policy instruments and the lengthening of the adjustment period. The Fund has been explicit in recognizing this argument and in recent years has sought a greater mix of demand management and supply-oriented measures in its programs, chiefly through its extended facility. However, the Fund has not found this a very successful experiment, and even the Fund's extended facility still concentrates largely on demand restraint (Killick, 1981 a).

Both of the other two stylized types of policy response could be viewed as attempting to redress limitations of the conventional approach. In the case of the new orthodox programs, a notable feature is the emphasis on improving the potential scope of traditional demand management instruments, particularly monetary instruments, while structuralist/populist programs concentrate on the supply side of the economy.

New orthodox programs

In new orthodox programs the short-term stabilization objective is pursued in tandem with the longer-term aim of moving the economy in a laissez-faire direction. Short-term policy relies heavily on the use of monetary, rather than fiscal, instruments while the longer-term objective is pursued through measures designed to reduce the size of the public sector, increase the efficiency of product and factor markets, and open the economy to trade and foreign capital. The dictates of the long-term objective tend to preclude the use of many policy instruments. For example, the commitment to increasing the efficiency of product markets rules out the use of price controls, opening up to foreign trade involves reduction of import controls, while reducing the size of the public sector precludes the use of public investment as a countercyclical tool. Moreover, the timing of financial, trade, and exchange rate reforms may have perverse consequences for short-run stabilization.

Financial reforms are introduced with a view to increasing the scope of monetary policy and promoting investment. Financial depression, indicated by negative real interest rates in the organized money market, is viewed as exacerbating the structural weakness of developing countries' economies and contributing to persistent disequilibria. Financial liberalization is designed to raise the real rate of interest in order to stimulate saving and to increase the share of reserves deposited in financial institutions. Such reforms may include the imposition of competitive conditions on the banking system, removal of interest rate ceilings, and narrowing of the spread between bank lending and deposit rates. Profitable investment opportunities are assumed to exist at the higher interest rates, but they discriminate efficiently between investments promising high or low rates of return. The financial reforms are intended to reduce excess demand for credit and to lower the average cost of borrowing for working capital and physical investment. Since interest rates in the organized capital market are typically lower than in the unorganized (curb or informal) market, both the volume and average cost of investment are expected to benefit as financial intermediation is extended and the informal market is formalized. Financial liberalization might be expected to lessen the adjustment costs associated with reducing instability, since the expansion of investment and aggregate supply would minimize the burden placed on the restriction of aggregate demand.

Although the favorable experiences of countries such as Korea are commonly cited, the histories of other countries reveal that efforts to develop financial markets can increase the difficulty of achieving the short-run stabilization objective. Drawing on the experience of Chile and Argentina in the mid-1970s, Foxley (1981) and Díaz-Alejandro (1981) have highlighted a number of ways in which a combination of financial liberalization, trade reforms, and exchange rate adjustments can undermine attempts to restore stability in the short run.

Interest rates in the organized market rise sharply following financial reforms of the type just described, increasing the cost of working capital and perhaps having a cost-push effect on prices. If, at the same time, demand is falling because of restrictive monetary policies, inventories will rise and firms will seek to minimize the effects of unwanted high-cost inventories by reducing output. The combined impact of freeing interest rates and restricting credit may thus lead to stagflation.

This same combination may result in undesired developments in foreign trade and payments. If the financial reforms result in interest rates above those prevailing abroad, domestic and foreign investors will tend to increase their holdings of local financial assets and local entrepreneurs will be more likely to look abroad to meet their credit needs. If interest rates are unrestricted, the results may be a substantial capital inflow and an appreciation of the exchange rate. The authorities, on the other hand, will seek to use currency devaluation as a stimulus to the production of tradables, so that, in such situations, there will be contradictions within the program. These may be resolved after a time, as the increased costs of servicing the foreign-owned external debt weaken the balance of payments and the exchange rate, but the transition may be quite prolonged and its cost, in terms of dysfunctional investment signals, may be substantial. Moreover, significant swings in the current account and in capital movements will destabilize the foreign-asset component of the monetary base, making effective monetary control all the more difficult to achieve.

The degree of conflict between short-run stabilization and structural transformation depends critically on the timing of the measures. In this respect, the program adopted in Chile in early 1975 exemplifies one extreme within the new orthodoxy. The Chilean program combined demand restraint with rapid financial and trade

liberalization. In this case, the extent and rapidity of financial liberalization had adverse effects even in relation to the longer-term aim.
For a variety of reasons, the resulting rise in interest rates at-
tracted funds to the short end of the market, discouraging investment in productive assets. The already low gross investment
ratio fell further to levels at which net investment was probably
negative. The choice of this kind of shock treatment approach is
based on a judgment that, while it may increase short-run economic
dislocation, it will facilitate the implementation of the program. A
gradualist approach, on the other hand, may lessen the chances that
the program will be fully implemented, given that there is likely to
be resistance from the groups most affected in the short run.

In the case of new orthodox programs, the priority accorded the
long-term objective tends to increase government toleration of
short-run costs. By contrast, structuralist/populist policies try to
achieve structural transformation while avoiding short-run stabilization costs.

Structuralist/populist responses

While financial and trade reforms of the kind associated with new
orthodox programs seek to supplement the traditional instruments
of demand management, the structuralist/populist tradition, by and
large, avoids using these instruments. The Latin American structuralist school disputes the appropriateness of these instruments,
and the neoclassical economic theory from which they derive, in
situations of dependent capitalism and offers a diagnosis of inflation
and payments disequilibria that stresses the structural features of
the supply side of the economy rather than the aggregate demand
side. Disequilibria are viewed as primarily the product of the pressure of growth on developing economic structures. Price signals do
not call forth appropriate supply responses because of resource immobility, market segmentation, and institutional rigidities. The resulting bottlenecks in the supply of food, foreign exchange, intermediate inputs, etc., force the economy to go through inflationary
cycles. Economic policy must therefore be directed toward the pre-
vention of such supply bottlenecks.

The major implication of this analysis for stabilization policy is
that the approach must be gradual. Preventing supply bottlenecks
involves reallocating investment. A stabilization program that fails
to take into account the long-term nature of this prime objective

can, in the structuralist view, succeed only in reducing one disequilibrium (such as a payments deficit) at the expense of accentuating another (such as unemployment). Faced with an immediate payments problem, structuralists would try to avoid adjustment through deflation, relying instead on exchange controls.

In practice, economic policies within the structuralist/populist tradition, such as those in Chile (1970–73) and Argentina (1973–76), have typically gone through two stages. The usual features of the first stage are increased public expenditure, across-the-board wage increases, money-supply growth, and increased government intervention, including extensive price and import controls. These expansionary policies, while often effective in bringing into use excess productive capacity, soon result in a higher-than-desired inflation rate or a payments crisis. The second stage has, therefore, typically involved a reversal of the policies of the first stage and a resort to traditional demand management measures.

To judge from Latin American experiences, the crucial weakness of structuralist-based policies in practice has been that the emphasis on the removal of supply bottlenecks has generally been accompanied by a neglect of short-run economic management. Traditional demand management techniques are rejected, but when price and exchange controls, which are essentially temporary expedients, are no longer practicable alternatives, structuralist-based policies have been unable to resolve pressing disequilibria within the necessary time span. The low priority accorded to short-run economic management hence jeopardizes the achievement of the longer-term aims. Income redistribution is usually an explicit goal of governments acting in this tradition, but typically the distributional gains achieved in the early days have been eroded by the end of the first stage.

While structuralist/populist responses are at one extreme of the spectrum for purposes of comparison, it is doubtful whether structuralism contains within it a coherent approach to short-term economic management. Structuralism is essentially concerned with medium-term and long-term policies designed to remove supply bottlenecks. Its main contribution to the debate about short-run stabilization is to highlight those structural features of developing countries' economies that constrain the efficacy and cost-effectiveness of traditional stabilization tools, rather than to set out a plausible alternative.

The apparent absence of a viable alternative set of policies means that the debate about least-cost methods of short-run adjustment is not one between orthodoxy and structuralism but rather concerns the range of options within orthodoxy; the relative merits of gradualism and shock treatment; the potential of eclectic approaches combining traditional demand management techniques with measures such as price guidelines, indexation, selective import controls, export subsidies, and restrictions on capital flows, as transitional devices; and the possibilities for controlling the distribution of the burden of adjustment. The scope for imaginative policy design and implementation narrows as the payments imbalance becomes critical, and the only viable policy option becomes crisis management by means of generalized demand restraint. Before this critical stage is reached, the priority accorded to stabilization and the range of instruments considered will, as has been seen, reflect long-run development objectives. It will also be influenced by short-run political constraints, which are discussed next.

Politics of stabilization programs

The apparent absence of a plausible short-term alternative to demand management in the face of economic disequilibria is all the more to be regretted because of the political difficulties with which conventional programs are associated. In general, a country faced with a nonviable payments deficit must reduce consumption or investment relative to income. To the extent that the burden falls on living standards, the interests of particular socioeconomic groups are adversely affected and the distributional implications of the program assume critical sensitivity. To the extent that the burden falls on investment, it raises an intergenerational issue: the choice between present and future consumption. In either case, stabilization programs are most unlikely to be distributionally neutral (although the Fund has traditionally treated this aspect as beyond its own sphere of competence), which adds to their political sensitivity. As an illustration of this sensitivity, there is Cooper's well-known finding (1971) that currency devaluation roughly triples the probability that the responsible finance minister will lose his job within the following year and roughly doubles the probability that the entire government will fall.

Many nations are marked by acute divisions, and their governments are commonly preoccupied with the maintenance of their own power and of social tranquility. Their task is frequently one of conflict management within a fragile political infrastructure. Such conditions make for instability and inconsistency of policies over time. Adjustment programs may be perceived as resulting in larger net political costs than the problems to which they are addressed. It may be for reasons such as these that there is a strong tendency for stabilization programs to become ineffective too quickly for them to achieve the desired results, so that it is often difficult to point to clear success stories. Thus, only 4 of 22 episodes studied by Krueger (1978) resulted in the sustained liberalization that was the objective in those cases. A stop-go cycle is fairly common, resulting in the worst of both worlds: the short-term losses of output and employment associated with demand restraint plus the continued uncertainties and dislocations of periodic payments crises and inflation.[12] If the cycle is prolonged, its effects on expectations can further reduce the chance of successful stabilization because there will be diminishing confidence in the efficacy of frequently announced policy changes.

To make matters worse, the effects of economic stagnation on saving and investment also undermine the prospects of successful adjustment on both the economic and political planes. Enlarged payments deficits and consequential slower growth in per capita income tend to reduce household and business saving. Economic stagnation is also likely to reduce perceived investment opportunities. It tends to worsen the public finances because, while government revenue is largely a function of national income, expenditures are to a considerable degree autonomous. For such reasons, the net per capita directly productive capital formation on which structural adjustment must be based is likely to decline rather than increase. Moreover, in an atmosphere of uncertainty and crisis, and in view of the political frustrations that are likely to accompany an economic slowdown, there is the danger of a poorer quality of policy decision making.

---

[12]Thus, Cole (1976, p. 158) cites in the Philippines a "four-year inflation-deflation cycle which was directly related to the election cycle. From Independence in 1946 to the discontinuance of normal electoral procedures in 1973, the Philippines experienced a pattern of financial profligacy at election time, which spilled over into inflation and foreign-exchange crisis in the following year. The next two years then encompassed a period of constraint and contraction to prepare the way and build up the financial resources for another election spree."

Approaches to stabilization cannot ignore these factors. It is not sufficient, for example, to diagnose a payments deficit and accelerating inflation as having been "caused" by the monetary consequences of large-scale deficit financing. It is necessary to inquire further into the political impulses behind the budget deficit and into the options that are realistically open to the government. The answers to these inquiries might tell more about the feasibility and design of stabilization programs than the most sophisticated economic analyses. But it is also important to remember that inaction in the face of a payments constraint may also have large political repercussions. What are called the political consequences of, say, a devaluation, or what is called an "IMF riot," may often more appropriately be laid at the door of a government that either preferred to suppress the symptoms of the problem for a while or simply drifted. If it is true that the popularity of governments is positively correlated with the performance of the economy, economic disequilibria undermine the government's legitimacy and *successful* stabilization can help to restore it.

CONCLUSIONS

Although this paper's original intention was not to dwell particularly on the difficulties of achieving stabilization, that is how it has evolved. Besides drawing attention to the size of the problem in many non-oil developing countries, it has had to emphasize the difficulties to be overcome before achieving a reasonable balance between financing and adjustment to the point of asking whether such a balance is feasible at all. And in looking at the three stylized illustrations of alternative responses to disequilibria, it has been easier to point to drawbacks than to positive virtues, just as it is easier to find real failures than successes. But somehow the problems have to be solved, and there is a responsibility not to be wholly negative. By way of conclusion, therefore, the following general propositions are suggested as perhaps pointing to the direction in which solutions may be found. However, no originality is claimed, and they are offered in a state of some perplexity.

1. For a large majority of non-oil developing countries, a policy of inaction is simply not viable. Accelerating inflation and, even more, the balance of payments constraint impose heavy penalties

on countries that fail to respond to the harsher world environment in which they must now live—penalties that undermine their political stability no less than their economic aspirations.

2. The standard position set out at the beginning of the paper remains the basis on which solutions must be sought. However, the following points need to be mentioned:

(a) In general, adjustment is feasible only over the longer term. Conventional programs, of the type with which the Fund is associated, have tried to achieve too much too quickly, thus producing the seeds of their own destruction.

(b) The options and the most appropriate combinations of instruments vary across country types—e.g., as determined by such variables as stage of development, oil dependency, composition of exports, size and openness of the economy, commercial creditworthiness, and the strength of the sociopolitical system. There can be no uniform approach to adjustment.

(c) It is a mistake to expect a great deal from country attempts at adjustment. Even in the longer run, it is bound to be a faltering and approximate business. Much of the problem is global in origin and hardly amenable to individual country correctives; the available policy instruments are weak relative to the magnitude of the disequilibria; fine tuning is out of the question.

(d) It is important to pay more attention than in the past to the task of minimizing the costs of adjustment. While demand management is often seen as the only way of dealing quickly with a crisis, it is also very likely to bring with it heavy losses of production and employment. Parallel measures to raise capacity utilization may in some situations go far to minimize the cost (see Daniel Schydlowsky's paper).

(e) Given the long-term nature of the adjustment task and its implications for the structure of production and demand, stabilization programs must be seen as inputs into the development effort and must be integrated into national development strategies. By inference, the underlying logic of the traditional division of labor between the Fund and the World Bank is losing force. It is becoming increasingly difficult to defend the view that the Fund's work is quite different from that of a development aid agency.

(f) The international provision of supporting finance is likely to be crucial to the success of many programs by helping to minimize the costs and extending the time available for adjustment, but the evidence suggests that policy conditionality is a necessary feature of this finance.

3. Present-day global conditions have shifted the desirable balance between financing and adjustment markedly toward the former. This not only follows from the size and exogenous nature of the payments imbalances but also from the more difficult circumstances in which adjustment must be attempted and from the severe limitations on the effectiveness of adjustment programs. The Fund has recognized this by considerably increasing the resources available in support of its programs, but it has not yet been able to go far enough in either extending the period over which programs are to be implemented or in modifying their policy coverage.

4. What was said earlier about the objectives of major country groupings being inconsistent with the achievement of an appropriate mix of financing and adjustment emphasizes the need for continued support for international institutions or gatherings in which national objectives can be reconciled. Global problems demand global solutions. There is a particular need for international financial arrangements that reconcile the objectives of OPEC surplus countries as investors with the financing needs of non-oil developing countries. However unpromising gatherings such as the 1981 Cancún (Mexico) summit[13] may be, there is in the end no alternative that does not threaten heavy welfare losses in the most vulnerable nations.

5. The unavoidably political nature of stabilization programs— and, therefore, of the international financing that supports them—must be stressed. More explicit recognition of this at the international level may promote a fuller understanding of domestic sources of economic instability and encourage greater sensitivity to such considerations in program design.

---

[13]Meeting of heads of state and government and other officials representing 22 industrial and developing countries, October 22–23, 1981. See *IMF Survey*, November 9, 1981, p. 349.

REFERENCES

Balassa, Bela A., "The Policy Experience of Twelve Less Developed Countries, 1973–1978," World Bank Staff Working Paper, No. 449 (Washington, April 1981).

Black, W. Stanley, "The Impact of Changes in the World Economy on Stabilization Policies in the 1970s," in *Economic Stabilization in Developing Countries*, ed. by William R. Cline and Sydney Weintraub, Brookings Institution (Washington, 1981), pp. 43–82.

Brandt, Willy, *North-South: A Program for Survival*, Independent Commission on International Development Issues (Brandt Commission) (London, 1981).

Brett, E. A., "The International Monetary Fund, the International Monetary System and the Periphery," International Foundation for Development Alternatives, Dossier No. 5 (March 1979).

Cole, David C., "Concepts, Causes and Cures of Instability in Less Developed Countries," in *Money and Finance in Economic Growth and Development*, ed. by Ronald I. McKinnon (New York, 1976), pp. 143–71.

Cooper, Richard N., *Currency Devaluation in Developing Countries*, Essays in International Finance, No. 86, Princeton University (June 1971). The paper is also reproduced in Ch. 9 of *International Trade and Money: The Geneva Essays*, ed. by M. B. Connolly and Alexander Swoboda (London, 1973), pp. 167–96.

Davis, Jeffrey M., "The Economic Effects of Windfall Gains in Export Earnings, 1975–78" (unpublished, International Monetary Fund, February 1980).

Dell, Sidney S., and Roger Lawrence, *The Balance of Payments Adjustment Process in Developing Countries* (New York, 1980).

Díaz-Alejandro, Carlos F., "Southern Cone Stabilization Plans," in *Economic Stabilization in Developing Countries*, ed. by William R. Cline and Sydney Weintraub, Brookings Institution (Washington, 1981), pp. 119–47.

Foxley, Alejandro, "Stabilization Policies and Their Effects on Employment and Income Distribution: A Latin American Perspective," in *Economic Stabilization in Developing Countries*, ed. by William R. Cline and Sydney Weintraub, Brookings Institution (Washington, 1981), pp. 191–233.

International Monetary Fund, Trade and Payments Division, *The Rise in Protectionism*, IMF Pamphlet Series, No. 24 (Washington, July 1978).

——, *World Economic Outlook: A Survey by the Staff of the International Monetary Fund*, IMF Occasional Paper No. 4 (Washington, June 1981).

Killick, Tony (1981 a), "IMF Stabilisation Programmes," Overseas Development Institute Working Paper, No. 6 (London, 1981).

—— (1981 b), "Extent, Causes and Consequences of Disequilibria in Developing Countries," Overseas Development Institute Working Paper, No. 1 (March 1981).

Krueger, Anne O., *"Foreign Trade Regimes and Economic Development: Liberalization Attempts and Consequences* (Cambridge, Massachusetts, 1978).

Little, Ian Malcolm D., Tibor Scitovsky, and Maurice Scott, *Industry and Trade in Some Developing Countries: A Comparative Study* (Oxford University Press, 1970).

Organization for Economic Cooperation and Development, *OECD Economic Outlook*, No. 29 (Paris, July 1981).

Overseas Development Institute, "OPEC Aid," Briefing Paper, No. 4, 1980, (London, August 1980).

Sharpley, Jennifer, "The Potential of Domestic Stabilization Measures in Developing Countries," Development Economics Research and Advisory Project, Working Paper A198 (Chr. Michelsen Institute, Bergen, March 1981).

Sutton, Mary, "The Costs and Benefits of Stabilisation Programmes: Some Latin American Experiences," Overseas Development Institute Working Paper, No. 3 (London, May 1981).

United Kingdom, *The Brandt Commission Report*, memorandum prepared by the Foreign and Commonwealth Office for the Overseas Development Subcommittee of the Foreign Affairs Committee, House of Commons (London, July 1980).

United Nations, *Yearbook of International Trade Statistics* (New York, 1979).

World Bank (1981 a), "Structural Adjustment Program," Background Note for the Press (December 7, 1981).

_____ (1981 b), *World Development Report, 1981* (Washington, August 1981).

Economic Management and International Monetary Fund Conditionality

MANUEL GUITIÁN

The International Monetary Fund was established to promote economic and financial cooperation among its member countries in order to facilitate the expansion and balanced growth of world trade. In fulfilling this broad mandate, the Fund has come to play a central role in the international monetary sphere.[1] An essential aspect of this role is the provision of financial assistance to members facing potential or actual balance of payments difficulties. In this area, the Fund's Articles of Agreement include the general norms that should be followed in making Fund resources available to members. Briefly, these norms are that the Fund should adopt policies on the use of its resources that assist members in overcoming their balance of payments problems in a manner consistent with the purposes of the Fund and that provide adequate safeguards to ensure that the use of the resources by members is temporary.[2]

Drawing on the experience gathered from a long and close relationship with a varied and growing membership, the Fund has developed a pragmatic and flexible body of policies and procedures to govern the use of its resources in a manner that will fulfill the prescriptions of the Articles of Agreement. Invariably, these poli-

---

[1]For a detailed exposition of the history and activities of the Fund, see Horsefield (1969) and de Vries (1976).

[2]See Article I(v) and Article V, Section 3(a) of the Fund's Articles of Agreement (IMF, 1978).

73

cies have been aimed at supporting members' adjustment efforts through the adoption of economic policy measures that would be compatible with the particular member's interests as well as with those of the Fund membership as a whole. The set of policies that govern the use of Fund resources has come to be widely known by the term *conditionality*.

While the principle of conditionality applies under most circumstances, its practical implementation has to be adapted in response to changes in the world economic environment. The need for the practices of conditionality to evolve has been widely perceived and discussed in the past decade, a period in which the evolution of the world economy was generally characterized by the prevalence of large payments imbalances, historically high rates of inflation, and faltering growth rates, particularly in industrial countries. This paper examines the principle and practices of conditionality as they are currently being applied. It first discusses the rationale of the concept of conditionality, bringing out its theoretical underpinnings as well as its economic policy implications. It then traces the recent practices for its implementation that have been developed to assist members in adjusting to a particularly difficult environment. Finally, the paper discusses a series of issues that have arisen in the context of the application of conditionality and their implications for the choice of policy instruments, the setting of policy objectives, and the interpretation of results.

THE PRINCIPLE OF CONDITIONALITY

Broad aspects of conditionality

From the very inception of the Fund, conditionality proved to be a controversial subject, mainly because it is the key determinant of members' access to Fund financial assistance. As such, conditionality is subject to close scrutiny both inside the Fund and in outside circles. Its controversial nature is based on a recognition that the design and the adaptation of policies on the use of Fund resources encompass a large number of complex issues and involve important elements of judgment on which consensus is not always easy to attain.

Except for a brief period after the Fund came into existence, however, there has been agreement among Fund members that the

Fund's financial assistance should be conditional on the adoption of adjustment policies. This was felt to be a necessary requirement to preserve the revolving character of the Fund's resources called for by the temporariness in their use as prescribed by the Articles of Agreement. In any examination of the rationale of the concept of conditionality, a key feature of the international adjustment process needs to be underscored—that external payments imbalances have to be adjusted whenever they are permanent or irreversible. Under most circumstances, adjustment will take place, with or without policy action, in the sense that claims on resources eventually have to be limited to those resources that are available. The issue at stake, therefore, is not whether adjustment will be carried out—because it will be—but whether it will be carried out efficiently, that is, without involving unwarranted welfare losses.

Conditionality is a means to ensure the efficiency of the international adjustment process to the benefit of all the Fund's membership (Witteveen, 1978). It also constitutes an essential aspect of the contribution the Fund makes toward easing the balance of payments difficulties of member countries. The main objective of the Fund's financial assistance has been to help members to attain, over the medium term, a viable payments position in a context of reasonable price and exchange rate stability, a sustainable level and rate of growth of economic activity, and a liberal system of multilateral payments. The concept of a viable balance of payments typically means, especially for many developing countries, a current account deficit that can be financed, on a sustainable basis, by net capital inflows on terms that are compatible with the development and growth prospects of the country and, therefore, with its debt carrying capacity.

The provision of resources by the Fund helps to extend the period during which adjustment is to take place, thereby making the process less severe than it would otherwise have to be. The strategies to finance and to adjust external imbalances are closely interwoven and form the core of the Fund's policies on conditionality, which seek to strike an appropriate balance between the two. Conditionality is based on an assessment of the *need* for adjustment, which—in the light of the financing available from the Fund and from other external sources—helps to determine the size and the pace of the required adjustment *effort*. It is frequently argued that adjustment and financing are alternative or substitute strategies.

This can only be true in the abstract sense that adjustment would not be necessary if financing were available indefinitely, and conversely, that adjustment would have to be immediate in the absence of financing. Either of these extremes hardly ever occurs in reality and, in most practical instances, adjustment and financing are joint and mutually supporting strategies.

Strategies of adjustment may vary according to the particular situation of the country requesting support, but there are two principles that the Fund seeks to uphold in all programs that involve the use of conditional resources: the principle of uniformity of treatment among members and the necessity that the Fund's policies on conditionality take into account the institutional characteristics and the particular circumstances of different countries. It is, therefore, necessary to strike a delicate balance between uniformity and flexibility of treatment, even though they may appear to be in conflict. The conflict, however, is more apparent than real because neither can the principle of uniformity be applied rigidly—that is, regardless of individual country circumstances—nor can individual circumstances be given such weight that uniform treatment loses all meaning. A common feature of the programs supported by Fund resources is the existence of an adjustment need, and the essence of conditionality is to ensure a commensurate adjustment effort. In general terms, uniformity of treatment requires that, for any given degree of need, the effort of economic adjustment sought in programs be broadly equivalent among members. Like all other aspects of the principle of conditionality, the achievement of uniformity of treatment necessarily involves a measure of judgment based on a consideration of the particular features of each case.

Basis and implications of conditionality

The restoration of viability to a payments position often means the reduction and eventual elimination of the causes that gave rise to the difficulties. Balance of payments problems may be due to a variety of factors that are often distinguished according to whether they are external or internal and whether they are transient or enduring. The particular strategies of adjustment can vary, depending on whether the payments difficulties are due to developments inside a country's economy or to developments in the rest of the world. But the fundamental question of whether adjustment is actually required hinges more on the assessment of the permanent or temporary character of the disturbance. Deficits stemming from adverse transitory external (or internal) factors—that is, deficits that normally can be expected to be reversible or self-correcting—typically call for resort to temporary financing, either through foreign borrowing or use of international reserves, or a combination of both. Mechanisms have been devised in the Fund and elsewhere to cope with situations of this sort. The Fund's compensatory financing and buffer stock facilities are examples of such mechanisms.[3] However, if the deficits (whether of external or internal origin) are not likely to be transitory, a country needs to take appropriate domestic and external measures of adjustment. Simply restricting international transactions cannot be considered as an adequate adjustment strategy, because restrictions do not act on the causes of the difficulties but only repress and usually aggravate them.

The conditionality associated with the use of Fund resources requires the member to undertake a program to adjust its balance of payments. The general purpose of such a requirement is that the Fund's financial assistance should be used to support the implementation of economic policies that give substantial assurance that a viable payments position will be attained within a reasonable period of time, which in turn involves restoring a sustainable balance between the aggregate demand for, and the aggregate supply of, resources in an economy. The policies required to bring about this result depend, of course, on the nature and size of the existing and prospective balance of payments deficits. Moreover, the particular policy instruments to be used are designed in the light of the institutional setting and the organization of the economy, as well as the economic and social priorities of the country.

Domestic Financial Policies. Imbalances in an economy are usually reflected in the prevalence of inflation and balance of payments deficits, on the one hand, and low rates of employment and growth, on the other hand. These imbalances can be due to a variety of factors, but one common element that generally characterizes them is an excessive or unsustainable expansion in aggregate demand. In most instances, variations in aggregate demand and expenditure—

---

[3]For an explanation of the financial facilities available at the Fund, see Gold (1980). See also Goreux (1980) for a detailed exposition of the compensatory financing facility.

associated, as they often are, with a relatively stable aggregate supply function—are the major causes of short-run fluctuations in output, prices, and the balance of payments. These broad considerations are behind the demand management approach to stabilization policy, which is designed to monitor the performance of the economy over the short term in order to keep the level and the rate of growth of aggregate demand in line with the level and the rate of growth of the economy's productive capacity.[4]

Fiscal imbalances stemming from levels of expenditure that exceed the public sector's revenue raising capacity are often behind the unsustainable expansion in aggregate demand and consequent weakness in the balance of payments. Correction of imbalances of this sort normally entails the adoption of direct measures to restrain fiscal spending or raise fiscal revenues in order to limit the size of the resulting public sector deficit to the amount of financing that is available. This line of reasoning underscores the importance of the interplay of fiscal (e.g., spending and revenue measures) and monetary (e.g., developments in bank credit and money flows) policies for the specification of a sustainable pace of aggregate demand and, *ceteris paribus*, of a viable balance of payments position.

The relationship between aggregate demand and fiscal and monetary variables has been treated extensively in the literature.[5] A well-recognized problem in the discussion of the relative roles of fiscal and monetary measures has been the difficulty of distinguishing between them unambiguously, as most of the time both types of measures are at work together. This is because actions undertaken to influence public sector spending or revenues have a direct impact on the public sector borrowing requirement, in general, and on the public sector's need for domestic bank financing, in particular. Because of the link between monetary flows, public sector spending, and aggregate demand, domestic monetary policy became a key element for demand management and stabilization purposes. For a relatively long period, however, propositions of monetary theory were derived from analytical models that were

---

[4]For expository purposes, this line of thought can be used to distinguish stabilization policy from development and growth policies; while the former is concerned with aggregate demand, the latter are aimed at influencing the level and rate of growth of aggregate supply.

[5]For example, see Friedman (1970) and Johnson (1973). For a recent and comprehensive treatment of some of these subjects, see Bryant (1980).

based on the assumption of a closed economy. These propositions served to establish relationships between the rate of monetary expansion and the evolution of nominal income in broad terms, and more specifically, the rate of inflation. In this approach, the linkages between monetary variables and the balance of payments via the interplay of conditions in the money market were generally overlooked. As a result, the policy conclusions derived from this analytical framework ignored the existence of international transactions but they still found their way into the analysis of open economies.

Conceptually, this procedure may be valid when the open economy operates under a completely flexible exchange rate, thus precluding the emergence of balance of payments surpluses or deficits and severing the link between the domestic money supply and international transactions.[6] From the standpoint of policy, it may also be justified in nearly self-sufficient economies where the balance of payments does not impose any serious constraint on the implementation of domestic economic policies. However, from a theoretical perspective, economic policy designed for open economies seeking to attain the internal objective of a measure of price stability at full employment and the external objective of a viable balance of payments position (or alternatively of a realistic and stable exchange rate) has to be based on an analysis that takes into account explicitly the role of international transactions. Recently, monetary theory has moved in this direction by focusing on the interdependence between the money supply and the balance of payments. This development has not involved essential modifications to the basic propositions of traditional monetary theory, but it has brought up the constraints that open economies face in the design of monetary policy in terms of its conduct and scope.[7]

For purposes of economic policymaking, the general argument is based on the proposition that the rationale and the effectiveness of monetary policy is contingent on the existence of a stable demand for money. In the context of traditional (e.g., closed economy) mon-

---

[6]This is particularly the case with Milton Friedman's monetary policy framework, which needs to be interpreted in the light of his article, "The Case for Flexible Exchange Rates," in Friedman (1953).

[7]See International Monetary Fund (1977) and Frenkel and Johnson (1976) for collections of theoretical and empirical articles on the monetary approach to the balance of payments. See also Frenkel and Mussa (1981).

etary theory, this proposition led to the empirical issue of the appropriate definition of money in order to identify an observable variable that would be useful for the purpose of policy formulation. In summary terms, the policy guideline that was derived from this approach was basically limited to a suggestion that the path of the supply of money (however defined) be kept in line with that of the demand for money.

This policy guideline implied that the money supply is within the control of the monetary authorities, an implication that is not valid in an open economy. In an economy of this nature, with a fixed (or not totally flexible) exchange rate, the nominal quantity of money can be changed through international transactions, that is, through balance of payments surpluses or deficits. These surpluses or deficits can be seen as equivalent to imports or exports of domestic currency, so that any disparity created internally between the demand for and supply of money can be eliminated by the balance of payments. In this environment, the monetary authorities have no direct control over the total quantity of money but only on that part which is supplied internally through domestic credit expansion, particularly by the central bank. When the exchange rate is perfectly flexible (or the equivalent, in a closed economy), an argument can be made that the quantity of money is under the control of the monetary authorities; but the practical importance of this argument is limited because the money supply continues to be endogenous (that is, subject to influences from the rest of the economy and from abroad) as long as the authorities are concerned about the impact of their policies on the stability of the price level and the exchange rate.

This line of reasoning makes it clear that monetary policy in any open economy needs to be formulated in terms of domestic credit expansion (the internal supply of money) to attain overall financial balance.[8] When the exchange rate is fixed, domestic credit policy is necessary to make the public's demand for money compatible with the authorities' demand for international reserves. When the exchange rate is flexible, domestic credit policy is required to satisfy the public's demand for money and the authorities' objective of exchange rate and price level stability. These theoretical proposi-

---

[8]See the discussion in Johnson (1972), Mundell (1968 and 1971), Guitián (1973 and 1977), and Selden (1975).

tions on the importance and role of domestic credit for purposes of macroeconomic and external payments balance provided the basis for the formulation, in financial arrangements involving use of Fund resources, of monetary policy commitments in terms of domestic credit expansion either by the central bank or by the banking system as a whole, depending on the structure of the financial sector in the economy in question. These domestic credit policy guidelines have become a uniform characteristic of arrangements with the Fund.[9]

External Debt Management. The design of domestic monetary policy, therefore, needs to take into consideration the importance of the interplay between domestic credit expansion and a money demand forecast for the determination of the overall balance of payments. While it is true that the concept of the overall balance of payments is important for economic policymaking, particularly in the short run, it must also be recognized that it addresses only one dimension of the concept of external balance—that is, the level and movements of net international reserves. Over a longer time frame, however, economic policy needs to focus also on the composition or the structure of the balance of payments—that is, on its current and capital account components (Salop and Spitäller, 1980; and Dornbusch and Fischer, 1980).

The link that exists between the overall balance of payments and the management of international reserves is a particular instance of a more general relationship that can be established between the current account of the balance of payments and the management of external debt in its broadest sense. These relationships are important factors for the assessment of consistency among policy measures. For example, domestic credit policy will not generally be sufficient to attain a desired balance of payments objective—in terms of both its overall level and its composition—if it is formulated without regard to potential foreign borrowing. Under most circumstances, domestic credit and foreign credit are substitutes for each other, so that domestic credit policy needs to be complemented and supported by foreign borrowing guidelines to ensure that the flow of total (i.e., domestic and foreign) financial resources available to the economy is compatible with the objectives sought not only for the

---

[9]See Gold (1970). For an illustration of financial programming exercises, see International Monetary Fund (1981 a).

balance of payments but also for the rate of economic growth and for inflation. In principle, given an economy's productive and absorptive capacity, there is a level of aggregate demand that is consistent with a desired path for those three target variables; in other words, the attainment of objectives with respect to the balance of payments, growth, and price performance requires that the flow of total financial resources be in broad alignment with such a level of aggregate demand. Thus, macroeconomic policy programming involves some broad specification of the link that exists between a desired aggregate demand-supply relationship, on the one hand, and the total financial resources available to the economy, on the other.

These arguments show the need for consistency between external debt management and domestic financial policies and bring to the surface their close relationship with international reserve management. Like domestic credit expansion, foreign borrowing is also an important factor for developments in the overall balance of payments and, thereby, in the money market (Loser, 1977; and Keller, 1980)—that is, over the short run the relationship between domestic credit expansion and a forecast money demand path can result in different balance of payments results, particularly with respect to the current account, depending on whether or not foreign borrowing takes place. In general, when imbalances are present in an economy, foreign borrowing provides an alternative to the use of international reserves for their financing.[10] From this standpoint, both external debt and international reserve policies are important aspects of an economy's overall portfolio management strategy.

The argument made so far emphasizes the relationship between foreign borrowing and demand management policies by pointing to the substitutability between foreign and domestic financing. However, the argument has to be taken one step further to bring out perhaps the most important of its ramifications. Domestic borrowing is a means to transfer resources from surplus to deficit sectors within an economy. In the absence of foreign borrowing and given a country's resource endowment, output and growth depend on the propensity to save and the efficiency of investment in the economy.

---

[10]Types of foreign borrowing range from foreign loans resembling closely international reserve liabilities, at one extreme, to loans approaching grants and aid, at the other. In general, however, all foreign borrowing adds to a country's foreign liabilities and, in that sense, represents an alternative to the use of foreign assets, including international reserves.

The possibility of borrowing abroad adds to the resources that are available to the economy. Thus, although all macroeconomic policies can influence supply by their impact on the efficiency of resource allocation, foreign borrowing, in addition, acts directly on the global availability of those resources and it thereby allows the economy to attain higher expenditure levels, providing in certain circumstances for higher growth rates than would be the case in its absence. Viewed from this perspective, it is clear that a medium-term framework is required for the formulation of macroeconomic policies in general, and external debt management policies in particular, thus linking, through the current account of the balance of payments, demand management with the saving-investment process and the longer-run evolution of the economy. This linkage makes clear the reasons for the concern in programs supported by Fund resources with the attainment of a sustainable balance of payments position, which is equivalent to seeking an appropriate relationship between savings and investment to ensure the realization of the economy's growth potential.

Role of the Exchange Rate. Imbalances between aggregate demand and supply are frequently brought about, and are always made possible, by the pursuit of macroeconomic policies that are not compatible with the economy's capacity to produce. If financing is available for the imbalances, it is not uncommon to see them last for protracted periods. In the process, the imbalances result in patterns and movements of domestic prices and costs that diverge substantially from those prevailing abroad. The competitiveness of the economy is thereby eroded and the efficiency of resource allocation is impaired by the creation of distortions in the structure of relative prices. At this stage, the typical situation is characterized by the prevalence of high open inflation rates (at times combined with ad hoc attempts to repress price increases), faltering growth and employment rates, excessive recourse to foreign borrowing, losses in international reserves, and very often resort to restrictions on international transactions as well.

One of the options that is usually considered in these circumstances in the process of designing a set of corrective measures involves an adjustment in the exchange rate. Experience has shown that an exchange rate change is not only a highly visible but also a controversial step that is often strenuously resisted (Cooper, 1973). At times, the resistance is rationalized by arguing that, from a theoretical standpoint, an imbalance created by unduly expansionary financial policies could, in principle, be redressed by a package of sufficiently strict policy measures. In the abstract, such an argument is indeed correct. However, to be relevant, it needs to be taken one step further to answer the question of the cost of correcting an imbalance in this manner. To a large degree, this is an empirical question for which a priori answers are not easy to provide. In the presence of imbalances, there is an important theoretical proposition to keep in mind—that there is no lasting trade-off between a devaluation and restrictive domestic financial policies. The trade-off is that between the exchange rate adjustment and the degree of restrictiveness of domestic policies. Other things being equal, the correction of a given imbalance is likely to require a less strict domestic policy stance when a currency devaluation is part of the strategy than when it is not.

Thus, it is clear that an important factor in the choice of a policy strategy will be the size of the imbalance in the sense that the margin for avoiding resort to a change in the exchange rate actually declines as the size of the imbalance rises. It can be established that when domestic prices and costs (or their rates of increase) are rigid in the downward direction, a strategy that relies exclusively on demand management measures is likely to be unnecessarily costly in terms of employment and output. Such a strategy entails the use of domestic financial policies to bring about a decline in domestic prices and costs (or in their rates of increase) to restore them to a balanced relationship with foreign prices and costs. Given the downward rigidity of the former, however, domestic employment and output will have to bear the brunt of the adjustment, an outcome that is likely to be the more pronounced the larger the decline needed in the level (or rate of increase) of domestic prices and costs. The alternative is to accompany the demand management measures with an adjustment in the exchange rate; this amounts to restoring equilibrium to relative prices by raising the domestic currency price of internationally traded goods rather than by lowering the price of domestic goods, as in the previous case.[11] Since this strategy does not require a decline in the level (or the rate of increase) of domestic

---

[11]For a recent collection of essays on exchange rates, see Frenkel and Johnson (1978). See also McKinnon (1981). The effects of exchange rate changes on output have been discussed explicitly in Almonacid and Guitián (1973) and Guitián (1976).

prices, the required adjustment in output and employment is likely
to be less pronounced.

In many respects, the usefulness of a devaluation lies in its broad
and pervasive effects on the economy. In the first place, by raising
the price of international goods relative to domestic goods, the exchange rate adjustment shifts demand from the former to the latter
(the expenditure-switching effect). At the same time, by reducing
the real value of nominal assets—thereby creating an excess in their
demand—the devaluation lowers the level or rate of growth of aggregate demand for goods and services (the expenditure-reducing
effect) and shifts the flow of spending toward the restoration of
balance in the market for nominal assets. This effect, by reinforcing
the impact of demand management measures, renders them less
strict than they would otherwise have to be.[12]

In general, when imbalances have been allowed to prevail for long
periods of time, an exchange rate adjustment is likely to be an
important, if not critical, ingredient of a corrective policy. This is
the case because the exchange rate is not only an instrument to
balance the external accounts and to monitor domestic absorption
but is also a key variable for the allocation of resources between the
domestic and the external sectors. From this perspective, there is a
counterpart in the field of exchange rates to the concept of a viable
balance of payments position discussed earlier. A similar concept
can logically be expressed just as well in terms of the exchange
rate—that is, a viable or realistic exchange rate; this concept would
certainly seem to be appropriate as a policy objective in an international environment characterized by broad flexibility of exchange
arrangements.

RECENT DEVELOPMENTS IN
CONDITIONALITY PRACTICES

On the basis of the broad propositions discussed in the preceding
section, the Fund developed practices and procedures to guide the
provision of its financial assistance to members. These practices
were adapted in the light of the growing experience gathered by the

---

[12]For an excellent discussion of the expenditure-reducing and expenditure-switching
effects, see Johnson (1958).

Fund in its relationship with members, as well as of the changing
international economic environment.[13] Recently, important issues
for the management of the international economy have been raised
by the resurgence of large payments imbalances associated with a
new round of sharp increases in world energy prices (de Larosière,
1980 a). The nature of the imbalances did not appear likely to be
short-lived, and the Fund has reacted to those issues by adapting its
conditionality practices in order to increase their resilience in assisting members to undertake the required adjustment efforts.

Nature of the adjustment

The size and intractability of the payments problems faced by
many member countries led the Fund to the conclusion that the
establishment of special facilities to provide resources subject to
limited conditionality or none at all would not be an appropriate
response. A more comprehensive approach was necessary, for two
main reasons: (1) for an important number of countries, payments
difficulties had not only worsened but they were superimposed on
long-standing imbalances, and the situation required more decisive
policy action than had been taken until then; and (2) although the
causes of the increasing deficits were for the most part external in
origin, they were not likely to be transitory; a realistic assessment
of the medium-term perspective called for timely and resolute adjustment efforts to cope with the adverse external environment.

Need for Structural Adjustment. From the beginning, a consensus developed that the Fund should be able to respond to the
needs of members in particularly difficult circumstances; there was
also general agreement that the payments imbalances prevailing in
the international economy were structural in nature and therefore
not amenable to correction over a short period of time (de Larosière,
1980 b). Adjustments to disequilibria of this sort were likely to
require extensive changes in members' economies, in particular
those of the oil importing countries, if the restoration of viability to
balance of payments was not to jeopardize their development and
growth prospects over the medium to long term.

---

[13]For an explanation of the practices developed in earlier periods, see Mookerjee (1966)
and Guitián (1980 and 1981).

The economic environment rendered the necessary adjustments more difficult. Inflation and inflationary expectations had become entrenched in many countries, raising the probability that sustained anti-inflationary policies—which on all counts were essential— might dampen growth rates further at a time when they were already well below historical levels. These developments, in turn, could slow down or even reduce the volume of world trade, thereby complicating the task of adjustment even further. These considerations formed the basis for moving toward a relatively long time frame for the adjustment effort to allow for changes to take place in the patterns of production and demand—changes that could be effected only gradually.

The basic purposes of the Fund were not altered by the disturbances that beset the international economy in the recent past, but these made attainment more challenging. In this context, the broad demand management policies usually included in programs supported by the Fund—particularly in the fiscal and credit areas— will continue to be needed, perhaps even more than before, to hold aggregate domestic demand down to a level consistent with the global availability of resources. These policies will still provide an appropriate framework for development and growth through the mobilization of domestic savings and the efficiency of resource investment. But recent events have also called for attention to be given to complementary measures aimed directly at bringing about an efficient utilization of resources to strengthen an economy's productive base.

Supply Management. Strictly speaking, interest in supply is not a new development in the Fund. While demand management measures and financial stability may have been *proximate* instruments and objectives of Fund policies, the full attainment of the supply potential has always been the *ultimate* aim. The novelty is the emphasis now openly found in the Fund and elsewhere on the effects of adjustment policies on resource utilization and therefore on production. It is as difficult to distinguish between demand and supply measures as it is to determine which blade of a pair of scissors does the cutting, to borrow Alfred Marshall's classic analogy. Policy measures have an impact on both demand and supply, and for the distinction to be useful, the measures need to be cataloged according to where they have their greatest effect.

The longer adjustment period allowed under the Fund's new guidelines for conditionality partly explains the current explicit accent on supply. On the one hand, measures to stimulate supply through productivity increases and high investment rates tend to show results only over the medium to long term. On the other hand, more time for adjustment requires the mobilization of resources in amounts larger than would be needed for shorter periods; it then becomes imperative to ensure that those resources are productively used to attain the supply potential.

The relationship between demand and supply management is illustrated by several factors that normally constitute a part of the design of a domestic stabilization program. In many instances, programs incorporate foreign borrowing strategies that directly enlarge the amount of resources available to the member. As a result, higher levels of expenditure can be achieved, as well as higher growth rates over the medium term. In the formulation of an adjustment program, it is also common to have a number of important policy understandings that provide the basis on which the feasibility of the domestic financial policies is predicated. These understandings can be critical for the attainment of financial balance and sustainable growth rates. They normally include public sector policies on prices, taxes, and subsidies that can contribute to eliminate financial imbalances and to promote efficiency in public sector activities, interest rate policies that foster the generation of domestic savings and improve intertemporal resource allocation, exchange rate policy that helps to control absorption and the external accounts but is also a powerful tool for development; and incomes policies that keep claims on resources from outstepping their availability.

Actions in these policy areas are of direct interest to the Fund because they foster savings and investment—the basis for expanding the supply potential and for developing a sound economy. Measures of this type elicit supply responses on two levels: by ensuring appropriate pricing in the broadest sense, the flow of output out of a given stock of resources is maximized, and by fostering the mobilization of savings and the efficiency of investment, the medium-term to long-term growth rate of output is enhanced.

Collaboration with the World Bank. Both the World Bank and the Fund share a concern over the economic and financial policies followed by member countries (Wright, 1980; and Landell-Mills, 1981).

Within this broad common interest, substantial scope exists to distinguish areas of primary responsibility for each institution. In general terms, it has long been agreed that the Fund is primarily responsible for balance of payments adjustment policies and the Bank for development programs and project evaluation. Over time, the two institutions have collaborated effectively in providing consistent policy advice to members while maintaining their distinct character and separate functions.

The complementary roles of the Fund and the Bank have become increasingly important in the current world environment, with the sharp increase in energy costs, the emphasis on appropriate supply responses, and the need for productive investment flows. At a time when the Fund has extended the time frame of its arrangements and has enlarged the scale of its assistance, the Bank has undertaken a program of lending for structural adjustment to provide support to countries with balance of payment difficulties that require structural changes; this kind of lending will be an important complement to Fund assistance.

These recent Fund-Bank initiatives call for additional measures of coordination. The range of subjects where coordination is required includes the structure and functioning of money and capital markets, the generation of domestic savings, the financial implications of development programs, and external debt management.[14] In providing policy advice, the Fund continues to focus on macroeconomic and balance of payments adjustment policies, while the Bank concentrates on the quality and effectiveness of development plans and investment priorities. This division of responsibilities remains essential; nonetheless, an increasingly close consultation between the two institutions is being developed as more members enter into adjustment programs supported by financial resources from both agencies.

The need for financing

Scale of Fund Assistance. Both the size and structural nature of the current account imbalances, on the one hand, and the emphasis on inducing adjustment and promoting supply responses, on the

---

[14]For a discussion of issues dealing with external debt management, see Nowzad, Williams, *et al* (1981).

other, provided a basis for a consensus by the Fund's Executive Board to continue lending resources in substantially larger amounts and for longer periods than before. Several interim steps were undertaken for these purposes.[15]

Soon after this consensus was formed, the Fund's Seventh General Review of Quotas was completed, raising members' quotas by 50 per cent. Guidelines on maximum commitments of Fund resources (excluding those under the compensatory financing and buffer stock facilities) in the context of the new quotas were adopted by the Fund's Executive Board; in general terms, the guidelines provide for commitments of Fund resources of up to an average of 150 per cent of quota a year within a maximum of 450 per cent of quota over a three-year period. These guidelines, which will be subject to periodic review, were supplemented by a maximum limit on total cumulative access to Fund resources, net of scheduled repurchases or repayments, of 600 per cent of quota. Such a maximum absolute limit was necessary to take into account past use of Fund resources, so that members would be treated uniformly, regardless of whether or not they had used the Fund resources before the adoption of the new guidelines.

Flexibility was built into the guidelines to accommodate the special circumstances of a member without impairing the principle of uniformity of treatment. Amounts in excess of the guidelines could be allowed in clearly exceptional cases—for example, when there is general recognition that a member's quota is unusually low in relation to the size of its economy or when an exceptionally strong and wide-ranging adjustment program is undertaken involving, inter alia, dismantling of controls and other restrictions that would require large financial support, at least in the initial stages.

The Fund as Catalyst. In its collaboration with individual members in the context of the design of adjustment programs, the effectiveness of the Fund as an institution goes far beyond its provision of resources. One of the most important aspects of the Fund's financial assistance to members in balance of payments difficulties—if not the most important one—is the close and predictable relationship between the provision of the assistance and the adoption of comprehensive programs of economic policy action. A critical side

---

[15]For a description of this interim period, see Guitián (1981).

effect of the mix of adjustment and financing that is typically built into the programs supported by Fund resources has been to help members attract flows of capital from sources other than the Fund. In the past few years, the major sources of financing for a large number of countries have been the international capital markets, and, in particular, foreign commercial banks in their important role as intermediaries.

In this manner, the Fund has contributed both to the efficiency and sustainability of resource transfers among members. Generally speaking, an arrangement with the Fund has traditionally been useful for members seeking to tap the capital markets because it tends to reduce uncertainty by providing a clear indication of the domestic policies to be followed and the objectives sought. The complementarity between the resources from the Fund and those from the private international capital markets is likely to become more important in the years to come, as countries face increasingly serious constraints and difficult policy choices.

A number of members have a relatively substantial and continuing dependence on flows of aid and concessional loans to finance their development efforts. Here again, the technical and financial assistance from the Fund and other multilateral agencies has encouraged donor countries to provide funds for members with a limited resource base and at a low level of development.

At the present juncture, the problems of adjustment faced by member countries are very complex, and they are likely to remain so. Large imbalances in the current accounts of the balance of payments will probably persist for some time. Appropriate adjustment policies will therefore continue to be needed to justify and encourage sustainable flows of capital on both concessional and commercial terms. In this context, the importance of the role of the Fund as a catalyst for other sources of financing cannot be overstressed.

SOME ISSUES IN THE CONTEXT OF CONDITIONALITY

Assessments of adjustment programs supported by Fund resources have been undertaken regularly at the Fund, both on a case-by-case basis and on a general level. The guidelines on conditionality that were adopted by the Executive Board in 1979 called for periodic studies "to evaluate and compare the appropriateness of the programs, the effectiveness of the policy instruments, the observance of the programs, and the results achieved."[16] The purpose of these studies was to obtain insights from the varied experience gathered from numerous financial arrangements in order to improve the methods and techniques of framing adjustment programs. By necessity, the observations derived from these studies cut across a wide spectrum of countries with diverse characteristics with respect to the institutional setting, level of development, and degree of openness to international trade. For this reason, the inferences drawn from such a diversity of experiences can only be of a general character.[17]

The issue of the length of the period to be covered by stand-by arrangements was discussed at the Fund as early as 1966, when the possibility of having two-year stand-by arrangements was proposed. The proposal was not followed up at the time, partly because in a sense its purpose was attained in practice by member countries entering into successive one-year stand-by arrangements for periods of several years. Since the mid-1970s, however, an increasing number of financial arrangements supported by Fund resources have involved policy programs formulated to cover periods longer than the one-year norm.

The adjustment period in extended and stand-by arrangements was lengthened in recognition of the prevalence of situations characterized by structural problems, slow growth rates, and relatively large payments imbalances. The mid-1970s and late 1970s witnessed, together with sharp terms of trade variations, the emergence of rigidities in many economies in an unfavorable world economic environment that tended to make adjustment, in some sense, more strenuous than in earlier periods. The issues that have arisen in this context are complex and interrelated; from many perspectives, they still remain unresolved. In this section, some general issues related to the adjustment process are discussed; to facilitate the presentation, the issues are organized in terms of the implications of the adjustment process for (1) policy objectives, (2) policy instruments, and (3) the interpretation of actual results.

---

[16]See paragraph 12 of Executive Board Decision No. 6056-(79/38) in *Selected Decisions of the International Monetary Fund and Selected Documents*, Ninth Issue (IMF, 1981 b, p. 22). See also Gold (1979) and Mookerjee (1979).

[17]For general studies of financial arrangements in the 1960s and early 1970s, see Reichmann and Stillson (1978) and Reichmann (1978).

Policy objectives and the period of adjustment

The tendency toward longer periods of adjustment essentially meant that economic policy programs, even if they were to be implemented on an annual basis, had to be formulated in the context of a medium-term horizon. Such a framework brought to the surface the various dimensions of the broad objective sought by programs supported by Fund resources—that is, the restoration and maintenance of viability to the balance of payments in an environment of price stability and sustainable rates of economic growth.

Economic Activity and Growth. In general terms, an inference that may be drawn from the experience of many recent arrangements with the Fund is that an economic environment characterized by uncertainty and by large imbalances tends to hamper the ability or the willingness of countries to adjust rapidly. This may be because the perceived cost—in terms of output and employment—of correcting payments imbalances and controlling inflation has risen, compared with what it was in relatively more stable environments. To put it differently, it is not inconceivable that a deterioration may have taken place in the trade-off frequently thought to exist in the short-run between balance of payments deficits and inflation rates, on the one hand, and levels of employment and rates of growth, on the other.

Apart from the implications for the requisite financing, the lengthening of the period of adjustment reduces the number of economic variables that can be considered exogenous for purposes of policy formulation. This is particularly the case with the effects of policy on economic activity and the rate of real economic growth, which for short periods of time can be disregarded as being either nonexistent or of small order of magnitude.[18] Such assumptions lose plausibility when the time frame is extended. The experience of countries undertaking an adjustment effort with respect to their rates of growth is generally mixed. In a large number of cases, this was perceived as a problem area and it led to the question of whether, in the process of adjustment, too much emphasis was placed on demand management measures and whether the appropriate strategy would be to supplement them with measures directly aimed at improving the allocation of resources and stimulating the growth of productivity and aggregate supply.

---

[18]For a discussion of this point in another context, see Mundell (1965).

This line of reasoning underscores the need for a better understanding of the relationship between growth and other economic policy objectives so as to minimize the cost of a given adjustment effort that has to be made over a foreseeable period. The experience of a large number of stabilization programs is that growth rates in the short run may fall below their previous trends. Such an outcome should not be surprising in cases where expansionary policies were pursued to stimulate economic activity and growth beyond sustainable levels, because logically a reversal of those policies is likely to have temporary effects that might be perceived at first as adverse. Available evidence shows that there is little scope to avoid outcomes of this sort; typically, unsustainable growth rates can be reached at the expense of international reserve losses or of increases in foreign indebtedness, either of which cannot be resorted to indefinitely.

The Rate of Inflation. Inflation control and the attainment of price stability are also among the major objectives of an adjustment effort. Experience in this area indicates that the adoption and implementation of corrective policy measures generally stops inflation from rising; outcomes with respect to a reduction in the rate of inflation, however, can be quite varied. This raises the issue of the appropriate way to set an inflation target. In earlier periods, policies supported by Fund resources were aimed at bringing inflation to a level compatible with exchange rate stability; this basically meant setting on the rate of inflation a ceiling broadly equivalent to that prevailing abroad. In cases where the domestic inflation rate was so high that it could not be realistically expected to be brought down to international levels over a short period of time, gradual reductions were programmed instead, together with a strategy of flexible exchange rate management. This strategy was based on the argument that the elimination of the inflation differential was not essential for balance of payments viability because the latter could be attained and maintained by an appropriate degree of exchange rate flexibility.

There is an element of truth in the argument that exchange rate flexibility can isolate the balance of payments from the adverse impact of inflation. However, the argument does not, by any means, end there. In the first place, such an argument overlooks the fact that inflation is not conducive to efficiency in resource allocation, that it generally has a real resource cost, and that, on both of these accounts, it clearly tends to impair the performance of the balance of payments. From this perspective, a flexible exchange rate may keep the balance of payments viable, but it may do so at an unnecessarily high cost. In the second place, while the argument could be considered, in some sense, valid from a single country standpoint, it loses value when applied to the world economy as a whole because, in such a context, the argument would be tantamount to accepting that the world rate of inflation cannot be made subject to control.

All of these reasons make inflation control, over a reasonable period of time, a desirable objective of economic policy. In this context, it would seem important to distinguish between an inflation target—the policy objective or desired outcome—and an inflation forecast—the likely outcome. The two need not (indeed, in most instances, they will not) coincide any more than a desirable outcome typically coincides with a probable result. In general, corrective policy programs should aim at reductions in the rate of inflation that are perceived as significant—even if they do not appear particularly realistic—in order to influence expectations in the right direction.

The Balance of Payments. The length of the period of adjustment has implications for the choice of the balance of payments objective. When the period under consideration is relatively short, an appropriate balance of payments target can be set by reference to the overall balance; in effect, this amounts to aiming at a certain desired development in net international reserves that is to be brought about by any combination of outcomes in the current and capital accounts of the balance of payments.

As the period for formulating policies and setting objectives expands, the particular combination of outcomes on current and capital accounts stops being a matter of indifference. A viable payments position over the medium term to long term calls for a sustainable structure or composition of the balance of payments. As a result, a variable such as the current account of the balance of payments becomes a legitimate policy objective in itself because it measures the rate at which the economy accumulates liabilities or assets vis-à-vis the rest of the world; alternatively, the focus on this variable ensures a sustainable relationship between aggregate demand and supply—that is, between investment and savings.

Like growth and inflation rates, the balance of payments can be both a result and an objective of economic policy. In contrast to them, however, the balance of payments has an additional dimension: it is equivalent to an economy's budget constraint vis-à-vis the rest of the world. As such a constraint, in a sense, it always has to be met, regardless of policies. From this perspective, a perceived improvement in the balance of payments, such as a reduction in the current or the overall deficits, need not reflect a policy improvement; it may be the result of a financing constraint imposed by the lack of foreign exchange. This characteristic of the balance of payments at times has contributed to the impression that policies supported by Fund resources were excessively biased toward balance of payments results because these seemed to be attained more often than price and growth targets.

Policy instruments and the period of adjustment

The lengthening of the period of adjustment also has implications for the choice of policy instruments, if only because it tends to increase the range of endogenous variables—that is, of the variables that can be expected to respond to policy action. One question that has been raised in the context of policy formulation concerns the appropriateness of the mix between measures to control aggregate demand and measures to stimulate domestic supply.

Demand and Supply Measures. Stabilization programs typically aim at controlling aggregate demand through constraints on the availability of financial resources. At that stage, the principal objective is to keep the level or the rate of growth of demand within broad limits judged to be sustainable. The issue of the source of origin of aggregate demand—that is, whether it comes from the public or private sectors—or of its composition—that is, consumption or investment—is not of immediate concern for the formulation of domestic financial policies. As the time horizon for policy formulation expands, however, the issue of whether demand is composed mainly of consumption or of investment becomes increasingly relevant for the future performance of the economy. In many instances, there is also concern about the source of origin of demand and expenditure.

It is generally accepted that, except in the very short run, both the level and the composition of aggregate demand are important considerations for the design of economic policies. In the abstract, it is conceivable to have an acceptable level of demand whose composition, however, is inappropriate. This is a purely transitory situation, since a suboptimal demand composition will impair the level of demand that would be sustainable in the future. This line of thought is related to the argument made earlier in the context of the balance of payments objective, where it was contended that a given deficit in the current account of the balance of payments is compatible with an indefinite number of combinations of savings and investment, not all of which are sustainable.

From this perspective, it is not a matter of indifference whether an adjustment sought in aggregate demand in general, or in the fiscal position in particular, is brought about through a curtailment in consumption or in total or public sector investment. Given the importance of productive investment for the future performance of the economy, the question may be raised about whether adjustment through reductions in investment is an appropriate strategy; the restoration of short-term financial balance to an economy (a proximate objective of demand management) needs to be attained by means that do not jeopardize its medium-term to long-term growth prospects. While, in this context, total investment is what matters, in many countries public sectors are the largest investors and their capital spending dominates total investment activity. In this respect, it is important that adjustment programs seek the generation of public sector savings to ensure that investment financing is available domestically on a sound basis and on the required scale.

Another area that calls for attention in designing adjustment programs is an assessment of the scope that is available to improve resource allocation in order to raise the flow of output out of the existing stock of factors of production. This assessment hinges on judgments about the appropriateness and realism of the structure of relative prices both within the economy and in comparison with those prevailing in the rest of the world. It is not infrequent that, to attain its objectives, an adjustment effort requires modifications in key prices in the economy, including the exchange rate and interest rates. In many instances, such measures are necessary conditions for the implementation of global macroeconomic policies.

Macroeconomic and Microeconomic Variables. A recurring distinction in discussions of programs supported by Fund resources is the one between macroeconomic and microeconomic variables.[19] In some sense, this distinction is related to those that are frequently made between demand and supply measures, on the one hand, and

---

[19]See paragraph 9 of Executive Board Decision No. 6056-(79/38) in *Selected Decisions of the International Monetary Fund and Selected Documents*, Ninth Issue (IMF, 1981 b, p. 21) and Gold (1979).

between short-run and medium-to-long-run measures, on the other. While it is generally agreed that the term "macroeconomic" conveys the idea of globality and aggregation, agreement is less clear with respect to its concrete definition and scope. Overall credit and fiscal policies aimed at demand management, and whose impact is generally short-term, typically are formulated on the basis of variables classified as macroeconomic. Measures that affect variables such as particular prices in the economy are normally considered microeconomic; rather than directly influencing aggregate demand, they affect resource allocation, productivity, and hence supply, and they tend to yield results over the medium to long term.

Several broad observations can be made on the subject of macroeconomic and microeconomic variables. First, there is the danger of overstressing the relevance of the distinction between the two types of variables. The distinction is useful for certain purposes and in certain contexts, but like most distinctions in economics, its usefulness or validity is by no means universal. At times, it has been used to support the proposition that microeconomic variables, such as relative prices, do not affect macroeconomic variables, such as the level of income, the rate of inflation, and the balance of payments. Such an argument, as a minimum, requires perfect price and cost flexibility in the economy, a flexibility that does not prevail in most cases. As a result, microeconomic variables can have considerable macroeconomic impacts; therefore, the distinction becomes less useful from an operational point of view.

Second, microeconomic variables do affect resource allocation and, hence, the distribution of income. In this context, programs aimed at redressing financial imbalances without impairing medium-term growth prospects need to include microeconomic measures to remove distortions and to improve resource allocation. Measures of this type are at times difficult to undertake because they are not universally popular in their short-run effects, but they can be essential for the success of the adjustment effort.

Assessment and interpretation of results

From a very general standpoint, it can be said that, in most instances, the policy programs supported by use of Fund resources tend to steer the economies in the directions that were originally intended. This being said, it must be recognized that the experiences under stand-by and extended arrangements have taken place under a wide variety of circumstances and settings; the experiences can be subject to a variety of interpretations and they indicate that the relationship between policy instruments and policy objectives—though well established in terms of the direction of events—is by no means clear-cut and precise. For all these reasons, not many observations can be made that would apply to all cases; however, useful inferences may be drawn for the assessment of outcomes and measurement of performance. These inferences reflect a particular, but by no means unique or universally agreed, interpretation of events based on the theoretical framework described above.

Standards of Measurement. A variety of standards can be thought of for purposes of assessing policy results and economic performance, all of which can be useful, depending on the nature and intent of the assessment. These possible standards can be classified into three broad categories. First, a positive or practical standard would measure performance under adjustment programs by comparing their results to the situation that prevailed in the economy prior to the introduction of policy measures; this positive standard amounts to a measure of *what is* relative to *what was*. Second, a normative standard would measure performance by comparing actual results under programs to the targets specified in those programs; this second standard compares, in a sense, *what is* with *what should be*. Third, a standard that might be called conjectural or judgmental would compare actual performance to the outcome that would have taken place in the absence of a policy program; this third standard focuses on a comparison of *what is* versus *what would have been*. Needless to say, this third standard is the most controversial one, if only because of its basically hypothetical nature, which makes the observations based on it a matter of conjecture, at least to some extent.

Inferences drawn by using the first standard are generally the least controversial because they simply compare sets of factual information. This characteristic is the main advantage of the positive standard; the counterpart is that the standard does not provide insights into areas such as the quality or degree of implementation of policies or such as the transmission mechanism between policy instruments and targets. From the standpoint of this standard, the general experience has been that in terms of the three main objectives (balance of payments, growth, and inflation), the degree of disequilibrium after the introduction of policies had been reduced relative to what it had been before—that is, in most instances the economic activity, balance of payments, and prices had improved as a matter of fact. In comparative terms, the more favorable outcomes were registered for the balance of payments, followed by inflation and growth, in that order. As hinted above, however, this standard of measurement does not allow for more than these factual statements.

The second standard, which compares results to targets, allows for a measure of judgment, if only because views may vary about the adequacy of the targets. Precisely because judgment needs to be exercised, this normative standard can be the subject of controversy. While experience is less amenable to generalization under this standard than under the first, there is a degree of consistency in the evidence provided by the two of them in the sense that, in comparing results to targets, the experience is broadly more favorable for the balance of payments than for the other two objectives. However, an important number of caveats need to be made with respect to comparisons based on this standard. An immediate one was already stated earlier when the particular dimension of the balance of payments was pointed out as a budget-type of constraint, which eventually limits the size of the possible deficits. The constraint is independent of the quality of policies, but its elasticity is not, in the sense that the more inadequate the policies, the tighter the constraint—a relationship that, *ex post* and factually, may lead to the impression of a balance of payments improvement because it either kept the deficit from rising or even reduced it. A second caveat, perhaps more elusive though not less important, is that targets should not be confused with forecasts. In most circumstances, targets are not attained and, as a matter of strategy, they are overachieved or underachieved. Frequently, targets are formulated with a view to influencing the actual results, particularly with expectations; the demonstration effects of policy changes and of the announcement of policy targets are important influences on their formation. This argues in favor of setting "ambitious" (that is, "unrealistic") targets even when it seems, a priori, clear that their complete attainment is unlikely. A comparison between targets and results in these circumstances would not be meaningful or even relevant. This being said, it needs to be borne in mind that a balance must be sought between the realism and ambitiousness of targets.

The third or conjectural standard is even more controversial, and yet it can be argued that, from some perspectives, it would be the most appropriate. What would be interesting to know, in gauging performance under an adjustment program, are the developments that would have taken place if policy action had not been undertaken. In general, a need for adjustment calls for an effort to steer the economy from its current and eventually unsustainable path toward one that can be sustained over time. Lack of policy action in these circumstances is likely to bring about disruptions created by severe foreign exchange constraints, rising inflation rates, and faltering growth rates. Compared with such a prospect, adjustment would appear to be desirable, even though it may involve a short-run cost by some measurements.

Problem Areas and Unresolved Issues. Problem areas abound in the field of economic policy implementation, to a large extent reflecting the fact that policies are intended to reverse situations characterized by excesses of claims over availability of resources. In most instances, these conflicting situations were created by the pursuit of a set of objectives which, while plausible in its components, was unsustainable in its totality. As a result, the adoption of adjustment measures is correctly perceived as a means to scale down the objectives and therefore is resisted as contrary to the country's priorities.

An area of policy implementation to which increasing attention must be paid is the relationship between macroeconomic and microeconomic variables. In many programs, the implementation of certain macroeconomic policies, such as those in the credit and fiscal fields, is contingent on the adoption of certain microeconomic measures dealing, for example, with particular prices in the economy, with taxes or expenditure patterns of the public sector, and the like. If these are not undertaken, the global basis for the program is undermined. The linkage between the global and specific aspects of economic policymaking is a function, inter alia, of the size of the required adjustment. The smaller the adjustment that has to be made, the more likely it is that macroeconomic policies will bring the economy back on a sustainable path.

A second area of interest in this context is the rapidity of the required adjustment effort. This issue, generally referred to as the choice between a "shock" and a "gradual" approach to the adjustment process, has not been conclusively resolved. Such a choice is usually constrained by the relationship between the availability of finance and the size of the imbalance, but it is also affected by the resolve and rapidity of policy response to emerging difficulties. The issue remains unresolved because it is not at all obvious that a gradual adjustment is preferable to a rapid one in all circumstances. The choice between shock and gradual strategies is only available with respect to policies because, as far as results are concerned, there is no option but to accept gradualism. In the policy context, the choice of strategy must distinguish between policies that have a time dimension—that is, flow type of policies such as credit expansion, borrowing, and expenditure—and policy steps that are of a once-and-for-all nature, such as a price adjustment or an exchange rate change. A gradual approach to policy formulation is likely to fit the former much better than the latter. Policy measures of a once-and-for-all nature are best undertaken as soon as they become necessary, if only because delays, *ceteris paribus*, will require that larger adjustments be made to attain a result of a given size.

REFERENCES

Almonacid, Ruben D., and Manuel Guitián, "The Optimal Rate of Devaluation," in *The Economics of Common Currencies*, Proceedings of the Madrid Conference on Optimum Currency Areas, ed. by Harry G. Johnson and Alexander K. Swoboda (London, 1973), pp. 281–97.

Bryant, Ralph C., *Money and Monetary Policy in Interdependent Nations*, Brookings Institution (Washington, 1980).

Cooper, Richard N., "An Analysis of Currency Devaluation in Developing Countries," in *International Trade and Money: Geneva Essays*, ed. by M. B. Connolly and Alexander K. Swoboda (London, 1973), pp. 167–96.

de Larosière, J. (1980 a), Address by the IMF Managing Director to the Economic and Social Council of the United Nations, Geneva, July 4, 1980. The address is reproduced in the *IMF Survey*. See "Managing Director Tells ECOSOC He Foresees Sufficient Resources for Expanded Recycling Role," *IMF Survey*, Vol. 9 (July 7, 1980), pp. 202–206.

———— (1980 b), Address by the IMF Managing Director to the 1980 Annual Meeting of the World Bank and the International Monetary Fund, Washington, September 30, 1980. The address is reproduced in the *IMF Survey*. See "de Larosière Explains Policies for Financing and Adjustment," *IMF Survey*, Vol. 9 (October 13, 1980), pp. 311–15.

de Vries, Margaret Garritsen, *The International Monetary Fund, 1966–1971: The System Under Stress*, International Monetary Fund (Washington, 1976).

Dornbusch, Rudiger, and Stanley Fischer, "Exchange Rates and the Current Account," *American Economic Review*, Vol. 70 (December 1980), pp. 960–71.

Frenkel, Jacob A., and Harry G. Johnson, eds., *The Monetary Approach to the Balance of Payments* (London, 1976).

————, eds., *The Economics of Exchange Rates: Selected Studies* (Reading, Massachusetts, 1978).

Frenkel, Jacob A., and Michael L. Mussa, "Monetary and Fiscal Policies in an Open Economy," *American Economic Review, Papers and Proceedings of the Ninety-Third Annual Meeting of the American Economic Association*, Vol. 71 (May 1981), pp. 253–58.

Friedman, Milton, *Essays in Positive Economics* (University of Chicago Press, 1953).

———, *The Counter-Revolution in Monetary Theory*, Occasional Paper No. 33, Institute of Economic Affairs (London, 1970).

Gold, Joseph, *The Stand-By Arrangements of the International Monetary Fund: A Commentary on Their Formal, Legal, and Financial Aspects*, International Monetary Fund (Washington, 1970).

———, *Conditionality*, IMF Pamphlet Series, No. 31 (Washington, 1979).

———, *Financial Assistance by the International Monetary Fund: Law and Practice*, IMF Pamphlet Series, No. 27 (Washington, Second Edition, 1980).

Goreux, Louis M., *Compensatory Financing Facility*, IMF Pamphlet Series, No. 34 (Washington, 1980).

Guitián, Manuel, "The Effects of Changes in the Exchange Rate on Output, Prices, and the Balance of Payments," *Journal of International Economics*, Vol. 6 (February 1976), pp. 65–74.

———, "Credit Versus Money as an Instrument of Control," *Staff Papers*, Vol. 20 (November 1973), pp. 785–800. The article is reproduced in International Monetary Fund (1977), pp. 227–42.

———, "Dutch Monetarism: A Comment," *Journal of Monetary Economics*, Vol. 3 (July 1977), pp. 379–81.

———, A series of three articles on "Fund Conditionality and the International Adjustment Process" that appeared in *Finance and Development*: "The Early Period, 1950–70," Vol. 17 (December 1980), pp. 23–27; "The Changing Environment of the 1970s," Vol. 18 (March 1981), pp. 8–11; and "A Look into the 1980s," Vol. 18 (June 1981), pp. 14–17. The series was reprinted as a single paper—Manuel Guitián, *Conditionality: Access to Fund Resources*, International Monetary Fund (Washington, 1981).

Horsefield, J. Keith, *The International Monetary Fund, 1945–1965: Twenty Years of International Monetary Cooperation*, International Monetary Fund (Washington, 1969).

International Monetary Fund (IMF), *Selected Decisions of the International Monetary Fund and Selected Documents*, Eighth Issue (Washington, May 10, 1976).

———, *The Monetary Approach to the Balance of Payments: A Collection of Research Papers by the Staff of the International Monetary Fund* (Washington, 1977).

———, *Articles of Agreement*, Second Amendment (Washington, 1978).

——— (1981 a), IMF Institute, *Financial Policy Workshops: The Case of Kenya* (Washington, 1981).

——— (1981 b), *Selected Decisions of the International Monetary Fund and Selected Documents*, Ninth Issue (Washington, June 15, 1981).

Johnson, Harry G., *International Trade and Economic Growth: Studies in Pure Theory* (London, 1958).

———, *Inflation and the Monetarist Controversy* (Amsterdam, 1972).

———, *Further Essays in Monetary Economics* (Harvard University Press, 1973).

Keller, Peter M., "Implications of Credit Policies for Output and the Balance of Payments," *Staff Papers*, Vol. 27 (September 1980), pp. 451–77.

Economic Management and Conditionality

Landell-Mills, Pierre M., "Structural Adjustment Lending: Early Experience," *Finance and Development*, Vol. 18 (December 1981), pp. 17–21.

Loser, Claudio M., "External Debt Management and Balance of Payments Policies," *Staff Papers*, Vol. 24 (March 1977), pp. 168–92.

McKinnon, Ronald I., "The Exchange Rate and Macroeconomic Policy: Changing Postwar Perceptions," *Journal of Economic Literature*, Vol. 19 (June 1981), pp. 531–57.

Mookerjee, Subimal, "Policies on the Use of Fund Resources," *Staff Papers*, Vol. 13 (November 1966), pp. 421–42.

———, "New Guidelines for Use of Fund Resources Follow Review of Practice of Conditionality," *IMF Survey*, Vol. 8 (March 19, 1979), pp. 82–83.

Mundell, Robert A., "A Fallacy in the Interpretation of Macroeconomic Equilibrium," *Journal of Political Economy*, Vol. 73 (February 1965), pp. 61–66.

———, *International Economics* (New York, 1968).

———, *Monetary Theory: Inflation, Interest, and Growth in the World Economy* (Pacific Palisades, California, 1971).

Nowzad, Bahram, Richard C. Williams, *et al*, *External Indebtedness of Developing Countries*, IMF Occasional Paper No. 3 (Washington, 1981).

Reichmann, Thomas M., "The Fund's Conditional Assistance and the Problems of Adjustment, 1973–75," *Finance and Development*, Vol. 15 (December 1978), pp. 38–41.

———, and Richard T. Stillson, "Experience with Programs of Balance of Payments Adjustment: Stand-By Arrangements in the Higher Tranches, 1963–72," *Staff Papers*, Vol. 25 (June 1978), pp. 293–309.

Salop, Joanne, and Erich Spitäller, "Why Does the Current Account Matter?" *Staff Papers*, Vol. 27 (March 1980), pp. 101–34.

Selden, Richard T., "A Critique of Dutch Monetarism," *Journal of Monetary Economics*, Vol. 1 (April 1975), pp. 221–32.

Witteveen, H. Johannes, Address by the IMF Managing Director to the 1978 Euromarkets Conference, London, May 8, 1978. The address is reproduced in the *IMF Survey*. See "Fund's Conditional Assistance Promotes Adjustment Programs of Members, Witteveen States," *IMF Survey*, Vol. 7 (May 22, 1978), pp. 145–50.

Wright, E. Peter, "World Bank Lending for Structural Adjustment," *Finance and Development*, Vol. 17 (September 1980), pp. 20–23.

Alternative Approaches to Short-Term Economic Management in Developing Countries

DANIEL M. SCHYDLOWSKY

The standard prescription for short-term economic management of balance of payments or inflationary problems consists of devaluation, demand restriction (both in terms of government expenditure and of credit to the private sector), and usually import liberalization.

This package has become less and less acceptable to a wide variety of constituencies. Some critics complain that it leads to unnecessary losses in output and growth. Others point to increases in unemployment. Still others claim that the package is self-defeating by leading to stagflation. Finally, others point to the political disruption that often follows its implementation. Whatever the merit of these or other criticisms, the availability of alternative approaches to short-term economic management would certainly be advantageous, even on the most narrow grounds of the traditional welfare economics of expanded choice.

Because managing a balance of payments problem is inherently different from managing an inflationary situation and in order to make the search for alternatives more manageable, balance of payments management will be taken up first and the management of inflation and price stabilization will be dealt with later.

BALANCE OF PAYMENTS MANAGEMENT

The need for alternatives arises because the techniques usually applied seem to yield a mix of balance of payments improvement that is based far too little on the growth of exports and far too much on the reduction of imports. Moreover, the reduction in imports results far too much from reduction in economic activity and far too little from changes in relative prices and the consequent substitution of domestic goods for importable goods in production and consumption.

The theoretical expectation derived from standard international trade models does not afford much basis for this empirical concern.[1] It is well established that supplies and demands in international trade are residual ones. Thus, the supply curve of exports is the difference between the supply curve of exportables in the domestic economy and the domestic demand curve for them (see Figure 1). Consequently, the price elasticity of the supply of exports is equal to the weighted sum of the price elasticity of the production of exportables and the price elasticity of demand for those exportables in the domestic market. Similarly, the demand for imports is a residual demand, arising from the difference between the domestic demand for importables and the domestic supply of such importables. Correspondingly, the price elasticity of the demand for imports is the weighted sum of the elasticities of domestic demand for and domestic supply of importables.

In an economy in which traded and nontraded goods are substitutes for each other, the level of imports and exports should adjust to relative price changes (e.g., devaluation) without any change in the domestic level of activity. As relative prices change, expenditures and the production mix would both be switched, the quantity supplied for export would rise, and the quantity of imports demanded would fall. Principally, price elasticities would be at work, with income elasticities playing a definitely secondary role. However, if nontraded goods are poor substitutes for traded goods and if they require an import component, then it is quite possible that an improvement in the balance of payments will require that the demand for nontraded goods fall below productive capacity, particularly if factor prices are less than fully flexible downward in real terms.

---

[1] What follows reflects an elasticities-absorption approach; a monetary approach would provide even less basis for the concern at issue.

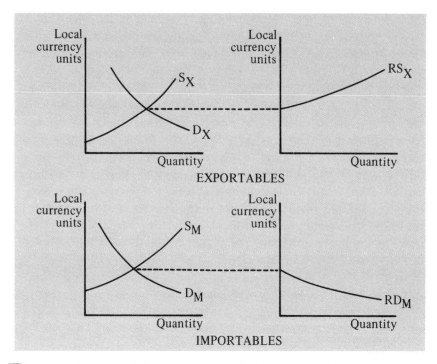

FIGURE 1. THE SUPPLY AND DEMAND CURVES OF EXPORTABLES AND IMPORTABLES

In the context of the model just outlined, the dissatisfaction expressed with the outcome of the usual balance of payments management techniques can be traced to the consequences of two elements of reality: (1) low elasticity of supply and demand for exports and imports, respectively, and (2) a too large nontraded goods sector in the economy. Correspondingly, alternative approaches to balance of payments management would need to focus on ways for raising these elasticities and for reducing the size of the nontraded goods sector, for only if these "structural" elements could be dealt with, would the balance of payments adjustment mechanism come closer to its desired functioning.

Before pursuing the line of approach just suggested, it is worth noting that the supply and demand model discussed in the preceding paragraph presents some difficulties for the most common explanation of the existence of balance of payments problems in developing countries—namely, that of generalized "overheating" of the economy. This model explains the existence of imports precisely because some sectors are "overheated"; that is, there is excess demand in these sectors. Correspondingly, export sectors are always "underheated." Only the nontraded goods sectors should be "precisely heated." But surely, the sense of generalized overheating goes beyond the mere overheating of the nontraded goods sector.

While in a single-sector aggregate model with a clearly defined supply capacity, overheating has a clearly specifiable meaning, in the context of a multisectoral model, which distinguishes exports from imports and from nontraded goods, overheating as a general category becomes meaningless. It is, therefore, probably more useful to focus on the shifts of specific goods and specific production activities between the categories of imports, exports, and nontraded goods as a result of changes in the conditions of international trade and the remuneration of domestic factors. What matters then is the mix of overheated and underheated sectors and their capacity to sell abroad and to procure from abroad.

Price elasticities in the foreign trade of developing countries

Let us look first at exports and then at imports.

Price Elasticity of Export Supply. Most developing countries have a wide variety of potential products to offer on world markets. For convenience, these may be grouped into mining products, agricultural products, and industrial products. Mining products typically have high fixed investment and a substantial component of rent in their average cost; their marginal costs are low compared with average costs, but they rise sharply when full capacity output is attained. Marginal cost consists mainly of skilled labor; moreover, there is usually very little domestic demand for the product, or none at all.

In agriculture, it is important to distinguish industrial agriculture from food agriculture. The former is usually fairly capital-intensive in addition to generating an important component of rent in its average costs. Domestic demand for the industrial crop is usually quite limited. Food agriculture is usually found in small plot sizes and typically uses less capital in the process of production. Domestic demand for food crops is substantial and in some instances exceeds supply capacity. Marginal cost in both types of agriculture is rising because of the decline in the marginal product of land as additional variable inputs are added. The input structure consists of fertilizers, pesticides, and a few other materials in addition to labor. Marginal costs in agriculture are typically higher than they are for most of the feasible range of output in mining.

Industry typically has a much higher ratio of marginal to average costs and also usually higher absolute marginal costs than these other two sectors. Moreover, the input structure is usually dominated by materials, many of which are imported. Marginal costs in industry are usually constant in the short run but sometimes decline as a result of economies of scale. Domestic demand for industrial products is considerable but typically falls short of installed productive capacity.

To develop an aggregate supply curve of exports, it is necessary to sum the supply curves of each of the individual products. To this end, it is useful to define a standard unit of output as a U.S. dollar's worth of product at international prices and to define marginal costs in local currency units per U.S. dollar's worth of output. The summation process is shown graphically in Figure 2. It becomes immediately apparent that this summation is not as straightforward as it

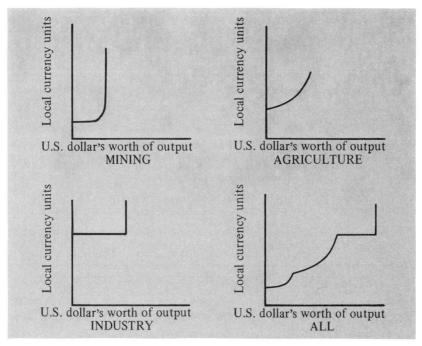

FIGURE 2. MARGINAL COSTS OF EXPORT PRODUCTS
(in local currency units per U.S. dollar's worth of output)

seems, for there is considerable question about how to interpret the price variable on the vertical axis. The conventional approach would be to use the exchange rate on the vertical axis. However, the exchange rate affects not only revenue but also costs whenever there are material inputs that are imported or that compete with imports and whenever domestic factors have supply prices defined in real terms and translated to current prices on the basis of a cost of living index that includes importables. Moreover, the different sectors have production structures that differ precisely in this crucial respect: mining has minimal importable inputs, agriculture has some importable inputs, and industry has a large amount of such inputs. On the other hand, mining and industry typically have wage structures closely tied to "modern consumption goods," which by their nature are linked closely to the exchange rate; this is less the case in agriculture, although differences exist between industrial and food agriculture.

Aggregation can proceed if the price variable is defined as the number of local currency units per U.S. dollar's worth of any output, with domestic costs assumed to be unchanged. The implication is that the domestic currency receipts from a dollar's worth of exports could change without changing the domestic currency costs of a dollar's worth of inputs. It should be noted that this implies conceptually the adoption of a multiple exchange rate system. However, this implication is not as shocking as it might at first appear, since if the cost structures are closely examined, it is found that each of the sectors is affected differentially by such exchange rate substitutes as tariffs, taxes on wages, differential interest rates, differential taxes on output, and profits—and, indeed, differential wages themselves. Thus, an implicit multiple exchange rate system already exists on the cost side,[2] and the construction of the export supply curve requires only the analogous adjustment on the demand side.

The result of the aggregation is an S-shaped curve, with a fairly inelastic portion in the area of mining and industrial agriculture, an intermediate, somewhat more elastic, segment for food agriculture, and then a very elastic segment corresponding to industry. The vertical cost distances between these different segments of the

---

[2]Calculations of effective protection recognize this situation by taking differential protection of inputs explicitly into account.

supply curve are fundamentally determined by the extent to which economic policy and institutional circumstance discriminate between economic activities. For example, if the incidence of tariffs on industrial inputs is higher than the incidence of the corresponding levies on agricultural and mining costs, then industrial costs will of course be much higher per U.S. dollar's worth of output than mining or agricultural costs. It should be noted that what matters in this case are the tariff rates, as well as the fact that industrial production has a much higher component of intermediate inputs than either agriculture or mining; thus, even under equal import tax rates, the incidence of the tax is higher in the case of industrial production. Cost differentials are also affected when agriculture is offered a preferential interest rate. Such a policy lowers the cost of credit to the agricultural sector, in comparison with other sectors, and thus affects the cost of production correspondingly. Wages have a similar impact. Insofar as industrial wages are higher than wages in the primary sector, either because of legislation, cost of living differentials, or different strengths of union labor; and insofar as fringe benefits differ between the sectors, industry will have higher costs than it would otherwise have had.

Under these circumstances, the definition of a supply elasticity of exports is ambiguous. The supply elasticity with regard to the sales price is different from the supply elasticity with regard to the exchange rate, and both of these are different from the elasticity with regard to a differentiated export subsidy of a particular description or from the elasticity with regard to tax measures affecting input costs.

The elasticity that is traditionally defined refers to the exchange rate. However, changes in the exchange rate affect costs as well as revenue, albeit differentially across sectors. In the primary sectors, the major impact of the exchange rate on costs is through the adjustment of nominal wages, which may respond to an increase in the cost of living caused by a devaluation. The extent to which this occurs depends naturally on the extent of unionization as well as on the nature of the supply curve of labor in the primary sector. In industry, the cost-push of devaluation works through the wage rate as well, but also operates through material inputs that are either imported or compete with imports. Furthermore, the impact on the costs of the different sectors is further differentiated because of the presence of rent in the average cost of mining and agriculture but not in industry. As a result of these factors, devaluation is less effective in making industrial production internationally competitive than in the case of primary production.

To what extent each sector contributes to the aggregate elasticity depends on each sector's share of total exports at the initial exchange rate, as well as on each sector's exchange rate elasticity. Since there are usually no industrial exports at the initial exchange rate and since industrial exports do not respond much to devaluation, the aggregate elasticity of exports with regard to devaluation depends principally on the supply elasticity of mining and industrial agriculture with regard to devaluation. As a result, the aggregate elasticity is rather low.

If, however, there was computed an elasticity of exports for a differentiated exports subsidy that would, for instance, provide symmetry on the export side to tariff protection in the domestic market, a drastic change would occur in the profitability of industrial exports while it would not noticeably affect the profitability of mining or agricultural exports. Therefore, the elasticity involved would result principally from the supply elasticity of industrial production, which is by far the highest. As a result, the elasticity of exports with regard to subsidies will be high indeed.

In summary, in a single exporting sector, using no intermediate inputs, the definition of the price elasticity of the supply of exports is unambiguous and can be undertaken directly with regard to the exchange rate. But when intermediate goods are used in production and the proportions of such goods vary across sectors, and when domestic factor incomes respond to changes in the cost of living that in turn are induced by devaluation, and when there are also significant differences in the prices at which comparable inputs are acquired for different economic activities—i.e., there exist wage differentiation, tariff differences, etc.—the elasticity of export supply with regard to price is no longer unambiguous but needs to be specified explicitly as being related to the exchange rate, export subsidies, changes in the tax regime, and so on. It follows that *different ways of affecting export profitability operate on different segments of the export supply curve and therefore are not faced with the same elasticity.* This finding is crucial for policy design and provides the fulcrum that will be used later on to suggest alternative balance of payments management techniques.

Price Elasticity of the Demand for Imports. At constant output levels, the response of the quantity of imports demanded to changes in the exchange rate depends essentially on two elements: (1) the extent to which the devaluation causes changes in relative prices between importables and domestic goods, or within importables, and (2) the underlying price elasticities themselves.

In the absence of intermediate goods, what is at issue is the substitution between an imported good, the price of which is entirely specified in foreign exchange, and a domestic good, the price of which results entirely from domestic factor returns. Where domestic factor prices are not responsive to changes in the exchange rate, there is no difference between the elasticity of import demand with regard to a devaluation and the elasticity of import demand with regard to relative price changes, because relative price changes are identical to the devaluation. However, when imported goods require some complementary domestic value added in order to be marketed in internal markets—such as port labor, transportation costs, wholesaling, and retailing—and when domestic goods in turn require an import content, then exchange rate elasticity and relative price elasticity are no longer equivalent.

Let us consider, for example, the case where all goods sold on the domestic market have the same import content. Under such circumstances, a devaluation would cause no change at all in relative prices and thus the exchange rate elasticity would be zero, whereas the price elasticity might still be other than zero. It is quite easy to see, therefore, that the more similar are the import components of the goods offered on the domestic market, the lower is the exchange rate elasticity. Furthermore, the more responsive domestic factor remunerations are to changes in the exchange rate (a link typically existing through the cost of living impact of devaluations), the lower is the exchange rate elasticity.

The above case can be usefully illustrated by the examples shown in Table 1, which portrays the change in relative prices of two goods sold in the domestic market as a result of a 50 per cent devaluation. The cost structures have purposely been specified to be very different; product A might well be a backward-integrated domestic industrial good, while product B might well be an import. Domestic factor remunerations are assumed in all cases to rise less than the exchange rate, except for managerial-entrepreneurial wages in Case I. Nonetheless, this large devaluation of 50 per cent produces

Table 1
EFFECT OF CURRENCY DEVALUATION ON RELATIVE PRICES[1]
(per cent)

Cost Structures		Product A		Product B
Imported inputs		20		60
Production labor cost		50		20
Managerial-entrepreneurial cost		30		20

Effect on Relative Prices

Case I				
Devaluation	50	Increase in P_A		40
Production wage increase	30	Increase in P_B		46
Managerial-entrepreneurial wage increase	50	Relative change P_B/P_A		4.3
Case II				
Devaluation	50	Increase in P_A		34
Production wage increase	30	Increase in P_B		42
Managerial-entrepreneurial wage increase	30	Relative change P_B/P_A		6
Case III				
Devaluation	50	Increase in P_A		26
Production wage increase	20	Increase in P_B		38
Managerial-entrepreneurial wage increase	20	Relative change P_B/P_A		9.5

[1]These examples assume that there are no pure profits. Nonetheless, accounting profits may well exist as a way of paying managerial-entrepreneurial wages.

a change in relative prices ranging from under one tenth to under one fifth of its size. If devaluation does not change relative prices much, it cannot generate much substitution based on relative price changes.

Since the cost structure and the import content of goods offered for domestic sale are so crucial, it is worth noting that they depend on a number of factors. One of these is certainly technology, which determines the material input content. Another is economic policy, which has much impact on the source of the material input. Policy also affects the share of costs that accrues to imports because, given an elasticity of substitution, tariffs and taxes affect the share of import costs in total costs. Wage-setting mechanisms also contribute to import intensity; when unions or government regulations generate higher wages, if the elasticity of substitution is less than unity, the domestic value-added component rises and, correspondingly, the import component falls. The same is true of interest rate policy; given an inventory requirement, the higher the interest rate, the greater the domestic value added and the lower the import component. Finally, a very important element is the market organization of the importing sector. To the extent that this sector is oligopolistic, it will charge higher margins and thus lower its import content while simultaneously raising the extent to which domestic producers are able to charge a higher value added over their own import content. It is useful to remember in this connection that, in the long run, domestic prices and therefore value added in domestic import-competing activity are determined by the margins in the importing business. In the short run, the opposite may well be true, if there are short-run supply inelasticities in procuring additional imports for the economy.

Size of nontraded goods sector

The theoretically sound definition of nontraded goods refers to them as those goods with domestic prices between the import and export points. It is therefore expected that these points will differ, and this difference is usually explained to be the result of the existence of such factors as transportation costs. It has been recognized for some time, however, that the spread between the import and export points can also be affected by policy.[3] Thus, import duties raise the import price, and export taxes lower the export price. As these tools of commercial policy are increasingly applied, or others with similar effects are used, the range of nontraded goods expands. It has thus become fashionable to distinguish within the nontraded goods sector between tradable and nontradable goods, with the latter being those that are not susceptible to trade (e.g., some services).

A large part of the economic policy followed by developing countries consists precisely of manipulating import duties and export taxes. Indeed, a major proportion of today's developing countries are applying or have applied an import substituting industrialization (ISI) policy.[4] This policy consists of raising the import point of a wide variety of goods well above the free trade level. Thus, import-competing production is expanded and, when import protection becomes prohibitive (either because tariffs are very high or quan-

[3] For an early discussion of this point, see Díaz-Alejandro (1965).
[4] For a general discussion, see Little et al (1970).

titative restrictions are used, or because domestic production has become more efficient over time and has thereby made existing tariffs unnecessarily high), a significant number of tradable goods become nontraded goods on the import side. Simultaneously, however, these tradable nontraded goods are not exportable because the ISI policy typically involves a low exchange rate (in terms of local currency units per U.S. dollar) for exports and because a large part of the import protection is absorbed in higher real factor remuneration made possible by policy-assisted segmentation of factor markets. Thus, the tradable products that have become nontraded goods on the import side by policy fiat have also been made nontraded goods on the export side by the same policy. As a consequence, the tradable nontraded goods sector may comprise as much as a third of gross national product (GNP)—all industrial production, for example.

It is useful to elaborate briefly on the policy structure that is involved in ISI. To do so, it is useful to consolidate the exchange rate and the commercial policy into its multiple exchange rate analogue,[5] as is done in Table 2, which shows a typical structure for an advanced ISI country.

Table 2
TYPICAL EXCHANGE RATE SYSTEM OF A SEMI-INDUSTRIAL DEVELOPING COUNTRY
(local currency units per U.S. dollar)

Product	Market	Financial Rate	Trade Taxation	Total Rate
			(per cent)	
Primary export	Domestic	10	—	10
	Export	10	—	10
Financial	—	10	—	10
Raw materials	Domestic	10	20	12
	Export	10	—	10
Semimanufactures I	Domestic	10	35	13.5
	Export	10	—	10
Semimanufactures II	Domestic	10	50	15
	Export	10	—	10
Finished products	Domestic	10	80	18
	Export	10	—	10

[5]This approach was first used in CARTTA (1966), Schydlowsky (1967 and 1971), and Diamand (1973).

It should be noted that, as industrialization has proceeded in successive stages of backward integration, tariffs have been raised in a cascade fashion. As a result, prices and costs have both risen, compared with free trade levels; however, while costs are above world prices, prices are also sufficiently high to allow sales for the domestic market to be profitable. Thus, for example, the typical industrial producer has costs based on an exchange rate of 12 for his material inputs, 14 for his semi-industrial components, and 13 for his wages (a mix of 10 on food and 18 on finished goods), thus making an average cost exchange rate of about 13. Since the sales exchange rate ranges from 13.5 to 18 on the domestic market, production is profitable (and, of course, imports do not come in). On the other hand, for export, no protection similar to that available for the domestic market is usually included; thus, while production must operate on a cost exchange rate of 13, the export exchange rate is only 10, which clearly does not allow profitability. Producers in this situation are locked out of export trade by policy design.

It is also worth pointing out that, in this policy context, the normal comparisons of production efficiency are misleading. It is not legitimate under these circumstances to take domestic costs and divide them by the financial exchange rate in order to compare the result with the c.i.f. price of imports. Producers' costs are not based on that financial exchange rate; rather, they are based on the applicable higher "commodity exchange rate," which incorporates commercial and other policies affecting costs. Whenever comparison is undertaken through simple division by a financial exchange rate, an "industrial inefficiency illusion" is introduced, which will be stronger the older the ISI policy and the deeper it has gone. If a cost of production figure is computed in dollars by dividing local currency costs by the applicable cost exchange rate, the result would be considerably closer to a proper measure of productivity. Even so, however, the result would at best represent only private x-efficiency (or x-inefficiency). A proper evaluation of social productivity would require the use of shadow prices for the domestic factors. Such prices are likely to differ significantly from the market prices, since unemployment is usually a major feature of the developing economy and thus the shadow price of labor would be expected to be well below the market price of labor. At the same time, if that situation obtains in the labor market, the shadow price of capital must be above its market price. However, in the market for capital, a further element needs to be taken into account—namely, the distinction between installed capacity and new fungible investment resources, with the former having a marginal social cost equal to the user cost and the latter having a shadow price equal to the opportunity cost of new savings.

Because the tradable nontraded goods sector has grown in an ISI setting and thus has been designated the leading growth sector by policy, it has typically accumulated an excessively large installed capacity relative to the needs of the market. This excess capacity is the consequence of a variety of policies leading to underutilization of plants within the hours worked, a low use of shift work throughout the day, and numerous days of idleness throughout the year.[6] The consequence for the supply elasticity in the tradable nontraded goods sector is significant. For a range, supply responds at constant prices to increases in demand. Additional capacity utilization can thereafter only be brought into use as a result of higher product prices or changes in the factor markets. Since these in turn can be affected by economic policy, the elasticity of supply of this sector varies significantly with regard to the specific policies used to change the price structure of the producer. Once again the same ambiguity is encountered as that found in discussing the aggregate price elasticity of exports.

Policy alternatives for balance of payments management

The purpose of an alternative approach is to boost the contribution of increased exports to balance of payments improvements, to raise the impact of the change of relative prices, and to contain the fall in the level of activity. The preceding discussion indicates that, in order to achieve these goals, policy must aim at operating on the elastic upper section of the supply curve of exports, and it must also change into traded goods as high a proportion of the tradable nontraded goods as possible.

When discussing the aggregate supply curve of exports, it was pointed out that its form depends crucially on the policy package for which it is designed. Thus, the elasticity of the supply of exports with respect to generalized conventional devaluations is very low.

---

[6]For further discussion of excess capacity and its determinants, see Schydlowsky (1979 b).

On the other hand, the supply of exports is quite sensitive to measures that change the local currency revenue from export of industrial goods that are currently subject to a strong tax as a result of the general anti-export bias of the ISI growth policy.[7]

A policy to boost the contribution of export growth to balance of payments management should, therefore, consist of a differential devaluation that would raise the local currency revenue from the export of industrial products by setting the rate for each output at a level at least comparable to the total exchange rate affecting industrial costs. Such a differential devaluation would bring the structure of exchange rates on the sales side into line with the implicit structure created by the trade restrictions and other policies on the cost side. As a result, the cost differences that cause the export supply curve to be S-shaped would be offset and the kink in the export supply curve would disappear, making the curve as a whole much more elastic and providing a much greater response to any future changes in the basic financial exchange rate.[8]

The same differential devaluation would make the previously tradable nontraded goods become traded goods, for it would suddenly open the possibility of penetration of export markets to the wide variety of goods restricted to the domestic market by the ISI policy. Essentially, the differential devaluation raises the export point and places it in the vicinity of the import point. Since many commodities have tariffs that are at an unnecessarily high level and since short-run marginal cost is often below long-run marginal cost and below short-run average cost, an export point even close to the import point often generates sufficient market profitability for exporting to make domestic goods into export products.

The differential devaluation suggested above can be categorized in different ways as:

(a) a policy action designed to offset the existing implicit multiple exchange rate structure on the cost side, thereby making the whole exchange rate system more efficient;

(b) a policy measure that provides symmetry in commercial policy, complementing import restriction with export promotion;

---

[7]Quantification of this anti-export bias can be found, for example, in Balassa, *et al* (1971).

[8]For a two-digit sectoral comparison of domestic and export sales exchange rates with cost rates for Argentina, see Berlinski and Schydlowsky (1982).

(c) a policy that provides the needed vent for surplus of the excess capacity accumulated over the years in the ISI policy; and

(d) a policy that allows unemployed capital and labor to be put to work in order for the economy to overcome its balance of payments problem.

There are at least as many alternatives for implementation of a policy of differential devaluation as there are interpretations of what it fundamentally means. Each of the policies compensates for the initial circumstance that caused the low elasticity of export supply with regard to devaluation and compensates for the excess size of the nontraded sector. Three alternative approaches to implementation are discussed below.

Compensatory Export Bounties. This is the simplest policy of all. At the time of export, every dollar's worth received is assigned a certain amount of compensatory export bounty—for example, a tax cancellation certificate. In this way, the export exchange rate is selectively and differentially modified for each potential export in accordance with the appropriate compensation.

Two main problems and one objection arise in connection with this approach. The problems consist of deciding at what rate to set the bounty for each commodity and how to finance the requisite disbursement from the treasury. The objection is that the bounty affects goods only and does not affect invisibles.

The rate-setting problem is by far the more important. The simplest method for setting the rates is to have a uniform across-the-board bounty on the value of exports, but it is sure to set the rate too high for some products and too low for others. As a result, a number of tradables that should be traded will continue to be non-traded goods; on the other hand, windfall profits will be generated that have the danger of allowing negative value added in export activities. A second rather straightforward approach consists of applying a symmetry rule, using existing import tariff rates as the appropriate rates for the export bounty. While this is superior to the across-the-board rule, it assumes that the tariffs themselves have been set at a proper level. The third alternative, and certainly the most difficult one, is to set ad hoc rates after careful study of each individual product, perhaps involving negotiation with the respective producers. This alternative allows taking into account such factors as the cost exchange rate involved, the domestic resource cost of foreign exchange in the productive process at issue, the divergence between market and shadow prices, and so on. It does, however, have the drawback of some arbitrariness and of an enormous laboriousness in design.

The fiscal costs issue is relatively more straightforward. Without question, the export bounty implies a disbursement from the treasury when exports under the system actually take place. At the same time, however, these new exports set in motion a foreign trade multiplier, absorbing existing installed and underutilized capacity together with unemployed labor. The result is an expansion in the tax base, with corresponding new revenue for the treasury. Whether the new collections fall short of, or are in excess of, the original disbursements represented by the bounty is an empirical matter. It would be expected that the more closed the economy is, the more likely it is that the collections will exceed the bounty. The same is true of the extent to which domestic costs are close to world prices and of the extent to which the tax system is elastic to the level of output. The few empirical calculations that exist in this regard all indicate very sizable tax collections resulting from activation, but this indication does not guarantee that it would be so in all cases.[9]

The objection that the export bounty affects only merchandise trade and does not affect invisibles is not fully valid. Undoubtedly, it could be extended to such invisibles as tourist flows, and it could also quite easily cover freight charges. However, far more fundamentally, it must be borne in mind that these export bounties are compensatory and that therefore the major proportion of the invisibles—namely, the financial transactions—are not candidates for such reimbursement because they have not been subject to the corresponding tax.

Compensated Devaluation. This is a more sophisticated way of implementing an across-the-board compensatory export bounty. It consists of simultaneous and offsetting modifications of the financial exchange rate and the trade taxation system.[10] In essence, the cost-increasing effects of a devaluation are compensated by offsetting tariff reductions (or import subsidies) and export taxes, whereas such compensation does not take place for the nontraditional ex-

---

[9]See Urdinola and Mallon (1967), Schydlowsky (1971), and Gonzalez-Izquierdo (1981). While tax revenue grows as output expands, what is at work is a Keynesian foreign trade multiplier rather than a Laffer curve.

[10]See CARTTA (1966), Schydlowsky (1967), and Diamand (1973).

ports that it is desired to promote, nor for financial transactions. A comparison of the numerical results of a uniform compensatory export bounty and of a compensated devaluation is shown in Table 3. Examination of the table shows that difficulties accrue under compensated devaluation when food is an import (export) product because compensatory import subsidies (export taxes) would then be needed. If these are not feasible or are not adopted, there will be some differences in the effect of a compensated devaluation and of a uniform compensatory export bounty. Naturally, a compensated devaluation cannot alone reproduce the effects of a differentiated compensatory export bounty; however, both measures can certainly be combined to produce any desired mix.

Domestic Tax and Price Measures. As an alternative to operating on the revenue side, it is possible to operate on the cost side, reducing selected elements of cost in a manner destined to make exports more competitive. Thus, for example, it is possible to give tax credits to exporters on a variety of items, such as social security and other fringe benefits payable on wages, some or all of the wage bill, additional depreciation on installed capacity put to work, financial costs incurred in export, and working capital. It is also possible to proceed directly to the provision of inexpensive finance to the exporting activities or to tie tax rates to the level of exports or to the rate of capacity utilization. Finally, it is possible to use public utility rates, port charges, and transportation rates to achieve the same end.

All these domestic policy measures are essentially alternatives to a differentiated export bounty and have the same difficulties of implementation as the differentiated export bounty.

MANAGEMENT OF INFLATION AND PRICE STABILIZATION

Once again, it is useful to begin by stating reasons for concern and for the search for alternatives. Price stabilization policy in its current mainline form is essentially a policy based on reducing demand. Its consequence is often to depress the level of activity.[11] Thus, in the best cases a considerable cost is paid in terms of real income and

---

[11]For a discussion of why this happens, see Schydlowsky (1979 a) and Taylor (1980), for instance.

Table 3
ALTERNATIVE MODIFICATIONS TO THE EXCHANGE RATE SYSTEM
(local currency units per U.S. dollar)

Product	Market	Initial Situation			Uniform Export Subsidy			Compensated Devaluation		
		Financial rate	Tax	Total rate	Financial rate	Tax or subsidy	Total rate	Financial rate	Tax or subsidy	Total rate
			(per cent)			(per cent)			(per cent)	
Primary export	Domestic	10	—	10	10	—	10	12	16.6	10
	Export	10	—	10	10	—	10	12	16.6	10
Financial	—	10	—	10	10	—	10	12	—	12
Raw material	Domestic	10	20	12	10	20	12	12	—	12
	Export	10	—	10	10	50	15	12	25	15
Semimanufactures I	Domestic	10	35	13.5	10	35	13.5	12	12.5	13.5
	Export	10	—	10	10	50	15	12	25	15
Semimanufactures II	Domestic	10	50	15	10	50	15	12	25	15
	Export	10	—	10	10	50	15	12	25	15
Finished products	Domestic	10	80	18	10	80	18	12	50	18
	Export	10	—	10	10	50	15	12	25	15

economic welfare for slowing the rate of price increase; in less successful efforts, the loss of real income occurs, but stabilization of prices is not achieved. Yet inflation is traditionally defined as a situation in which too much money is chasing too few goods and thus the options for stabilization are few; it is necessary either to reduce the amount of money doing the chasing or to increase the amount of goods being chased. As the latter alternative usually takes too much time, demand restriction seems to be the only short-run alternative. This conclusion is overly pessimistic for several reasons that are given below.

In the first place, it is rather simplistic to state that inflation is always an excess demand phenomenon. The ambiguity of the meaning of overheating has already been discussed in the context of balance of payments problems; the same arguments apply to the view of simple excess demand. Once the excessive aggregation of the single-sector macroeconomic model is abandoned, an open economy always has sectors in which there is excess demand; otherwise imports would not exist; by the same token there are always sectors in which there is excess supply or exports would not exist. In addition, it has been well recognized for a long time that inflation may also be of the cost-push type. And, although it may be true that in the long run a cost-push inflation is not sustainable without validation from the demand side, that long-run period may be so long that it makes the intervening costs of breaking a cost-push inflation through demand restriction quite prohibitive. Discussion of the management of inflation and price stabilization therefore needs to start by looking at different types of inflation that have commonly occurred in developing countries—of which demand-pull inflation and cost-push inflation are only two types.

Before proceeding, however, it is also useful to mention that the assumption made by the standard approach—that output cannot be expanded in the short run—is also empirically questionable. If capacity is fully utilized in all economic sectors, output could expand only as a result of new investment. As is well known, investment requires a gestation period; thus, output could increase only some time after the initial investment. However, it has already been noted that many developing countries have considerable excess capacity in their industrial sectors—and often in the rest of their nontraded goods sectors as well.[12] This capacity can be mobilized

---

[12]See evidence cited in Schydlowsky (1979 b) and Hughes (1976).

without any gestation period for investment, since the physical plant and equipment are already in place. Naturally, mobilization of this potential additional supply is not instantaneous, but neither is demand restriction. Thus, in the realistic situation of many developing countries, there is scope for expansion of supply in very much the same time frame as there is scope for reduction of demand. This discussion of economic management of inflation and price stabilization therefore deals in part with the question of how to use this potential to contain price increases.

Types of inflation

It is useful in the context of most developing countries to distinguish four different kinds of situations in which domestic prices rise faster than international prices: (1) demand-pull inflation, (2) domestic cost-push inflation, (3) exchange rate inflation, and (4) spiral inflation. Let us discuss the characteristics of each in turn.

Demand-Pull Inflation. This is the best-known type and the one regarded as most usually present in developing countries. Demand-pull inflation is characterized by excess demand in all sectors of economic endeavor except the traditional export sectors. In other words, the quantity demanded from the economy's productive facilities exceeds the capacity to produce these quantities at or near the prices of past years. As a result, prices rise. If the economy is an open one, operating with tariffs but no quantitative restrictions, prices would not be expected to rise past the import points; rather, the excess demand obtaining for domestic productive facilities would spill over into imports and the inflation would be contained at the expense of balance of payments deterioration. For the import points to be the upper level that domestic prices can reach, however, it is necessary to have an infinitely elastic supply of imports in the domestic market. It is generally assumed that, if a country is small, this condition will obtain. However, the small country assumption states only that the prices at which the rest of the world is willing to sell to the small country do not depend on the quantity that this country buys. In other words, the *c.i.f. port of entry price* is constant and there is an infinitely elastic supply of foreign goods to the importing country's port. This is quite different from saying that the elasticity of the supply of imported goods in a country's *domestic* markets is infinite. Considerable domestic value added intervenes between the port of entry and the domestic marketplace—transportation, port labor, wholesaling, retailing, storage, and so on. While the supply of pure imported goods at the entry point may be infinitely elastic, it is not at all clear that the supply of the domestic complementary factors needed for bringing those imports into the domestic market is in infinitely elastic supply. On the contrary, the evidence indicates that when the demand for imports grows very rapidly, the prices of importables rise, even when no foreign exchange scarcity obtains (as occurs, for example, in the various oil surplus developing countries). If demand grows slowly enough, then import supply expands and the demand-pull inflation generates a balance of payments deterioration that may eventually lead to a devaluation, which in turn will raise the price of importables, with all import-competing goods following. The circle is thus closed, and the higher prices caused by the demand-pull inflation are brought about. In a demand-pull inflation, prices tend to rise ahead of wages, and in most cases the share of government in GNP rises as well.

Domestic Cost-Push Inflation. This is quite a different phenomenon. It is typically set off by demands for higher real incomes, usually wages, backed by the bargaining power of unions or the political power of organized labor. When wages go up, businesses attempt to pass on these wage increases to their buyers by raising prices. Along the way, an effort is made to maintain real profits by anticipating the price increases that will result from the wage-push inflation. Thus, it is not uncommon for a wage-push inflation to be accompanied by a profits-push inflation.

Another kind of cost-push inflation that is also increasingly common has its origin in financial liberalization. When long-standing controls on the interest rate are relaxed or removed altogether and the cost of money borrowed from banks rises, this typically affects the cost of "modern" business, which finds that its inventory and other financing costs have gone up and that target rates of return on investment must also be adjusted accordingly.[13] The attempt to pass on these cost increases to customers sets off the interest-push inflation.[14] Any one of the different kinds of cost-push inflation can

---

[13]For a discussion of the role of credit in inflation and stabilization, see, for example, Aspe (1978), Cavallo (1977), and Schydlowsky (1979 a).

[14]Note that the increase in interest costs may be a one-time price increase or may be a repeated one if the liberalization is staggered. Its propagation to the prices of goods and services, however, may occur over a number of periods. Thus, while the increase in interest rates will not by itself generate a sustained inflation, the price increase during the adjustment period is not distinguishable by economic agents from a lasting inflation.

occur independently of the degree of utilization of capacity; indeed, it is conceivable that demands for higher wages come about as an offset to lesser overtime or shorter working hours. More commonly, profit margins are increased to compensate for a fall in volume of production and sales; thus, it is commonly found that profit-push inflation is associated with a recession.

Domestic cost-push inflation does not feed as directly into a balance of payments deterioration as demand-pull inflation does, since it needs to work through relative price changes and substitution.[15] However, under cost-push inflation, the domestic cost of importing also rises. Thus, whether or not a balance of payments problem ensues depends very much on the extent to which costs have risen in importing activities in comparison with similar costs in domestic production. Under cost-push inflation, typically the real income of the factor pushing inflation rises, and the government is likely to lose in share of GNP.

Exchange Rate Inflation. This occurs when a devaluation is forced by a shortage of foreign exchange that coexists with an ample supply capacity of goods demanded on the domestic market and that also coexists with absence of cost pressures from the factor supply side. Such a balance of payments crisis could come about when domestic demand expands to utilize more fully domestic installed capacity, and this leads to an increase in demand for imported inputs without a parallel increase in the supply of foreign exchange. Such a situation reflects an imbalance in the economy between the sizes of the traded and nontraded goods sectors and may be the result of earlier erroneous allocation of investment resources over time or the result of an erroneous commercial policy that has created a large number of tradable nontraded goods, or the result of both. In any case, the precipitating factor of the inflation is the change in the exchange rate that produces price rises for all imports, competitive price increases in import-competing goods, and cost pressures in all other sectors of production that require imported inputs and inputs of goods whose prices in turn are related to the exchange rate. The real incomes of wage earners, profit receivers, and government all decline in this type of inflation, and the only gainers are the producers of exports, whose returns increase.[16]

---

[15]It should be noted that imported cost-push inflation is quite different. For example, an oil price increase affects domestic prices and the balance of payments at the same time.

[16]To the extent that different income receivers are protected by indexing, these distributive effects are reduced.

It is important to distinguish exchange rate inflation from the latter phase of a demand-pull inflation in which a devaluation also occurs. Under demand-pull inflation, the devaluation results from excess domestic demand spilling over into the balance of payments and causing a shortage of foreign exchange. In an exchange rate inflation, there is no excess demand in the domestic market; rather, supply capacity exceeds the quantity demanded and the shortage is felt only in the foreign exchange market because of an imbalance between the demand for foreign exchange at full capacity utilization and the capacity to supply that foreign exchange.

Spiral Inflation. This ensues when any one of the three other types of inflation (or imported inflation) has taken hold and all economic agents attempt to protect themselves from the consequences of the initial price increase. Thus, for example, if a demand-pull inflation starts prices rising, it is not unlikely that a cost-push inflation will follow as factor income receivers attempt to defend their real incomes. This may well, in turn, cause the government to expand its deficit financing in an attempt to maintain its real purchases. If the inflation starts with a wage-push, this may lead to a fuller utilization of capacity and thereby may set off an exchange rate inflation as a second stage, which may well be followed by further cost-push inflation as wage and other income receivers attempt to avoid the lower real income resulting from the devaluation.

Inflationary spirals are particularly pernicious because they increase the homogeneity of the price system. The longer an inflationary spiral continues, the less money illusion there is among the economic agents in an economy, the more everybody learns to operate in terms of real relative prices, and the less anybody is willing to accept a cut in real income relative to anybody else. As a result, once inflation has reached the spiral stage, it may no longer matter very much how it got started.

Alternative management of inflation and price stabilization: prophylaxis

"A stitch in time saves nine," according to an old saying; avoidance of inflation is the best technique for its management. In the cases of demand-pull and cost-push inflations, such insight is not very novel or useful, since economists have been preaching for a long time that government should not generate nor permit excess demand and that laborers and others should not demand income increases in excess of rises in productivity. However, the context in which this advice is of considerable practical import is that of exchange rate inflation.

In the case of a balance of payments problem that is the consequence of a specific scarcity of foreign exchange and not the result of demand generally exceeding the installed capacity in the economy, a devaluation will set off inflation and cause a recession, while alternative ways of dealing with the specific scarcity of foreign exchange can avoid the inflationary consequences altogether. The respective techniques are those that have been discussed before in the context of alternative forms of managing a balance of payments problem—essentially, using the excess supply in the sector of tradable nontraded goods to earn foreign exchange and alleviate the specific scarcity threatening to generate inflation. Thus, differential devaluation, implemented in any of its diverse forms, is a first-rate prophylactic for exchange rate inflation.

It is worth noting that this prophylactic approach to exchange rate inflation is useful in contexts that have elements of demand-pull inflation and cost-push inflation. For example, as demand-pull inflation begins to gather strength and begins to strain capacity in some sectors, there will still be other sectors that have plentiful excess supply and that can be mobilized to break the bottleneck arising in the balance of payments as a result of the expansion in demand. Likewise, as cost-push inflation increases factor incomes and thus domestic aggregate demand and capacity utilization, pressure on the balance of payments is likely to be of the specific sectoral kind (before becoming general) that once again can be dealt with through the techniques appropriate for avoiding exchange rate inflation. Nonetheless, it should be clear that prophylaxis has its limits and will not prevent all types of inflation from occurring.

Alternative management of inflation and price stabilization: therapeutics

It is useful to consider separately two kinds of inflation: (1) low-grade inflation, ranging up to perhaps 20–25 per cent, and (2) virulent spiral inflation, typically 50 per cent and higher and of several years' duration. An inflation between 25 per cent and 50 per cent can fall in either category, depending principally on how long it has gone on at that rate.

Low-Grade Inflation. This kind can be managed with a simultaneous application of two different techniques. The first of these consists of drowning excess demand in increased supply. A differential devaluation is deliberately applied in order to provoke export-led capacity utilization in the tradable nontraded goods sector. As this sector begins to generate exports, it pulls the rest of the economy with it through the foreign trade multiplier. In the process, new fiscal revenue is generated for the treasury, which partially or wholly wipes out the pre-existing deficit. Simultaneously, the higher income generates a demand for additional financial assets on the part of the private sector, thus enlisting the monetary balance of payments adjustment mechanism in the service of stabilization.

The second technique available is particularly useful in the face of cost-push inflation. It consists of breaking the inflationary spiral by weakening the link between wage increases and cost increases. Three instruments can be used for breaking this link: economies of scale attendant on fuller utilization of installed capacity in the context of export-led growth; increased x-efficiency resulting from higher and more stable volumes of production; and substitution of payroll taxes and other cost-raising levies by alternative revenue sources (such as taxes on Ricardian rents). It should be noted that all three instruments imply increases in productivity and thus represent once-and-for-all gains. They are likely to be quite large, however, and thus may well be sufficient to bring a low-grade inflationary spiral under control. Because of their one-time nature, however, their suitability for dealing with rapid inflation is much more limited.

Virulent Spiral Inflation. Virulent spirals are bedeviled by the curse of homogeneity. All economic agents attempt to maintain their real incomes, and none of them are willing to let their terms of trade deteriorate. Economic agents perceive themselves as being in a zero-sum game and are all determined not to lose.

The logical approach to this situation is to develop an incomes policy that freezes relative income shares but reduces the inflation by agreement. However, the usual problem is that wages are easier to control than prices and therefore the labor sector is reluctant to enter into this kind of agreement. The textbook response is to use import competition as a mechanism for price control, opening up the economy through the reduction of tariffs and the elimination of quantitative restrictions and using an active crawling exchange rate as the tool to regulate price increases.

The combination of incomes policy and active crawl has the elements that should make for success—control on wages by agreement and control on prices through regulated import competition. Nonetheless, it is not without pitfalls and dangers. If the economy has been closed for a long period of time, import competition will not be very strong initially. Rather than domestic prices of imports being governed by the ceiling given by the import point, prices of imports are likely to be held at domestic levels, with rents accruing to importers. This is the result of short-run inelasticity in the supply of importing services, which was discussed above in the context of demand-pull inflation. If domestic prices continue their upward movement, however, the exchange rate becomes overvalued, giving rise to expectations that the policy as a whole is unsustainable and that a major devaluation is going to be undertaken in the future. Such expectations undermine the rest of the incomes policy, thus reinforcing the divergence between domestic inflation and the trend in world prices. In the context of the zero-sum game, the expectation that the incomes policy will have to be abandoned is enough to guarantee its lack of success.

The time frame for slowing down the virulent spiral therefore becomes fundamental. If enough time is allowed for the link between domestic prices and import points to be solidly established, the policy has a chance of succeeding in terms of its conception. However, with a long time horizon, there is the risk of losing the patience of the economic agents who have agreed to the domestic part of the incomes policy. On the other hand, leaning too soon on the slender branch of import competition, before it has become a trustworthy bough, dooms the policy quite certainly.

A major change in the prospects for the stabilization of virulent spirals can take place if the context of the effort is changed from a zero sum to a positive sum. If the economic agents felt that they had something to gain by stabilizing as opposed to merely avoiding losses, agreements would last longer, individual time horizons would be lengthened, and the winding down of inflation could proceed at a pace at which it is more likely to be sustainable. In order to transform the context into that of a positive sum, attention must be paid once again to the supply side. By including a differential devaluation in any of its forms in the policy package, some export-led growth can be generated based on the use of capacity and unemployed labor in the tradable nontraded goods sector, thus providing increases in real income to labor and economies of scale and productivity gains to business—thus putting downward pressure on the spiral. When this supply element is added to incomes policy and an active crawl, economic agents see that expanded real incomes and less inflation can go together. The willingness to take a risk for stabilization increases, and the possibility of individual loss is seen in terms of less improvement rather than in terms of an absolute reduction in real income.

EMPIRICAL APPLICABILITY OF ALTERNATIVE MANAGEMENT TECHNIQUES

Two conditions must be satisfied for the empirical applicability of the alternative short-term economic management techniques discussed above:

(1) Unutilized productive capacity must either exist in the economy or must be created as a result of the demand-side policies being adopted; and

(2) This unutilized productive capacity must be mobilizable by policy.

Countries evidently differ with regard to both conditions.

The existence of unutilized productive capacity in semi-industrialized developing countries is increasingly documented. Data now exist on shiftwork and the number of days of the year that plant and equipment are utilized for a dozen or more countries spanning the developing world. Moreover, some research has been done on comparisons of current output with past peaks. Nobody disputes the existence of abundant employable labor in these countries, and there is also evidence that skills can be learned quite quickly. Thus, countries that have an industrial sector that has progressed at least somewhat into the ISI phase are most likely to satisfy the first condition.

However, industry is not the only place where developing countries accumulate excess capacity. Studies show how multiple cropping throughout the year can raise the productivity of land, but there is no conceptual difference between multiple cropping and multiple shifting. Thus, in many a country excess capacity exists in agriculture as well.

Finally, demand-side policies generate excess capacity automatically by depressing the level of activity. Thus, even in the case where there is no excess capacity initially, as soon as the level of activity becomes depressed, there is scope for supply-side measures.

It can be concluded, therefore, that condition (1) will be met in a large number of countries. Nonetheless, the potential contribution varies by country, depending on the importance in the economy of the excess capacity sectors. A direct relationship with the level of development and industrialization is likely in this case. In the least developed of the developing countries, alternative management techniques may consist of making a few white elephants gray; for the more developed developing countries, a major growth spurt may be involved.

The satisfaction of condition (2) depends to a large extent on the flexibility of the policy structure and the extent to which policy-makers are willing to adopt measures that will elicit the desired response, independent of ideological prejudice. It must be recalled that policy response elasticities are, after all, the reactions of individuals to stimuli; in many developing countries, the number of individuals reacting is quite small. As a result, policymakers generally do not deal in the impersonal world of the statistical aggregate; they deal with the very personal reactions of a small number of individuals, who can often be identified by name. Under these circumstances, policy reaction can always be obtained; it may often be only a matter of making the appropriate political transaction.

Finally, some concerns of a welfare theoretic nature need to be raised. Let us assume that capacity exists and that it is mobilized. Almost invariably, the measures adopted will imply discrimination between sectors and will entail short-run activation of economic production that it would not be desirable to maintain for the longer run because short-run social marginal cost on installed capacity is likely to be much lower than long-run marginal cost. Trade-offs then apparently arise between long-run static welfare optimization and short-run needs. The best solution is to develop a phased policy that takes into account the gradual growth of short-run policy into long-run policy. This would imply activation incentives that are different from investment incentives, for example. The stark choice of achieving short-run gain at the cost of long-run loss can thus be avoided with appropriate policy design. Should such a desirable policy not be feasible for some reason, then, of course, the short-run to long-run trade-off has to be faced. Given the size of the potential GNP lost both from cyclical as well as from secular underutilization of capacity and any reasonable discount rate, the gains from long-term improved allocation must be very large to outweigh the short-term losses. However, since these are magnitudes that can be estimated,[17] a priori conviction should yield to empirical research.

REFERENCES

Aspe, Pedro A., "Microfoundations and Monetary Stabilization Policies: A Further Look at Liquid and Working Capital" (unpublished doctoral dissertation, Essay II, Massachusetts Institute of Technology, 1978).

Balassa, Bela, and Associates, *The Structure of Protection in Developing Countries*, International Bank for Reconstruction and Development (World Bank) and Inter-American Development Bank (Johns Hopkins University Press, 1971).

Berlinski, Julio, and Daniel M. Schydlowsky, "Argentina," in Bela Balassa and Associates, Part II, "Incentive Policies and Economic Development: Case Studies," in *Development Strategies in Semi-industrial Economies*, World Bank (Johns Hopkins University Press, 1982), pp. 83–122.

CARTTA (Cámara Argentina de Radio, Televisión, Telecomunicaciones y Afines), "Proyecto de Modificación de la Estructura Arancelaria-Cambiaria" (Buenos Aires, September 1966).

Cavallo, Domingo, "Supply of Commodities and Credit Conditions in the Short Run" (unpublished doctoral dissertation, Harvard University, 1977).

Diamand, Marcelo, *Doctrinas Económicas, Desarrollo e Independencia* (Buenos Aires, 1973).

Díaz-Alejandro, Carlos F., *Devaluation of the Exchange Rate in a Sub-Industrialized Country: The Argentine Experience, 1955–1961*, M.I.T. Economics Monograph Series, Vol. 5 (M.I.T. Press, 1965).

Gonzalez Izquierdo, Jorge, "El Efecto Fiscal del Certex: Una Evaluación del Año 1979," *Perú Exporta* (March 1981), pp. 15–20.

Hughes, Helen, "Capital Utilization in Manufacturing in Developing Countries," World Bank Staff Working Paper No. 242 (Washington, September 1976).

Little, Ian M. D., Tibor Scitovsky, and Maurice Scott, *Industry and Trade in Some Developing Countries: A Comparative Study* (Oxford University Press, 1970).

Schydlowsky, Daniel M., "From Import-Substitution to Export Promotion for Semi-Grown-Up Industries: A Policy Proposal," *Journal of Development Studies*, Vol. 3 (July 1967), pp. 405–13.

———, "Short-Run Policy in Semi-Industrialized Economies," *Economic Development and Cultural Change*, Vol. 19 (April 1971), pp. 391–413.

——— (1979 a), "Containing the Costs of Stabilization in Semi-Industrialized LDC's: A Marshallian Approach," Paper prepared for the Independent Commission on Inter-

---

[17]Some estimates can be found in Schydlowsky (1979 b).

national Development Issues (January 1979), reprinted in Discussion Paper Series, No. 36, Center for Latin American Development Studies, Boston University (December 1979).

———— (1979 b), "Capital Utilization, Growth, Employment, Balance of Payments and Price Stabilization," in *Short-Term Macroeconomic Policy in Latin America*, ed. by Jere Behrman and James A. Hanson, National Bureau of Economic Research, Other Conference Series No. 14 (Cambridge, Massachusetts, 1979), pp. 311–55.

Taylor, Lance, "IS/LM in the Tropics: Diagrammatics of the New Structuralist Macro Critique," in *Economic Stabilization in Developing Countries*, ed. by William R. Cline and Sidney Weintraub, (Brookings Institution, Washington, 1981), pp. 465–506.

Urdinola, Antonio, and Richard Mallon, "Policies to Promote Colombian Exports of Manufactures," Harvard University, Development Advisory Service, Center for International Affairs, Economic Development Reports, No. 75 (September 1967).

Roles of the Euromarket and the International Monetary Fund in Financing Developing Countries

RICHARD O'BRIEN

This paper is organized into three parts. First, it discusses the current position of the international banking system with respect to lending to developing countries. Second, it summarizes the principal issues regarding the relative roles of the International Monetary Fund and the private banking system in developing country financing, including observations on bank debt rescheduling and Fund conditionality. And third, it attempts to tackle the difficult issues of unequal access of developing countries to capital and credit markets, and the efficiency of international banks in recycling surplus funds to developing countries.

The paper attempts to reach an overall conclusion as to the present situation, to identify the key problems, and to suggest methods for tackling these problems. Written from a private bank economist's viewpoint, it primarily summarizes ideas and arguments with respect to the roles of the Euromarket and the Fund, rather than providing a detailed statistical analysis of the flow of funds.

POSITION OF THE BANKS IN 1981

The casual observer of international bank lending to developing countries can be forgiven if he regards international banking spokesmen as people with rather short memories. Approximately one year ago, international banks were sending out fairly clearly, and in relative unison, a message that developing countries could no longer rely on the international banks to finance their debt to the degree experienced in the past. Bankers were cited by aid lobbies (not traditionally a group with an apparent communality of interest) in their arguments for more aid and financing to developing countries. Now a similarly clear message is being sent out to the effect that banks are continuing to finance developing countries' deficits and that, while there may be some changes in pricing for selected countries, the banks' recycling of surplus funds will go on. Perhaps the degree of unity in the banking community can be over-emphasized. Some bankers claim that there is very little risk in lending to developing countries, particularly to governments. Others claim that lending to developing countries is leading the banks down a very treacherous path—one that is not only dangerous for borrowing countries' financial status but also for the health of the international banking system. A banker may, of course, try to influence the market by his statements in order to receive a higher reward for taking on such a risk. At the same time, he will be reluctant to admit that any of his clients really represent a high risk.

What, in fact, is the relationship of the banks and the developing countries today?[1] In 1980, bank lending to developing countries by means of syndicated credits fell dramatically over 1979. There were a number of special reasons for this decline. First, a few selected countries, for their own reasons, were less active (see Table 1 for data on seven key borrowers). Second, the crisis in Iran put a dampener on the market in early 1980 and raised questions of political risk for lenders and depositors. Third, record high U.S. interest rates had a dramatic effect on countries' debt servicing costs and probably had a discouraging impact on borrowing. It should be noted that the average cost of borrowing in 1980 was very much the same as in 1979; the main surprise was that interest rates stayed high, rather than coming down as the international recession deepened. And finally, the 1980 data looked rather low, compared with data for 1979, because the 1979 figures had been inflated by a great deal, perhaps as much as $12 billion,[2] in prepayment and refinancing of credits at the then lower spreads.

---

[1]For a fuller description of lending by private banks to developing countries, see O'Brien (1981 b).

[2]This estimate is taken from Morgan Guaranty and Trust Company of New York, *World Financial Markets* (June and November 1980).

Table 1
DEVELOPING COUNTRY BORROWING: SYNDICATED BANK CREDITS
(billion U.S. dollars)

	1979	1980	1981	Percentage Change from Previous Year 1980	1981
Two major borrowers[1]	3.0	1.0	1.8	−66.4	79.8
Other oil exporting developing countries	5.8	5.8	3.9	0.7	−33.4
Total oil exporting developing countries	8.8	6.8	5.7	−22.4	−15.3
Five major borrowers[2]	24.5	14.9	22.3	−38.9	49.0
Other non-oil developing countries	9.9	11.3	17.2	14.5	51.5
Total non-oil developing countries	34.4	26.3	39.4	−23.6	50.0
All developing countries	43.1	33.1	45.1	−23.3	36.4
Memorandum item					
Seven major borrowers	27.5	16.0	24.1	−41.9	51.0
Other developing countries[3]	15.7	17.1	21.0	9.4	22.8

Source: Organization for Economic Cooperation and Development, *Financial Statistics Monthly* (February 1982), Table I.31, pp. 13–15.

[1]Algeria and Nigeria.
[2]Brazil, the People's Republic of China, Korea, Mexico, and the Philippines.
[3]Excluding Yugoslavia.

Note: Components may not add to totals because of rounding.

In 1981 there has been an acceleration in lending to developing countries, although the trend is very different for different borrowers. The seven developing countries whose borrowing programs declined (Brazil, the People's Republic of China, Korea, Mexico, Algeria, Nigeria, and the Philippines) have increased their borrowing rapidly in 1981 (by 51 per cent, after a 41.9 per cent drop in 1980), and other developing countries have increased their borrowing by 22.8 per cent in 1981, after a 9.4 per cent increase in 1980. Both Argentina and Venezuela continued to borrow at previous levels. Total borrowing thus exceeded the previous record level of 1979, although the volume would be relatively lower if adjusted for inflation in 1979–81. In addition to syndicated credits, there is always a certain amount of nonpublicized credit being made available in the market, and private banking flows also include trade credits and other activities.

At the same time as lending is increasing, the number of countries having to reschedule existing bank debts is also increasing and a larger proportion of new financing is being used to refinance maturing debts. The latter phenomenon is not a complete surprise. In early 1977, it was calculated (*Amex Bank Review*, March 1977) that by 1980 one out of every two dollars borrowed would be to refinance maturing debt and that the ratio would rise to two out of every three dollars by 1985. The 1980 figure has been on target, and the ratio is rising.

Reschedulings, or debt difficulties, are less predictable, even though they often occur for similar reasons. In recent years, some 10–15 countries have rescheduled existing debt or undertaken major refinancing. Argentina, for example, refinanced its debt, after the collapse of the Perón regime, with extensive new Eurocredits. Turkey rescheduled its short-term convertible lira deposit debts into medium-term credits. Zaïre rescheduled some of its debts and rolled unpaid interest into capital. Other examples of debt repayment problems include Peru (1976–78), Jamaica (1979–81), Nicaragua (1980–81), Gabon (1978), Chile (mid-1970s), Indonesia (1975), Bolivia (1981), and Costa Rica (1981). Each incidence of refinancing has provided a new lesson in private bank debt, such as new rescheduling techniques. Two examples may be cited:

1. Banks cannot expect to write their own stabilization programs for countries (attempted in the case of Peru); this is the task of the Fund. All the banks can really do is to urge and cajole borrowers to take corrective action, which might include encouraging (as in the case of Jamaica) or even insisting (as in the case of Bolivia) that a country borrow from the Fund.

2. Governments do have a responsibility (if only to preserve a country's creditworthiness) to monitor and, if necessary, to take over the debts of their own state enterprises (as in the case of Indonesia's assumption of all Pertamina's debts).

The reschedulings and debt problems of Turkey, Gabon, and Nicaragua were also illustrative of the nature of debt problems. Turkish experiences showed how excessive short-term debts can damage creditworthiness as such debts become unmanageable; Gabon was an example of problems occurring even at relatively low debt service ratios when there are cumulative debts and budget cost overruns; and Nicaragua's "special case" was the first time in which banks faced the possibility of rescheduling debts at spreads effectively below the cost of funds as a result of the severe economic crisis (when any interest not being paid was rolled into new principal).

The terms and conditions of rescheduled debts (except for Nicaragua) have been at commercial rates, although the "locked in" position of the banks has probably meant that the spread has been below what a country in a similar position would then have obtained. In some cases unpaid interest or capital has been rolled into the new loans, and in other cases where there have been few payment delays, the new debt has merely ensured that debt problems are avoided. The success of rescheduling[3] depends on the future economic changes in the country. Where the economy's foreign exchange revenues have recovered, the success has lasted longer (as in the case of Peru, Indonesia, and Argentina). In other cases, further reschedulings have had to be discussed (as for Zaïre).

Despite these various problems, the lending activity continues. At the same time, flows from the Fund to developing countries have been increasing. But how much more can private banks lend to developing countries? It can be argued that banks were able to take up the recycling of surplus funds after the first oil crisis because banks were at that time already familiar with lending to developing countries, and the commodity price boom of the early 1970s had improved the creditworthiness of developing countries. Debts of developing countries were not nearly as high as they are today. But now, after the second oil crisis and in view of the problem of very high real interest rates, can recycling be carried out successfully once again? Other complications, such as the banks' declining capital ratios, have added to the doubts as to whether recycling can be done again as effectively through the Euromarket as it was in the 1970s.

To answer this question (of how much more private banks can lend to developing countries) with any real degree of accuracy, analysts should look at a number of banks' balance sheets worldwide. That is a long and laborious task, but analysis of different banking groups' exposures does reveal some information as to how exposed different national banking groups are to developing countries. American banks' share of the total Euromarket loans to developing countries has been declining steadily since 1975 (from 53 per cent of the market to 38 per cent by March 1981). There are two reasons for this. First, U.S. banks tended to be pioneers in the Eurodollar market and therefore what was happening in 1975–80 was that other banks were joining in. Second, it can be argued that the fact that American banks entered the market earlier meant that their build-up of developing country debt portfolios was more rapid than that

---

[3]See the final section of this paper for a discussion of access and efficiency with respect to rescheduling of debt.

for other banks. Thus, as country limits were reached earlier in the United States, there was some moderation in U.S. banks' enthusiasm to lend to developing countries even before other banking groups became averse to such risk.

In examining national banking groups' exposures in lending to developing countries, it can be seen that American banks are the most exposed, with 28 per cent of their international asset portfolio in loans to developing countries (Table 2). Loans by other major banking groups

Table 2
BANKING GROUP EXPOSURES IN LENDING TO DEVELOPING COUNTRIES
(end of 1980)

Location of Banks	Total Foreign Assets (billion U.S. dollars)	All Developing Countries	Nonmembers of OPEC	OPEC Members
		(as percentage of total foreign assets)		
United States	352.1	28.3	22.0	6.3
France	143.2	22.7	17.2	5.5
United Kingdom	106.2	23.4	16.9	6.5
Luxembourg	88.6	15.8	14.8	1.0
Germany, Fed. Rep. of	73.3	20.5	13.8	6.7
Netherlands	62.1	9.1	7.8	1.3
Other countries	497.6	14.8	9.6	5.1
Total Euromarket lending	1,323.1	20.0	14.7	5.3

Source: Amex Bank Review (September 1981), p. 3.

follow in the 20–25 per cent range (banks in the United Kingdom, the Federal Republic of Germany, and France), while loans by banks in Luxembourg and the Netherlands are below the market average of 20 per cent. Accurate portfolio figures for lending to developing countries by Japanese banks are not publicized, although it may be estimated that they are in about the same range as those of the larger banking groups, say 20–25 per cent.

The fact that non-U.S. banking groups' lending exposures are still below those sustained by U.S. banks in the past five years may mean that there is still the potential of more lending before these banking groups' desire to lend is satiated. Or, it may be that, with the higher risk perception of developing country debt now prevalent in the market, these banking groups will not want to move up to the U.S. banks' level of lending. The relationships between national banking groups and developing countries will, of course, affect the banks' desire for developing country business.

In addition to the positions of these banks, the rapid increase in Arab banks' participation in the syndicated credit market, as both lead managers and managers of credits, is important (Table 3). Not only have Arab banks been more active internationally, but the share of non-oil developing countries, non-Islamic countries, and nonmembers of the Organization of Petroleum Exporting Countries (OPEC) in their lending activity has increased from a low of 3 per cent in 1976 to over 30 per cent in 1980 and is still at 20 per cent for the first seven months of 1981.

Table 3
LENDING BY ARAB BANKS: DISTRIBUTION BY BORROWER
(percentage share of Arab bank lending)

	1976	1977	1978	1979	1980	1981[1]
Non-oil developing countries	3.0	10.6	6.6	7.6	32.0	21.2
OPEC members and others[2]	43.6	82.6	77.0	53.6	38.4	40.0
OECD members[3]	43.9	5.2	10.8	29.9	24.0	32.0
CMEA countries[4]	9.6	1.6	5.6	8.9	5.6	6.8
World percentage	100	100	100	100	100	100
Total amount (million U.S. dollars)	1,139	1,048	2,905	1,997	3,847	4,001

Source: *Amex Bank Review* (September 1981), p. 11.
[1]First seven months.
[2]Members of the Organization of Petroleum Exporting Countries (OPEC), other oil producing developing countries, and Islamic countries.
[3]Member countries of the Organization for Economic Cooperation and Development.
[4]Member countries of the Council for Mutual Economic Assistance.

It can be concluded that, at this stage, the Euromarket has already begun to diversify the number of banking groups involved in lending to developing countries. Most banking groups may soon be in the same position as the U.S. banks, and thus banks may wish to increase their developing country loan portfolios only slowly. But it is important to remember that, at the same time, the banking system is not static. The recent participation of Arab banks and the ability of more aggressive pricing to bring in banks that are less active in developing country lending can widen market participation by increasing the number of banks that are lending and thereby raising, in effect, the capital base on which developing country loan portfolios can be built.

To summarize the banking outlook, the key factors are the question of profit (the spread on developing country loans) and the quality of the loans to developing countries. In the past few years the spread on developing country loans has declined, and it has been suggested that only banks with special relationships with developing countries can absorb lending to developing countries at very low spreads (Wallich, 1981 a)—perhaps why the group of U.S. banks accounting for developing country loans has not widened within the United States. And in terms of quality, the increasing amount of loan reschedulings being arranged may lead the banks to require greater loan provisions (reserves) and to write off more developing country related debt than in the past (Wallich, 1981 b). If experience with loan losses has a significant impact on bank profits, there may well be more aggressive pricing of developing country loans (i.e., higher spreads) and then a real reluctance to extend further loans to countries that have a poor credit record.

BANKS AND THE FUND

At this point comments are in order on developing country lending by banks with respect to the role of the Fund. A number of proposals have been made in which bank lending could be supported in some way by official lending, but the practical obstacles are considerable (O'Brien, 1981 a). The private sector always welcomes support from governments, but the private sector also recognizes the dangers of distorting its role as a result of public sector actions, particularly if that distortion is in the form of persuading private bankers to lend where otherwise their judgment would suggest that they should not lend. Such distortion surely can lead only to high effective subsidies and a misallocation of resources.

The most important point that this paper can make is that, while the banks and the Fund are both contributing to the task of financing countries' balance of payments, their roles and responsibilities are very distinct. The banks in the past decade have been effectively increasing their international financing as a means of increasing profits and the volume of business. The Fund, on the other hand, plays an international governmental role with respect to the international monetary system. It therefore has a responsibility to ensure that liquidity is provided to meet shortages and to ensure that financing is made available on the right conditions in order to maintain stability within the international financial system.

Now the banks, having pursued the profit motive in lending to developing countries, must consider the full implications of the risks they are running in lending to them. Inevitably, banks are exposed in certain countries in rather large amounts, and on a rather longer-term basis, than the initial loan decisions may have envisaged. The Fund, meanwhile, has increasingly been playing a "policeman's role" and acting as a lender of last resort to countries in financial difficulty. A further extension of this role may dilute the Fund's effectiveness.

In the 1980s, therefore, the prospect is that while the 1970s have seen a valuable evolution of both the banking system and the Fund, it may not be healthy for the international financial system if this evolution continues at its present pace. The problem is how to ensure stability and maintenance of the status quo while maximizing flexibility and the ability to adjust to new economic conditions.

It is perhaps useful to examine the factors by which the roles of the banks and the Fund in recycling are judged, in the form of criticism and counter-criticism. Such an examination of both bank lending and Fund lending ensures that account can be taken of everyone's value judgments.

The banks

The first major criticism is that banks provide funds to countries with very few conditions as to the economic policies of the borrowers. Thus, no adjustment is forced on the country, and the banks—particularly with respect to sovereign borrowers—have very little leverage with which to ensure that the financing is used efficiently. This aspect also has a good side. Countries borrowing from the banks have access to a fast disbursing source of funds, without conditions that they may not wish to follow. Thus, borrowers can take steps toward economic adjustment on their own terms and conditions—that is, each country can pursue its own adjustment process and can react to individual circumstances.

The second problem with bank lending is that, while it is provided quickly, it is only too quickly withdrawn when the warning signals are seen. For example, when there are debt problems, banks may be quick to withdraw availability of future credit, thereby accelerating the financial problems and accentuating the costs. It is, however, also suggested (Hardy, 1981) that banks tend to lend to a country long after difficulties set in and are too slow to read the warning signals—an apparent contradiction of the first criticism. At this point, it should be noted that banks, as commercial institutions, can react quickly in either withdrawing or providing credit and are not bound by bureaucratic regulations often faced by multilateral institutions—a problem perhaps more associated with development banks than with the Fund.

The third criticism of the banks is that their lending of large sums to developing countries has threatened the stability of the international banking system—and, in turn, possibly the international financial system. But, equally, a similar point can be made in favor of banks—that the increase in bank lending internationally merely reflects the change in the world economic system and that, by reacting to these changes (i.e., in their recycling activities), banks have helped to avoid a problem for the international financial system.

The final major criticism of bank lending is that it is not well distributed among developing countries. It is frequently pointed out that six of the non-oil developing countries account for two thirds of the bank lending to developing countries. This point needs to be tempered by the fact that these six countries also account for one third of the merchandise export revenues of the non-oil developing countries. Thus, the maldistribution is not quite as startling as it first seems. It can also be pointed out that, with respect to Fund quotas, five countries account for 46 per cent of the quotas of non-oil developing countries. Excluding the People's Republic of China as a relatively new entrant, four major developing countries account for 37 per cent of the Fund's developing country quotas, while they account for only 24 per cent of developing country exports. These issues of distribution are obviously relevant to the discussion on unequal access to the banks. At this stage, suffice it to say that bank lending should not be equally distributed if banks correctly allocate their lending according to creditworthiness and not just according to demand. Not all borrowers are equally creditworthy.

The Fund

The factors for judging the role of the Fund partly mirror the factors for judging the role of the banks. The first criticism of the Fund is that its conditionality may not be appropriate to the individual country's problem. But, equally, it must be said that the presence of conditionality at least forces the country to make some adjustment, so that the balance of payments does improve over time (though the amount of success is clearly an important area of debate). One of the benefits of the Fund's role is that the international financial system does have a "policeman" applying certain standards to the financial system. When providing financing, the Fund can at least ensure in some measure that the existing balance of payments gap will be closed within a reasonable period of time.

The second criticism often made of multilateral institutions is that they are too slow to provide finance (and, as noted above, the benefit of bank lending is that it has been provided quickly). This is probably less a criticism of the Fund because it does act relatively quickly once the countries themselves have gone to it for financial support. Of course, the question of whether countries resort to the Fund for borrowing in time to solve their balance of payments problems is an important issue: the timing decision rests with the borrowing countries, but the terms of available Fund assistance (amount, rate, maturity, and policy conditionality) will be an important consideration in reaching this decision. The Fund has to perform the difficult balancing act of offering sufficient finance to make the policy conditionality acceptable.

The third criticism of the Fund is that it has been unable to do as much of the recycling as is needed because of a shortage of funds. On the other hand, it must be pointed out that the Fund has increased its financing rapidly, while it must always balance the obvious benefits of providing a large amount of finance with the need to ensure that adequate "conditionality" is applied.

The final major criticism of the Fund refers to its control by its creditors rather than by its debtors. But, surely, all credit institutions ultimately have to be responsible to their creditors, as they are the ones in the intermediary role of offering the investor a haven for his funds and of taking risks in lending out these funds.

With these standard criticisms briefly summarized, where are the changes in the banks and the Fund leading the international financial system? The banks are becoming more selective in their lending, with the proviso that being selective when also rescheduling is not an easy task. Inevitably, banks are now moving toward more effective accounting for sovereign risk losses in their balance sheets, even if this is not made public (Wallich, 1981 b). Once any sovereign risk losses, even if they are only opportunity losses, begin to affect profits, then there should be further realistic adjustment of the pricing differentials at which individual countries can raise money in the credit and capital markets. The Fund, meanwhile, seems to be moving toward the provision of more longer-term balance of payments support, with some easing in conditions as measured by loan terms rather than by policy conditionality.

The international financial system is now at a critical point. Reform of the Fund's lending facilities and operating guidelines was clearly necessary because its quotas and financing capabilities had been made rather inadequate by events during the 1970s. But now the Fund may have reformed these loan conditions adequately and may have increased its financing base sufficiently in order to play its required "policeman's role." If the Fund becomes too liberal in providing finance, then its role as lender of last resort may become diluted. As a result, the Fund's effectiveness as a "policeman" for the international financial system could decline, and the Fund may become merely a source of finance with which indirectly to rescue banks from difficult country positions.

The banks themselves are also at an important crossroads. A number of reschedulings have already occurred, with the emphasis always on maintaining the creditworthiness of the borrower and the banks usually increasing their loans outstanding with the borrower. Banks must now, however, tackle the problem of what losses to really account for in the reschedulings. If sovereign borrowers are supported by more and more credit without lenders and investors taking their losses, the inevitable result is likely to be a vast and inefficient credit mountain to insolvent borrowers.

Both banks and the Fund are thus facing a critical period. As both are apparently financing the same payments problems, it is tempting to seek a common solution that will bring the Fund and the private banks into concert. Discussions of guarantee systems and various other suggestions have proliferated since the late 1970s. Everyone seems to be looking for a way of financing developing country deficits without easing the conditions or reducing the credit standards. It is important not to confuse roles. It may be that getting the banks and the Fund to work in concert is not the solution to this problem. The banks must remain profit-oriented private institutions that together make up a market but remain individual entities. The Fund at the same time remains a public and international institution, responsible to institutional and governmental shareholders, and an institution that has a specific task in the international monetary system. Of course, the role of the Fund can be changed by multilateral government fiat, and thus perhaps the ability of the Fund to change its nature is greater than that of the banking system.

UNEQUAL ACCESS AND THE EFFICIENCY
OF RECYCLING METHODS

The question of unequal access to capital and credit markets is probably the most discussed question in international finance today. Inequalities are a fact of life, but in discussions on bank lending to developing countries the real question is whether bank funds are going to the countries that should be able to borrow from the private market and, if not, whether there is any way in which access can be widened for the countries that should have greater access to this market.

First, what determines the degree of developing country access to the private credit market? The major factor is, of course, the creditworthiness of the developing countries. This may sound like a tautology, but it is important to distinguish this factor from other aspects, such as legal restrictions, which often prevent developing countries from borrowing in national capital markets. With respect to the Euromarket, such restrictions are limited and thus creditworthiness effectively determines the access of the developing countries to this market.

What makes a developing country creditworthy? The primary factor is the assessment of whether the country will be able and willing to repay its debt on time. Thus, it is not surprising that a large proportion of bank lending goes to the countries with the highest capacity for earning foreign exchange. Creditworthiness may not necessarily reflect the overall economic development of the country, and it may have little relation to the size of the country or its population. Banks increasingly are adopting relatively structured approaches to assessing a country's creditworthiness and to allocating credit. The main task is to try and assess the economic and political risk of lending to the country—the first part of the equation determining loan policy; the other parts of the equation are the rate of return on lending to that country, the relationships of the banks there, and the banks' ability to obtain good business.

It is perhaps useful to consider the factors analyzed with respect to the economic and political creditworthiness of a country, using as an example the American Express Bank's country rating system. Eight major factors are analyzed for all countries, and these are assessed by means of a series of statistical ratios followed by judgmental analysis.

1. *Dependence on foreign capital for development of the country*. Indicators analyzed include the growth of external debt, compared with domestic growth, and the size of the current account gap, indicating the borrowing requirement.

2. *Import dependence and import compressibility of the country*. For example: How will the country be affected by a rapid increase in oil prices? To what extent will it be able to reduce its foreign exchange spending, by reducing imports, in a time of liquidity shortage?

3. *Vulnerability of export earnings*, particularly those related to the risks associated with reliance on a single commodity for foreign currency earnings.

4. *The debt servicing burden of the country.*

5. *Domestic monetary and fiscal control within the country*, focusing on its quality and the government's ability to control expenditure and inflation.

6. *Hospitality to private and foreign capital*, assuming that the more hospitable the country is to such capital the more likely it is that it will be able and willing to respect its international and financial obligations and to welcome other private sector activities.

7. *Comparative international importance of the country*, on the simple thesis that the more important the country is with respect to trade volumes worldwide, and also the higher the level of debt the country has with banks, the greater the efforts that will be made by the banking community, official institutions, and perhaps the country itself to achieve successful rescheduling when necessary.

8. *Political risks*. The rating system starts with a socio-economic analysis, followed by political judgments as to the risks and how they affect the potential creditworthiness of the country.

Credit analysis is geared not only toward determining whether the country will repay its debts but also toward how the country will solve any financial problems it encounters. Based on the number of reschedulings by the country in international financial markets in the past few years, distinctions can be made between those reschedulings that have gone relatively smoothly and those that have taken a long time to be worked out. The opportunity losses may tend to be higher as a result of a very difficult and lengthy period of rescheduling, compared with losses incurred in a smooth rescheduling where the business relationship continues without any interruption. Smooth rescheduling also enables a country to maintain its growth path. Debt problems over a long period lead to other problems; for example, trade credit becomes difficult to obtain, and the country may be able to trade only on a cash basis. This situation has a very deleterious effect on economic growth, political stability, and future earnings. Lengthy periods for rescheduling also affect the banks' earnings during the renegotiation and could have a serious short-term impact on liquidity and on the maturity of the banks' assets.

These basic criteria for creditworthiness are fairly standard among banks and are often reflected in the areas examined by the bank regulatory authorities. The criteria are unlikely to change, but it should be asked what effect their application has on the economic development of countries. The emphasis on foreign exchange earnings to repay debts means that countries need to emphasize their export sector more than they might otherwise wish. But if foreign savings are to be used to develop the economy, this bias must be accepted. A further problem, often raised, is that bank lending is of too short a maturity, and therefore necessary infrastructure projects do not receive financing. Again, it is very difficult to extend loan maturities much beyond ten years. Perhaps this is a fruitful area in which cooperation between banks and official institutions can ensure a steady flow of funds to important infrastructure projects, even if the cash flow does not support the financing. Financing of such projects may make more sense than large balance of payments financing.

There may be a case for improving the access to capital and credit markets for the countries that so far have borrowed very little. Of course, it is important to consider whether those countries that have not borrowed from the private market should be encouraged to borrow privately. Surely, the fact that they are not heavy debtors (because of their inability to service such debts) reflects an efficient allocation of financial resources. It may be quite healthy that only a third of the developing countries (in terms of their exports) receive two thirds of the credit, if loans to these countries yield the best rate of return on the investment and these countries have the highest growth potential.

Nonetheless, some developing countries still have to make their reputation in international financial markets. While they may borrow only very small amounts, the effort required to sell their creditworthiness in the market, compared with the financing obtained, may be rather costly. Therefore, there is a need for international institutions to try and help lesser known countries to tap the markets. This is already being done, and efforts by the World Bank to introduce countries to the financial market through seminars and presentations has clearly been fruitful (although, in some instances, an excellent presentation, made with the assistance of an official institution, has encouraged banks to lend and later the banks have had problems in terms of rescheduling).

A further reason for increasing the access of developing countries to the banks is that the transfer of banking skills might be accelerated. Otherwise, there seems very little reason, in terms of efficient allocation of resources, for actively encouraging the access of a greater number of countries to the market, apart from the fact that this would mean that these countries do not have to rely so heavily on aid. To repeat, if countries cannot service commercial debts nor prove creditworthy, they should not be encouraged to build such debts. Furthermore, it should be stressed that while it seems that access is very unequal, with a few countries obtaining most of the syndicated credits, bank lending to developing countries is worldwide and trade financing is carried on with all countries, even if the net flow is not great. Indeed, the best way of increasing bank activities among a wider range of countries may be to encourage export credit financing agencies to provide greater amounts of cover for less creditworthy countries. In that way, the greater amount of financing can both involve the banks and encourage trade, without leading to a deterioration in banks' portfolios.

The question of unequal access is clearly leading to the question of efficiency. Has the banking system proved an efficient conduit for recycling surplus funds, and can the Fund and the banking system make recycling more effective? This can be answered fairly briefly. First, bank lending has been an efficient route for recycling because it has been fast. Creditworthy countries that needed loans to cover balance of payments deficits have been able to obtain them with few conditions and with little delay. Second, it can be claimed that the banking system has been efficient because it has permitted the borrowers to determine the allocation of these financial resources, as the borrower should be the best judge of this allocation. At the same time, cases such as Turkey, which had excessive short-term financing, suggest that the market has not been particularly efficient, and this has led to debt servicing problems through inappropriate financing techniques. Financing through the banks has been efficient because it has offered OPEC surplus countries a reasonable rate of return with protection against risk while enabling higher-risk countries to borrow these funds. Also, it has been efficient because, through floating rate syndicated credits, the banking system has not had to take a massive interest rate exposure. As a result, the banks have been able to lend over the long term to countries that otherwise could not obtain long-term financing from capital markets (the banks, of course, still take a maturity-risk exposure). This floating rate aspect is very important: there is no way in which fixed rate finance could have been made available to new borrowers in such quantities.

What evidence of inefficiency exists? The number of commercial debt reschedulings suggests that not all lending is as healthy, and thus as efficient, as it might be. The fact that many of these debt problems have been successfully solved, however, also suggests that the markets have been able to cope with many of the problems that have arisen. Reschedulings do raise important questions as to equality of access and degree of efficiency. In a number of cases, banks have lent further money only after the country has carried out a Fund adjustment program. Fund programs have thus kept open the access of the country to the capital and credit markets, but this role of the Fund can perhaps be used only to a limited extent.[4] If all bank financing to developing countries, after the experience of a large number of reschedulings, became conditional on the operation of a Fund program in the country, the lending then becomes conditional lending, and banks would be implicitly supported by the Fund if the program was supposed to lead to an improvement in foreign exchange earnings. At the moment, the banks are at an important juncture where they still have to decide whether a Fund program will improve creditworthiness. There is no obligation on the part of

---

[4]It remains debatable (on a case-by-case basis) as to whether Fund programs and lending can trigger new large private capital inflows, but Fund programs have at least helped to restore the flow (e.g., Jamaica, Peru, Zaïre, and Argentina) and close liaison with the Fund has had an impact on Brazil's economic strategy and its continued high access to the bank credit market.

the Fund to support the banks if the country's policies do not improve the balance of payments. It is difficult to see how the banks can improve on that second-best solution. Every Fund program should be judged on its merits in the same way that all reschedulings are currently judged on their merits. The real problem comes if the Fund programs themselves begin to lose their effect, and here the discussion reverts to the questions raised about the future role of the Fund as a "policeman." If it is assumed that the "policeman's role" can be continued, there should be little problem if the banks continue to consider the Fund's operations in developing countries as one means of ensuring that money is lent to creditworthy countries.

CONCLUSIONS

On balance, it would be wise for the banks and the Fund to continue to have separate roles. Attempts to blend their relative responsibilities should be discouraged. The continued status quo, with a case-by-case approach, however inelegant, is probably the best path for the future. The persistent haggling over each country's problems, on a case-by-case basis, is probably healthy and is probably more efficient than the arrangement of a safety net or rescheduling system that all countries must follow.

But it must be recognized that there are a number of countries for which this solution is hardly satisfactory—countries that are not creditworthy and can do little about their oil deficits and for which access to private markets is limited. Here is the real problem. But this is a problem for governments; the problem for the developing countries that are not creditworthy is how they can continue to buy goods from industrial countries and maintain their political stability under increasing economic hardship.

The private banking community has become increasingly involved in development issues during the last decade. This has been most welcome. But it will be important not to try and push the private capital market into areas that are neither their responsibility nor, perhaps most importantly, their field of expertise. Private banking institutions are involved in developing countries in many ways, particularly through their branches that lend in local currency to companies in developing countries. Here very different risk-reward relationships are encountered. Here, perhaps developing countries really benefit from the transfer of technology from the banking system. But at the more global balance of payments level, it must surely be up to governments and international institutions to seek a more equitable solution if present financing conditions are judged unsatisfactory.

REFERENCES

American Express Bank International Group, "The Maturity of Debt: Financing LDC Development with Medium-Term Eurocredit," *Amex Bank Review*, Vol. 4 (March 1977), pp. 1 and 4–5.

_____, "Bank LDC Portfolios," *Amex Bank Review*, Vol. 8 (September 1981), pp. 1–12.

Hardy, Chandra S., "Rescheduling Developing Country Debts, 1956–1980: Lessons and Recommendations," Overseas Development Council, Working Paper No. 1 (Washington, 1981).

Morgan Guaranty and Trust Company of New York, "International Credit Markets," *World Financial Markets*, (June 1980), pp. 4–6; (November 1980), pp. 5–7.

O'Brien, Richard (1981 a), "Should Banks' Lending to Developing Countries Be Underpinned by International Institutions?" *Financial Times* conference paper (London, January 1981).

_____(1981 b), "Private Bank Lending to Developing Countries," World Bank Staff Working Paper, No. 482 (August 1981).

Wallich, Henry C. (1981 a), "LDC Debt—To Worry or Not to Worry?" remarks to the 59th Annual Meeting of the Bankers' Association for Foreign Trade, Boca Raton, Florida, June 2, 1981.

_____(1981 b), "International Lending and the Role of Bank Supervisory Cooperation," remarks to the International Conference of Banking Supervisors, Washington, September 24, 1981.

Some Issues and Questions Regarding Debt of Developing Countries

BAHRAM NOWZAD

External debt has traditionally not elicited the same amount of intellectual curiosity, nor received the same degree of analytical treatment, as other topics of relevance to developing countries. For instance, balance of payments adjustment has aroused more interest and controversy, as well as provoked a keener and more spirited discussion, than have debt problems facing developing countries. External debt, however, has come to the forefront recently, and external debt problems are now routinely discussed in virtually any conference or symposium dealing with current issues relating to developing countries. This paper briefly addresses two questions: first, Why has the topic of external debt become such an important issue? and second, What are some of the principal issues regarding developing country debt for the future?[1]

EXTERNAL DEBT AS AN IMPORTANT ISSUE

What has sparked the considerable interest in the foreign debt problems of developing countries in recent years is the increasing incidence of countries that have experienced debt servicing diffi-

[1]The factual material in this paper is based mainly on Bahram Nowzad, Richard C. Williams, *et al*, *External Indebtedness of Developing Countries*, IMF Occasional Paper No. 3 (Washington, May 1981).

culties. In theory, as long as the real rate of return on investments financed from external borrowing is equal to, or greater than, the real rate of interest, no debt problems should arise. This, however, does not appear to have been borne out in an increasing number of countries whose external debt obligations have exceeded their capacity to service them. Problems of debt servicing have arisen for a variety of reasons. The principal sources of debt difficulties can be traced to (1) overly ambitious government expenditure programs that have given rise to excessive borrowing, (2) investment of the resources from external borrowing in projects that have had inadequate rates of return, (3) lack of central control and monitoring of the contracting of external debt, and (4) general balance of payments problems (caused by domestic policies or exogenous factors, or both) that have reduced the foreign exchange resources available and thus have constrained the ability of certain countries to meet their contractual obligations on their outstanding external debt.

For these and other reasons, an increasing number of countries have been faced with debt servicing problems that have been dealt with through the imposition of restrictions, the compression of domestic expenditure, or the accumulation of arrears. In an increasing number of instances (see Table 1), debt servicing difficulties have led the debtor country to seek a rescheduling of its debt service obligations.[2]

During 1981 in particular, the number of multilateral debt renegotiations increased substantially. As Table 1 shows, eight Fund mem-

Table 1
MULTILATERAL DEBT RENEGOTIATIONS

1975	1976	1977	1981
May–Chile	May–India	July–Zaïre	Jan.–Pakistan
June–India	June–Zaïre	Sept.–Sierra Leone	Feb.–Togo
		Dec.–Zaïre	April–Madagascar
1978	1979	1980	June–Central African Republic
			July–Zaïre
May–Turkey	June–Togo	Feb.–Sierra Leone	Oct.–Senegal
June–Gabon	July–Turkey	July–Turkey	Nov.–Uganda
Nov.–Peru	Nov.–Sudan	Dec.–Liberia	Dec.–Liberia
	Dec.–Zaïre		

[2]Table 1 refers to debt renegotiations within the framework of the Paris Club—i.e., of debts that are official or officially guaranteed. In addition, a number of countries have engaged in a renegotiation or rescheduling of their debt to private banks.

ber countries sought debt relief—the greatest number in any year since the inception of multilateral debt renegotiations in Paris in 1956. With the exception of Pakistan's renegotiation (which, like India's renegotiations of 1975 and 1976, was used as an alternative technique for transferring resources for development assistance), all other debt reschedulings in 1981 were associated with an actual or imminent interruption of debt service payments. The total amount of debt service due in 1981 and rescheduled under the eight multilateral renegotiations is estimated at about $850 million, while arrears outstanding at the end of 1980 and rescheduled in this context amounted to about $95 million. In addition, outside the aegis of the creditor club, Bolivia, Jamaica, Nicaragua, Sudan, and Turkey renegotiated their debt outstanding to commercial banks.

In all cases, at the time of the multilateral renegotiation the debtor country had adopted an adjustment program supported by an arrangement for the use of Fund resources in the upper credit tranches. As in the past, the rescheduling typically covered government debts or debts guaranteed by official institutions in the creditor countries of over one-year maturity, as well as accumulated arrears on such debts. The principle of excluding the rescheduling of payments due on previously rescheduled debt was generally upheld.

Underlying developments

The recognition that external debt servicing is becoming an important issue for a growing number of developing countries has focused considerable attention and analysis on certain aspects of developing country debt.[3] The salient features of the current situation are the sheer size of the total debt, now surpassing half a trillion dollars (Table 2), the rapid growth in the stock of debt as well as in debt servicing obligations during the past decade, and the significant shifts in the structure of the debt, especially the shift to an increasing amount of borrowing at market rates from the international banking community (Table 3). An associated feature of the latter development is higher debt service obligations, reflecting largely the high interest rates in capital markets in recent years. Since much of the new borrowing is automatically linked to market rates through the mechanism of floating interest rates, much devel-

---

[3]These are surveyed in *External Indebtedness of Developing Countries*, and the following paragraphs thus concentrate on updating the factual information provided there.

Table 2
TOTAL EXTERNAL DEBT OF DEVELOPING COUNTRIES
(billion U.S. dollars)

	1979	1980
Medium-term and long-term debt of 150 developing countries and territories as reported by OECD	391.0	456.2
Short-term debt	85.0	100.0
Use of Fund credit	8.3	10.8
Arrears	5.1	5.3
Total	489.4	572.3
Of which[1]		
Medium-term and long-term debt of 99 developing countries[2]	363.1	414.5
Medium-term and long-term debt of 92 non-oil developing countries[2]	304.1	347.9
Public[3] medium-term and long-term debt of 99 developing countries[2]	299.2	340.4
Public[3] medium-term and long-term debt of 92 non-oil developing countries[2]	247.3	281.9

Sources: World Bank, *World Debt Tables;* OECD, Development Assistance Committee; and Fund staff estimates and projections.

[1]The number of countries covered here and referred to in the text is limited by the lack of comparable data. The main source of debt statistics is the World Bank's Debtor Reporting System (DRS), which collects information from debtor sources on public and publicly guaranteed debt, as well as nonguaranteed debt for 101 developing countries and territories. Two of the countries in the DRS are not classified as developing countries by the Fund, thus reducing the number of countries covered in this paper to 99. The exclusion of 7 countries defined as "major oil exporters" in *External Indebtedness of Developing Countries* results in a grouping of 92 non-oil developing countries.

[2]Not including outstanding use of Fund credit or arrears.

[3]Public and publicly guaranteed debt.

oping country debt has borne the full brunt of high and variable interest rates.

The total external debt of all developing countries—in the broadest definition, encompassing oil producers and including debt of less than one year—reached about $570 billion by the end of 1980, some $83 billion more than it was at the end of 1979. Of this grand total, about $350 billion related to medium-term and long-term obligations of non-oil developing countries.[4] This figure compares with $304 billion at the end of 1979 and less than $80 billion at the end of 1972. The increase of close to $44 billion during 1980 was a reflection of the expanded current account deficits accumulated by non-oil developing countries, but it represents a lower growth rate than that in the late 1970s. However, it must be noted that, similar to developments in 1974–75, these countries made heavy use of their own reserves and of short-term credit—a process that cannot be maintained over the medium term—so that a faster growth of

[4]See footnote 1 of Table 2.

Table 3
MEDIUM-TERM AND LONG-TERM DEBT OF DEVELOPING COUNTRIES
(billion U.S. dollars)

	1972	1973	1974	1975	1976	1977	1978	1979	1980[1]	Annual Compound Rate of Change (per cent)
Debt outstanding (end of period)										
Public debt[2]	72.5	88.9	108.5	129.9	159.5	200.1	253.6	299.2	340.4	21.3
Official creditors	47.1	55.1	64.9	75.2	87.2	103.4	122.7	138.6	158.3	16.4
Private creditors	25.4	33.8	43.6	54.7	72.3	96.7	130.9	160.6	182.1	27.9
Nonguaranteed debt	19.8	25.2	31.1	35.5	40.6	47.4	55.6	63.9	74.1	17.9
Total	92.3	114.1	139.6	165.5	200.1	247.5	309.2	363.1	414.5	20.7
Debt service										
Public debt[2]	8.3	11.3	13.9	15.4	17.9	23.7	35.6	47.4	54.1	26.4
Official creditors	3.6	4.4	5.0	5.8	6.4	7.8	9.5	11.7	14.3	18.8
Private creditors	4.7	6.9	8.9	9.6	11.5	15.9	26.1	35.7	39.8	30.6
Nonguaranteed debt	3.9	5.7	8.1	9.1	9.6	11.2	14.2	17.6	21.1	23.5
Total	12.1	16.9	21.9	24.5	27.5	34.9	49.8	65.0	75.2	25.7

Sources: World Bank, World Debt Tables; and Fund staff projections.

[1]Preliminary figures.
[2]Public and publicly guaranteed debt.

Note: Components may not add to totals because of rounding.

medium-term and long-term debt can be expected in the future. This reduced reliance on medium-term and long-term debt[5] was almost totally due to a much slower growth of outstanding debt to private creditors, which was about a third as rapid in 1980 as it was during the period 1973–79 (13.6 per cent, compared with 34.0 per cent). One consequence of this pronounced deceleration was that, unlike the experience of the 1970s, outstanding public debt to official sources grew faster than did outstanding public debt to private creditors (14.4 per cent, compared with 13.6 per cent). However, commercial bank lending (excluding Hong Kong and Singapore), inclusive of short-term loans, rose at about the same rate as during the period 1973–79 (26.8 per cent, as against 26.5 per cent during the earlier period).

As a ratio to gross national product (GNP), outstanding medium-term and long-term external debt declined to 23.6 per cent, reflecting the slower expansion of external debt. The continued expansion of the share of exports of goods and services in gross domestic product (GDP) brought the ratio of outstanding external debt to exports to 109.0 per cent, or about the same as in 1973. The burden of servicing this debt continued growing at a rapid pace, rising by 14 per cent to about $62 billion in 1980. Sharply higher international interest rates were the major force behind the rise of one third in interest payments in 1980, and these higher interest payments exceeded the increase in total debt service payments. As would be expected, low-income countries, with their higher proportion of concessional finance, experienced a smaller increase in their interest charges.

In 1980 and 1981 the very high interest rates (in real as well as in nominal terms) were of particular concern. These high interest rates reflected the interaction of restrictive monetary policies in many industrial countries with the momentum of ongoing inflation after a long period of generally inadequate fiscal restraint. But, notwithstanding the necessity of dealing with inflationary problems through policies of monetary and fiscal restraint, the very high real interest rates have created a drain on the international purchasing power of most net debtor countries. The non-oil developing countries face a particularly serious problem, since the impact of high interest rates is affecting them at a time when their international

---

[5]Excludes private nonguaranteed debt.

purchasing power is already eroded because of the deterioration in their terms of trade, weak markets for their exports, increasing protectionist pressures, and slow growth in aid flows to low-income countries.

Notwithstanding the rapid increase in debt service at the absolute level, debt service as a ratio to exports of goods and services showed a slight decline to 19.5 per cent in 1980, compared with 21.5 per cent in 1979. While this represents a departure from the increases in debt service during the 1970s, these aggregate data mask the markedly different patterns for various subgroups of non-oil developing countries, specifically net oil exporters, whose debt service ratio fell from 32.7 per cent in 1979 to 22.6 per cent in 1980, primarily because of their strong export performance, especially for petroleum products. The remaining non-oil developing countries experienced virtually no change in their debt service burden as the debt service ratio for major exporters of manufactures remained at about 20 per cent, for low-income countries at about 11 per cent, and for other net oil importers at about 18 per cent.[6] Within each of these subgroups, considerable variations can be seen in the debt service ratio for individual countries.

For 1981, the financing requirements of the non-oil developing countries were estimated in mid-1981 to be about $15 billion larger than in 1980. Although a shift toward greater longer-term financing is indicated, these requirements have continued to be satisfied by short-term flows, cessation of reserve accumulation, and reliance on reserve-related borrowing. The present unsettled conditions in the international financial markets and the high interest rates, however, may have discouraged longer-term financing. The major exception is the "net oil exporters" subgroup, which (at least through mid-1981) increased reserves mainly through long-term borrowing while avoiding the short-term borrowing that has characterized the oil importing developing countries.

Many bankers had expressed concern that private financial institutions would not be able to channel funds to deficit countries in

---

[6]Data presented here differ in coverage and classification from those of *External Indebtedness of Developing Countries*. The change in coverage is minor; however, the difference in classification has a more marked impact on the relevant magnitudes. This is due to the previous classification of India as a major exporter of manufactures (IMF, *World Economic Outlook*, May 1980). Subsequently, India has been reclassified as a low-income country, resulting in a convergence of debt service ratios for two of these groupings.

sufficient volume to cover their expected requirements. Thus far, it appears that these concerns were to some extent exaggerated, partly because the recourse to private financial institutions for longer-term financing was considerably less in 1980–81 than in 1979. However, looking ahead, there remains a danger that resources available to groups of non-oil developing countries that at present have access to the international capital markets may become constrained, especially as these countries are expected to shift from short-term borrowing and reserve-related financing to a more viable pattern of financing their current account deficits.

New focus on debt issues

The basic developments in external debt, as sketched above, and the attention that has been focused on debt issues of developing countries have led to the recognition that in a number of countries debt servicing problems may result from deep-rooted structural problems. This has prompted discussion about the sustainability of developing country debt over the medium term—that is, whether many of the debtor countries can continue to service their existing debt obligations, as well as whether they have the capacity to incur further debt. This reappraisal, whether open or implicit, has had an impact on the decisions of creditors.

The outcome of these developments—at the very time when the financing gap of developing countries is reaching unprecedented levels and at a point when developing countries need large amounts of external resources for developmental as well as for balance of payments purposes—is that increasing doubts have arisen about the ability of many countries to assume additional foreign debt or even to continue to service their existing debt obligations. In one way or another, virtually all developing countries have been affected by resource flow problems. Countries that have limited access to international capital markets, and consequently must depend on official development assistance (ODA), have seen a virtual stagnation of ODA flows. Countries that have access to international capital markets are experiencing an increase in interest charges on much of their outstanding debt and are being subjected to greater scrutiny by creditors. It has become increasingly recognized that any serious disruption in external flows would not only have immediate implications for short-term balance of payments prospects of the countries concerned but would also affect their development outlook and, in turn, external resource flows.

Issues for the Future

As no global debt problems have arisen, a cautious optimism has frequently been expressed that the necessary flows can continue. Several aspects of future financial flows and their external debt counterpart, however, must be examined closely.

Supply of financing

There is, first, the issue of the supply of financial resources. The answer to the question of whether the supply will be sufficient to meet the demand for financing is tautological in the accounting sense that balance of payments deficits cannot arise unless the financing for them is available. But the supply side is affected by other factors, especially as regards the supply of financing from international capital markets, which involves, in large part, questions of distribution, spreading of the lending burden (i.e., bank exposure, portfolio concentration), and the distribution of lending among borrowing countries (whether the supply will be adequate where it is needed). These questions cannot be answered abstractly in the aggregate. Nevertheless, they relate to points about which the international banking community and bank supervisory authorities in several countries are increasingly concerned. Any action to counter these concerns, such as a reduction in lending to a particular country or group of countries, would be implemented without publicity or fanfare, but the impact on the borrowing country could be far-reaching.

Demand factors

The main issue on the demand side for many countries is, as already indicated, whether they can sustain additional debts. The answer can only be given on the basis of individual countries. Virtually all analysts have expressed confidence that, at least for the immediate period ahead, developing countries as a group can absorb an increasing amount of external debt, but individual countries with significant debt obligations may encounter serious difficulties. Understandably, the international banking community has publicly expressed few worries on this score; indeed, any such concern by banks might tend to become self-fulfilling. There is, however, no doubt that, while there is little concern about the probability of a major default, the impact of a potential default on the part of a major debtor country is viewed much more seriously. Such a development would not only have direct implications for the individual country but could also have serious repercussions for the international financial system. One of the questions that needs to be addressed is what mechanisms and safeguards would be available to meet such an emergency. Would there be a lender of last resort? Would assistance be given to the defaulting debtor country, or would it be given to the creditor banks that encountered difficulties as a result of such default? Is it necessary to set up precautionary measures to contain the defaults, or would that only serve to precipitate more defaults?

The sheer size of the payments imbalances confronting non-oil developing countries, as well as the fact that the imbalances are expected to persist for some time, adds a dimension to the question of sustainability in the 1980s. In particular, the persistent nature of these imbalances distinguishes the current situation from the one immediately following the first oil shock of 1973–74. At that time, concerns centered on the ability of the international financial system to recycle funds from surplus to deficit countries. Because of the prolonged nature of present imbalances, a new concern must be added—that of the sustainability of these imbalances, both in terms of size and the use made of external borrowing.

It is clear that the current situation calls for financing to be reinforced by adjustment policies. The Fund is ready to play a more active role in both the adjustment and the financing efforts of its members than it did during the earlier period. While retaining the demand management element of its programs, which is crucial for their success, the Fund has adopted a more supply-oriented policy approach to promote the most efficient use of domestic and foreign resources. This twin approach is well suited to both reducing a member's financing requirement to manageable proportions and ensuring that the borrowed resources are utilized in a sustainable manner. Recognizing the importance of financing to any adjustment program, the Fund has recently increased the amount of resources that a member may draw over three years to 450 per cent of the newly increased quota, excluding resources with low conditionality, such as the compensatory financing facility.

Mechanism of transfer

A third issue for the period ahead that is frequently discussed relates to the effectiveness of the mechanism to channel external resources. This issue raises a number of questions. Will a mechanism that worked well in the 1970s be able to perform with the same efficiency in the substantially changed circumstances of the 1980s? If it will not, what is the reason and what must be done? Could the mechanism work in such a way as to increase and broaden the market access of countries that at present have limited access? Will it be possible to wean the so-called newly industrializing countries away from ODA and into the international capital markets? Is there a need for new guarantee mechanisms to enhance the access of marginally middle-income countries to private funds?

Criticisms of the institutional arrangements for recycling funds during the 1970s (e.g., through private financial institutions) are most often focused on the distribution and form of lending. Lending in the recent past has been concentrated in a small number of countries that account for the bulk of the total debt owed by developing countries. This concentration stems partly from the fact that private creditors have assumed a major role in the financing of current account deficits during the 1970s and have lent most heavily to those countries—primarily net oil exporters and major exporters of manufactures—where export prospects appear brighter. With this shift from official to private creditors have also come changes in the terms of the loans to shorter maturities and to market-related interest rates. It is also felt by some critics that the concentration of lending to a relatively small group of countries may have reduced the net transfer of resources to other non-oil developing countries, such as the low-income countries, and may have led to a situation where the strong get stronger and the weak get weaker. While not commenting on this view nor the various proposed solutions, it may be noted that the Fund expects in the coming years to lend its resources more heavily to the low-income countries and the other net oil importers among the non-oil developing countries. In addition, the Fund has also set up a subsidy account to alleviate the burden of high financing costs for many low-income countries borrowing under the supplementary financing facility.

The interest rate issue

Of the main issues confronting developing countries, the interaction of inflation and interest rates on debt service has received particular attention. This is not surprising because the combination of rapid inflation and monetary stringency in the industrial countries has recently raised interest rates in international capital markets to historically high levels (during the first half of 1981, the London interbank offered rate averaged about 17 per cent, compared with less than 7 per cent in 1974). Moreover, with the advent of variable interest rate loans and the increasing importance of financial flows from commercial banks, interest rate movements have acquired greater significance for the economic situation, particularly the external position, of developing countries.

The importance of variable interest rate loans, however, ranges widely among the subgroups of non-oil developing countries. By the end of 1980, major exporters of manufactures and net oil exporters (20 countries) had acquired an estimated 52 per cent of their total public external debt from financial institutions, compared with only 8 per cent for low-income countries. Not all loans from financial institutions are contracted under variable interest rate terms, but data on these loans provide an approximation of relative exposure. While a small number of countries are affected, these countries accounted for about 60 per cent of total public debt of non-oil developing countries in 1980 and a somewhat higher share of the outstanding public debt extended by financial institutions. Any decline in nominal interest rates in major financial markets would be very quickly reflected in the nominal value of interest payments on external debt by developing countries that rely heavily on market finance, because, as already indicated, a considerable proportion of the outstanding debt of these countries has flexible interest rates that are linked to market rates. Any such decline, however, would be short-lived if inflation and inflationary expectations are not curbed in the industrial countries. Given the imperative need to control inflation in these countries, there seems to be a strong prospect that real interest rates will remain well above the low or negative levels of the 1970s. This prospect implies that external borrowing will remain more costly in real terms than it was in the 1970s, and it underscores the need for prudent adjustment measures in many of the borrowing countries.

One of the major forces behind the rise in interest rates during the 1970s was the increasing inflation rate. With fixed interest rate loans, higher inflation results in a transfer of real resources from the creditor to the debtor (depressing debt service indicators). With variable interest rate loans, however, higher interest rates, which incorporate an inflation premium, may compensate for the deterioration in the real value of the loan (increasing debt service indicators). As actual interest payments on variable rate loans include a component reflecting the erosion in the real value of the loan, the loan is amortized at a faster rate in real terms than was originally expected.

So long as the real interest rate is unchanged, the underlying conditions influencing the sustainability of external debt are unaffected by inflation and higher nominal interest rates (although certain indicators, such as the ratio of interest payments to GDP, may give misleading signals). Even though the long-term viability and therefore the associated risks remain the same, the short-run prospects are altered by the faster effective amortization rate. Consequently, in the short term a country would require larger gross borrowing to maintain the same real net resource transfer (i.e., loan disbursements less debt service payments). Thus, a new debt manageability problem is introduced and a country's vulnerability to disruptions in capital markets or short-run fluctuations in exports is increased; and the maintenance of creditor confidence becomes more important.

Variable interest rate loans not only expose debtors to uncertainties as to the speed at which their debt will be amortized in real terms but also complicate investment decisions and the analysis of the future sustainability of external debt because a new factor must be considered—monetary policy in developed countries. In addition to their response to inflation, higher nominal interest rates also stem from more restrictive monetary policies, which have recently pushed real interest rates to relatively high levels and narrowed the range of economically attractive investment opportunities. Moreover, the viability of past investments may be endangered as higher real internal rates of return are required to match the increased real interest costs. The recent variability of real interest rates has further compounded the planning problems associated with external borrowing.

Suggested solutions to the problems associated with variable interest rate loans can be broadly classified into three types of indexation—financial, maturity, and price. Some of the main issues connected with each approach are outlined below, and it is explained why none of the solutions suggested significantly reduces debt service uncertainties.

Financial indexation would adjust amortization payments by an interest rate index. Such a technique, which has been used in certain countries with high inflation rates, has merit but still would not make the repayment schedule immune from the impact of inflation or monetary policy. In fact, during periods of high real interest rates, the lender would be overcompensated because movement in the interest rate index would outstrip inflation. Although the precise mechanism may differ, the principle behind maturity indexation schemes is the same—change the amortization schedule to offset the faster amortization rate. Thus, in effect, both the interest rate and the amortization schedule would be variable, with only the final maturity unchanged. While this technique would neutralize the impact of inflation in most, but not all, situations (as shown in Appendix II of *External Indebtedness of Developing Countries*), it would also add to the bookkeeping work and complicate further the analysis of a country's prospective debt situation. Price indexation of amortization payments, combined with constant or floating real interest rate loans, would eliminate the problem of faster amortization and has been utilized in some countries that were experiencing high inflation and interest rates. However, a great many technical issues would require resolution before this scheme could be extended to the international capital markets, such as the proper index (i.e., consumer prices, wholesale prices, export prices, or import prices), the appropriate real interest rate, and the timing in relation to price data. Even with price indexation, which would reduce the uncertainties associated with the real debt burden, nominal borrowing requirements would be difficult to predict and would be a potential source of debt management problems.

All these proposals have technical deficiencies, lack widespread support, and leave untouched the uncertainties connected with real debt service or nominal debt service and with real or nominal borrowing requirements—uncertainties caused by inflation and interest rate movements. None of the schemes can eliminate these uncertainties, although the risks can be shifted from one party to another, because risk is inherent in the present uncertain international economic environment. Only policy measures that succeed in reducing both the level and variability of inflation and interest rates can diminish the uncertainties associated with international lending and borrowing.

Framework for debt renegotiations

In view of current debt levels and balance of payments prospects, it seems probable that a number of countries will encounter debt servicing difficulties and will require a rescheduling of their obligations. Questions have therefore been raised as to whether the present framework for multilateral debt renegotiations is satisfactory. While it seems to be agreed that the framework for the renegotiation of official and officially guaranteed debts (i.e., the Paris Club) is adequate, there has been some discussion of increasing the cooperation between official creditors and commercial banks on debt reschedulings. The basis for such discussion is the conviction that successful debt rescheduling assists all parties: the debtor country, the official creditors, and the commercial banks. It has thus been asserted that, ideally, all debt renegotiations, whether official or commercial, should be seen in the context of a broader program to assist the debtor countries to be able to resume sustainable flows. A main question has been whether this would be feasible, given that the objectives, procedures, and methods of international banks are quite distinct from those of official lenders.

These questions by no means exhaust the issues relevant to the debt problems of developing countries in the 1980s. They merely highlight the broader conclusions of this paper—that, for a variety of reasons, the debt question has become an important issue and that continued vigilance is necessary in the years ahead. Moreover, there is also a need to keep under review existing procedures and mechanisms and, where necessary, to adapt them so as to ensure that individual debt problems do not threaten the entire international monetary system.

The Position and Prospects of the International Monetary System in Historical Context

BRIAN TEW

The developing countries—at any rate those not endowed with oil resources—have in recent years been attempting to develop in an environment that has become markedly less favorable than that of the 1960s. This deterioration must be attributed in part to the way the international monetary system has evolved during the last decade. In this paper, the course of events is explained in terms of the roles played by the main *dramatis personae:* the major industrial countries, organized as the Group of Ten; the International Monetary Fund; the non-oil developing countries; and the developing countries, as represented by the Group of Twenty Four.

ROLE OF THE GROUP OF 10

The ten members of the International Monetary Fund adhering to the General Arrangements to Borrow (GAB), which entered into force on October 24, 1962, came to be called the Group of Ten. They comprised Belgium, Canada, France, the Federal Republic of Germany, Italy, Japan, the Netherlands, Sweden, the United Kingdom, and the United States. Switzerland, a nonmember of the Fund, soon became associated with the GAB, so that the Group of 10 actually includes 11 countries.

The GAB represented an assumption of decision-taking responsibility by the signatories in that activation of the GAB re-

170

quires collective agreement under procedures laid down in the so-
called Baumgartner correspondence. But the establishment of the
GAB was only the first of a more extensive accretion of decision-
taking responsibilities by the participating countries. Since 1962,
the Group of 10 has met regularly, at both ministerial and official
levels, except for a gap of three years when it was recovering from
the bitter negotiations that concluded at the Smithsonian meeting in
December 1971. At its meetings crucial decisions have been taken as
to the operation and development of the international monetary
system—for example, large drawings on the Fund, increases in
Fund quotas, the negotiation of the special drawing right (SDR)
scheme, the introduction in 1964 of "multilateral surveillance" under
the auspices of the Organization for Economic Cooperation and Development (OECD), the operation of the gold pool and its eventual
termination in 1968, and so on. Admittedly, since September 1973
such weighty matters have been discussed in an even more exclusive
forum—the Group of Five, comprising France, the Federal Republic
of Germany, Japan, the United Kingdom, and the United States—
but meetings of this group have always been followed by Group of 10
meetings, at which Group of Five decisions are reviewed and, if
necessary, modified to ensure the consent of the other Group of 10
countries.

The importance of the Group of 10 is enhanced through the fact
that its membership is the same as that of Working Party No. 3, a
subcommittee set up in 1961 by the Economic Policy Committee of
the OECD (1966, p. 8n) to review on a regular basis "the effect on
international payments of monetary, fiscal and other policy measures." Working Party No. 3, consisting of senior government and
central bank officials, "established the practice of holding its meetings at six to eight-week intervals."

The smaller and poorer countries of the world came to regard the
meetings of the Group of 10 and of Working Party No. 3, sometimes
rather unfavorably, as alternative manifestations of the same rich
countries' club. Moreover, it did not pass unnoticed that the central
banks of the Group of 10 countries were represented at the monthly
meetings of central bank governors at the Bank for International
Settlements (BIS) in Basle. Such meetings in the 1950s had been
attended only by governors from the eight countries represented on
the BIS Board of Directors (Belgium, France, the Federal Republic
of Germany, Italy, the Netherlands, Sweden, the United Kingdom,

and Switzerland), but beginning in 1961 they were joined by U.S. representatives and somewhat later Canada and Japan were also represented.

There can be no doubt that the Group of 10 countries, meeting in their various forums, have usurped an important part of the decision-taking responsibility that the founding fathers of the Fund had intended to vest in the Fund's Executive Board. The Board, therefore, may on occasions be reduced to rubber stamping propositions put to it by the nine Executive Directors who come from Group of 10 countries, which control slightly over 50 per cent of the Board vote.

This partial usurpation by the Group of 10 of the responsibilities of the Fund's Executive Board has not diminished the role of the Fund's Managing Director and his staff, who attend both Group of 10 meetings and Fund Executive Board meetings. Moreover, the Group of 10, as distinct from Working Party No. 3, has no staff of its own and relies heavily on the Fund staff for expert advice, drafting reports and other documents, and undertaking research.

The losers in the *de facto* allocation of responsibilities would seem to be the Executive Directors from the developing countries, who are likely to be presented with a *fait accompli* whenever members of the Group of 10 consider their vital interests to be at stake and can agree on what action they want taken. On occasions, such has indeed been the case; for example, the developing countries have hitherto failed to overcome the Group of 10 countries' opposition to a "link" (an arrangement for issuing SDRs so as to provide development financing).

But on other issues the Group of 10 has not been so unyielding; for example, the early Group of 10 proposals for what eventually became the SDR scheme restricted participation to the richer countries alone, but on strong pressure from other Fund members the option of participation was finally extended to all Fund members. The pressure was exercised, inter alia, through the Group of Twenty-Four, made up of eight countries each in Africa, Asia, and Latin America and assigned by the Group of 77[1] to consider monetary affairs. The Group of 24 has subsequently met regularly to

---

[1]The Group of 77 is a creation of the first meeting of the United Nations Conference on Trade and Development (UNCTAD) in Geneva in 1964. It was established under a UN General Assembly resolution of December 30, 1964. The membership of the Group of 77 has now grown to well over a hundred members.

formulate developing countries' views and to further their interests; thus it operates in a sense as a counterpoise (though not usually a very weighty one) to the Group of 10.

Differences of opinion between the Group of 24 and the Group of 10 on the international monetary system arise for the most part because the two Groups view the system from very different perspectives. The Group of 24 represents countries that are relatively poor and that aspire to rapid economic development; hence it constantly emphasizes "the pressing need for a substantial increase in the transfer of real resources to the developing countries" (Group of 24, 1980) and seeks to use the international monetary system, as well as the development agencies, the General Agreement on Tariffs and Trade (GATT), and all other international economic arrangements, to further that end.

The Group of 10 countries, on the other hand, see themselves as bearing the whole responsibility for actually operating the international monetary system. They are aware that theirs are the world's major currencies. An overwhelming proportion of the world's stock of money and monetary instruments is denominated in the Group of 10 countries' currencies, some of which are in widespread use internationally as well as internally. Virtually all international trade is invoiced in their currencies. Almost all the large financial markets are located within their borders. Hence they are constantly preoccupied with the relative strength or weakness of their currencies, with speculation between one of these currencies and another, and with official measures affecting the interconvertibility of their currencies and the level and volatility of the rates of exchange between them. Such matters, they believe, are best discussed in the intimate forum of the Group of 10, or even the Group of Five, since other countries have little to contribute. Whatever actions the Group of 10 countries subsequently take, whether individually or acting in concert, must then be accepted by the smaller and developing countries as an aspect of their environment to which they have to adapt. How has this aspect of their environment been shaped by the decisions and actions taken by the Group of 10 countries in the 1960s and subsequently?

Restrictions on trade and payments

A stable and reliable feature of the environment resulting from the Group of 10's rules of the game has been the virtual absence of any restrictions on trade and current payments imposed by the Group for balance of payments reasons or as a remedy for general unemployment. Such restrictions are nevertheless imposed for other reasons, particularly to protect European agriculture and to prevent Group of 10 manufactures from being undercut by imports from the developing countries—the notorious "new protectionism," about which developing countries such as Korea and Singapore rightly complain.

Seven of the Group of 10 countries had participated in February 1961 in the concerted move from Article XIV to Article VIII status under the Fund's charter; the United States and Canada already had Article VIII status by then and presumably Switzerland would also have had it if the country had been a member of the Fund. That accounts for all Group of 10 countries except Japan, which moved to Article VIII status in 1964. The significance of the change from Article XIV to Article VIII status is that, under the transitional arrangements of Article XIV, Section 2 (IMF, 1978, p. 48),

> A member that has notified the Fund that it intends to avail itself of transitional arrangements under this provision may, notwithstanding the provisions of any other articles of this Agreement, maintain and adapt to changing circumstances the restrictions on payments and transfers for current international transactions that were in effect on the date on which it became a member.

On the other hand, under Article VIII, Section 2(*a*) (IMF, 1978, p. 29),

> ... no member shall, without the approval of the Fund, impose restrictions on the making of payments and transfers for current international transactions.

Since the early 1960s, it has been very rare for any Group of 10 country to seek a waiver of the Fund and GATT provisions against restrictions imposed on trade and current payments for balance of payments reasons.

The Group of 10 countries have also been increasingly reluctant to have prolonged recourse to restrictions on capital movements. Admittedly, the United Kingdom maintained restrictions on capital outflows continuously until 1979, and the United States also imposed restrictions on capital outflows from 1964 until January 1974; but these were the exception. Most Group of 10 countries imposed exchange controls or equivalent regulations on capital flows only for much shorter periods. In some cases—for example, the Federal Republic of Germany, Switzerland, and Japan—restrictions were on inflows; in other cases—for example, the United Kingdom and the United States—they were on outflows.

Most Group of 10 countries have been prepared to pay at least lip service to the undesirability of controls on capital movements on the grounds that such controls impede the optimum allocation of resources, but their reluctance to have recourse to such devices arose in practice much more from the realization that evasion of controls could not be prevented. Of course, such evasion has always been only partial. A comparison of U.S. dollar interest rates in New York and London over the period 1963–74 shows that the U.S. regulations must have been holding back at least some capital outflows; likewise, a comparison of deutsche mark interest rates in Frankfurt and Luxembourg shows that German regulations (when in operation) cannot have been wholly ineffective in deterring capital inflows. But in neither case were the regulations capable of retaining more than a limited amount of outflow, and leakages became progressively more serious with the passage of time.

Countries outside the Group of 10, especially the developing countries, have in many cases been much less reluctant to have recourse to restrictions on trade and payments for balance of payments reasons, as well as for other purposes. Many of them are still under Article XIV, and those under Article VIII often seek waivers for exchange controls and equivalent devices when in balance of payments difficulties. In particular, they make use of quantitative restrictions. They also frequently seek to restrict capital outflows by exchange controls; this may be more effective in a country whose currency is not in the same widespread use as are the currencies of the Group of 10 countries.

Though the intention of the original Fund and GATT charters was to apply the same set of rules of good behavior to all members, it has come to be widely accepted that such "universalism," as Richard Gardner (1980, p. 383) called it, was unrealistic and indeed undesirable. In particular, the Group of 10 countries seem to accept the fact that their own code of good behavior with respect to restrictions on trade and payments should not be imposed on the developing countries, even if it could be.

The Bretton Woods exchange rate regime

The "universalism" of the original Fund charter lasted until the early 1970s in respect of the original Article IV rules about exchange rates (IMF, 1945). In this case, it was the Group of 10 countries that disappointed the founding fathers by abandoning pegging in favor of floating exchange rates.

In the 1960s, the objectives set out in the original Article IV were achieved by the following three arrangements:

1. The U.S. authorities assured the interconvertibility of gold and the U.S. dollar by undertaking to trade gold against dollars with other countries' central banks at $35 an ounce. This undertaking was terminated by U.S. President Nixon in his famous speech on August 15, 1971.

2. The other Group of 10 countries assured the interconvertibility of each of their currencies and the U.S. dollar at a pegged rate by market transactions, all using the dollar as their intervention currency—the pegs being in principle adjustable, but in practice adjusted only as a last resort. These pegging arrangements broke down in the first three years of the 1970s, as the partners of the United States in the Group of 10 successively abandoned the practice of pegging to the dollar, the last defections being in March 1973.

3. Other countries pegged their currencies to one of the Group of 10 currencies, especially to the U.S. dollar, the pound sterling, or the French franc. Pegging was achieved by official transactions in the relevant intervention currency, backed up in some cases by recourse to exchange control. Pegging to sterling went out of fashion with the floating of sterling against the dollar in June 1972, but pegging to the dollar and, to a lesser extent, to the French franc has continued. Other countries outside the Group of 10 have moved to pegging to "baskets" of currencies, especially the SDR basket. In the opinion of the countries outside the Group of 10, and particularly of the developing countries, the abandonment of pegging to the dollar by the United States' partners in the Group of 10 represented a deterioration of their environment. John Williamson (1977, p. 92) in his study of the work of the Fund's Committee of Twenty (Committee on Reform of the International Monetary System and Related Issues) recalls that an area of debate

> where the developing countries displayed interest and tended to adopt a common position . . . was the exchange rate regime, where most of them supported retention of the adjustable peg quite forcefully. Even those developing countries that had themselves adopted a floating rate or crawling peg argued for retention of the adjustable peg by the developed countries,

for reasons which probably corresponded to those later put forward in the report of the Brandt Commission (Brandt, 1980, p. 207):

> The floating of the major currencies introduces uncertainties about real earnings from exports and real costs of imports since exports and imports are often invoiced in currencies which move against each other in unpredictable ways. This kind of uncertainty discourages allocation of resources to producing goods for export or for competition with imports, and introduces complications in external debt management.

Most of the smaller developing countries prefer to peg, rather than to float, their currencies (Lipschitz and Sundararajan, 1980, p. 25):

> In a world of generalized floating exchange rates, many countries have sought to peg their currencies to some relatively stable standard. By December 31, 1979, 94 out of the 140 Fund members were classified as having pegged rates; of these, 60 were pegged to a single currency; the rest were pegged to a basket of currencies. In 14 cases, the basket chosen was the special drawing right (SDR) .... The developing countries as a group have generally preferred some form of pegging arrangement, and an increasing number of them have abandoned single currency pegs and have fixed their exchange rates against currency baskets.
>
> There are various reasons for countries to peg the value of their currencies to some standard. Exchange rates are determined in an asset market—a market for different monies—and even in a relatively stable world, asset market prices tend to fluctuate sharply. It is widely believed that real economic costs are associated with such fluctuations; they inhibit trade, harm domestic price stability, increase uncertainty, and serve generally to frustrate economic decision-making. If there is not much international trading of a particular currency, so that occasional large transactions dominate the market, fluctuations of its exchange rate are likely to be even more volatile. Most developing countries fall into this category. In addition, these countries generally do not have well-developed forward exchange markets to allow transactors to protect themselves against future exchange rate changes. In this situation, the risks associated with international transactions are likely to discourage foreign trade. Also, as prices of traded goods are linked to the exchange rate, changes in the relative price of traded goods to home goods are likely to distort the allocation of investment within the local economy, and may lead to investment in less productive sectors. These factors are sufficient to induce many countries to peg their exchange rates. An additional, though less often discussed, argument for fixing the exchange rate is that a fixed rate system has a built-in cushioning effect that tends to reduce the impact of short-term real shocks. For example, in bad years when there are harvest shortfalls, the authorities will have to sell foreign reserves in the market to support the exchange rate. These reserves will be used to finance imports to make up the shortfall. In good years of bountiful supplies, the authorities will have to buy foreign exchange to prevent an appreciation of the exchange rate, and reserves will be built up against future needs. This cushioning mechanism is particularly important for stability in those developing countries in which domestic consumption and investment are extremely sensitive to output and market conditions for the few primary commodities that are produced and exported.
>
> While for many countries there are good reasons to fix the value of the currency, in most cases the appropriate standard is not apparent

since the increased instability of the relative value of the major currencies of the Group of 10 countries (the U.S. dollar, the deutsche mark, the yen, the Swiss and French francs, and the pound sterling) has typically made it more difficult to decide what currency to peg to. Sometimes the choice is easy. Some small countries have a dominant trading partner, whose currency is the obvious choice for pegging purposes—for example, the smaller countries of Latin America, which peg to the dollar, and francophone Africa, which mainly pegs to the French franc. The economies of such small countries may be so closely integrated with their dominant trading partner's economy that a change in the exchange rate has little effect on relative prices; hence, devaluation or revaluation is not a useful policy instrument for influencing the flow of imports and exports. However, more often the choice is not as easy:

1. Many countries do not have one dominant trading partner. This, of course, accounts for the increasing popularity of pegging to a basket of currencies.

2. The composition of the basket poses delicate problems, in that a country like Norway or Australia may find that, although the United States is ceasing to be its dominant trading partner, the dollar remains the dominant currency for invoicing purposes.

3. A country's dominant partner in its export trade may be different from its dominant partner in its import trade (e.g., Botswana).

The problem facing the smaller developing countries—that of deciding to which currency they should peg—is associated with another—that of deciding in what form to hold their reserves. The Group of 10 countries that abandoned pegging to the dollar have nevertheless continued to hold their foreign exchange reserves almost entirely in dollars. Membership in the Fund and the European Monetary System (EMS) has, of course, required them to hold SDRs and European Currency Units (ECUs) as well, but there has been little deliberate diversification into the SDR or the ECU, or into gold. Outside the Group of 10, however, diversification has already proceeded quite a long way. Sterling is now only a minor reserve asset among the countries previously in the sterling area. There has also been a move away from the dollar into the deutsche mark and the yen, and into gold. The move into gold by countries outside the Group of 10 has, however, been untimely, in that it occurred mainly after the rapid rise in the gold price over the period 1973–79. The main beneficiaries of the revaluation of official gold reserves have been the Group of 10 countries.

Floating by the Group of 10 countries

The problems of pegging referred to above are compounded by the apparent inability of the Group of 10 countries to decide how they want to float, so that their official actions cannot now be reliably predicted.

1. Should they float individually or jointly? Since the establishment of the EMS in March 1979, five of the Group of 10 countries have been floating their currencies jointly in the European "snake." However, before March 1979 the snake usually had a smaller and unstable membership; much of the time the Federal Republic of Germany, Belgium, and the Netherlands were the only Group of 10 countries in the snake.

2. Should the floating be clean or managed? So far, none of the Group of 10 countries has opted for clean floating of its currency, with no official transactions at all in the foreign exchange market. However, they have, by common consent, all eschewed aggressive intervention—that is, intervention to push the exchange rate in the direction in which it was already moving. Instead, their intervention has always been to lean against the wind—that is, to moderate, by official transactions, movements in the market value of their respective currencies. But should such official intervention be "light" (small in amount, and soon reversed) or "determined" (large in amount, and persistent)? The BIS *Annual Report* (BIS, 1977, p. 19) correctly made the generalization that in 1977 the dollar-deutsche mark rate alone was only lightly managed in practice, usually by the U.S. and German authorities acting in concert, with all other rates within the Group of 10 being managed in a much more determined manner, almost always by each of the countries concerned buying or selling its own currency against the dollar. The German authorities had "a foot in both camps"; they were light interventionists when acting in concert with the United States and determined interventionists as members of the snake. But the state of affairs reported by the BIS in 1977 had emerged only after a number of changes en route. In the first year of the floating pound sterling (mid-1972 to mid-1973)

intervention was light; it was only later in 1973 that there began three years of continuous and massive official support. The Swiss franc floated fairly freely until February 1975. The Canadian dollar was only lightly managed up to the time of the provincial elections in Quebec in November 1976 (BIS, 1977, p. 129). And after 1977 there were further changes. The dollar-deutsche mark rate was managed with massive, though short-term, intervention in the three years 1978–80, only to revert (according to U.S. Secretary of the Treasury Regan)[2] to very much lighter intervention under the Reagan Administration. The U.K. authorities have also changed course; having supported the pound sterling massively until 1976, they rapidly unwound their support in the first three quarters of 1977 and thereafter intervened in the market with a much lighter touch.

3. "Leaning against the wind" may not only be practiced by undertaking official transactions in the foreign exchange market; it can also be pursued by a suitable modification of the stance of fiscal and monetary policy. Deflationary policies—a tougher budget, credit restraint, and a rise in interest rates—serve to strengthen a weak currency in the market; reflationary policies tend to mitigate the appreciation of a strong currency. However, all of the Group of 10 countries have a marked tendency to set their fiscal and monetary policy by reference to what they judge to be the needs of the internal economy; only as a last resort will they sacrifice their internal objectives (say, maintaining employment or alternatively reducing inflation) to the external objective of moderating a rise or fall in the exchange value of their currency. Nevertheless, both the Federal Republic of Germany and Switzerland have on occasions been prepared temporarily to permit excessive monetary growth in relation to the target previously set as optimal for the internal economy,[3] in order to moderate the rise in the external value of their currencies. Likewise, a fall in the external value of a currency, if sufficiently sharp, may well provoke a reaction in the form of a more deflationary fiscal

---

[2]*Financial Times* (London), April 18, 1981.

[3]Both the German and the Swiss authorities tolerated an overshooting of their monetary targets in 1977 and 1978. In January 1979 the Swiss National Bank decided to refrain from setting a target for money supply growth for 1979, in case this should be incompatible with undertaking official sales of Swiss francs in the market to restrain the rise in the exchange rate.

and monetary policy, as was seen when the pound sterling fell catastrophically in 1976. The U.S. case is even more dramatic. The weakness of the dollar in 1978 provoked the deflationary Carter package of November 1, 1978, and throughout 1979 and 1980 U.S. fiscal and monetary policy was conducted with the strength of the dollar always in mind. With the strengthening of the dollar in 1981, U.S. Treasury Under Secretary Sprinkel began demanding that monetary policy should be set by reference to the need to restrain inflation, irrespective of how high the dollar rises in the exchange market.[4]

Practical monetarism

The unpredictability of the official actions of the authorities of the Group of 10 countries has been aggravated by their widespread conversion to what has come to be called "practical monetarism"— the adjective "practical" serving to distinguish it from "academic" monetarism. That practical monetarism should have made official actions less predictable is certainly ironical, since academic monetarists have always recommended their prescriptions as avoiding any need for "fine tuning," or indeed discretionary official action of any kind, so that the rules of the monetary authorities' behavior could be widely known and their behavior therefore could be predicted. Admittedly, the practical monetarists have not actually followed (or even tried to follow) the detailed prescriptions of academic monetarism in any of its varieties, but they were nevertheless convinced that one of the major advantages that would flow from the adoption of practical monetarism was that official policy would no longer be an arcane art but that, instead, everybody would understand where the authorities were heading and why.

That monetary policy could thus become so simple and transparent has always been rather implausible. Even in very general terms, the objectives of monetary policy—say, low inflation, full employment, growth, etc.—are ambitious in relation to the available policy instruments, which are few in number and weak. It would be surprising, therefore, if optimization did not require trade-offs and compromises that could not be encapsulated in simple rules. In more practical terms, this conclusion follows *a fortiori*, since the sectional interests that politicians must respect (e.g., the

---

[4]Samuel Brittan in *Financial Times* (London), April 21, 1981.

interests of exporters, housewives, house purchasers, trade unions, etc.) force them to perform a highly precarious balancing act all the time. Nevertheless, they have from time to time temporarily deluded themselves into believing that they could steer a direct course through the crosscurrents of conflicting interests and objectives by one or the other (or both) of two navigational aids: (1) *benign neglect*, which comprises a combination of two policies: leaving the exchange rate to float with a minimum of official intervention and directing fiscal and monetary policy exclusively to internal objectives, in particular the achievement of the monetary growth target; and (2) *monetary targets*.

Benign Neglect. This was U.S. policy from the collapse of the Bretton Woods system of fixed exchange rates until U.S. President Carter's turnabout in 1978. According to recent pronouncements by U.S. Treasury officials Regan and Sprinkel, this policy is apparently being embraced once again in the United States by the Reagan Administration. It was also U.K. policy in the year following the floating of the pound sterling in June 1972. Thereafter, it went out of favor with the U.K. authorities; sterling was given prolonged and massive official support in the market, and in 1976 the deflationary fiscal and monetary policies then adopted were undoubtedly precipitated by the perceived need to strengthen sterling. The Thatcher Administration in the United Kingdom brought a reversion to benign neglect, at any rate until September 1981.

The intermittent popularity of benign neglect with U.S. and U.K. statesmen appears to have been due less to the persuasiveness of monetarist literature than to the traumatic experience, in much of the 1960s, of having an overvalued currency under the Bretton Woods system. The demise of the Bretton Woods system in the early 1970s seemed like an escape from an irksome straitjacket; henceforth, fiscal and monetary policy could be set by reference to the health of the internal economy, and a floating exchange rate would dispose of what had come to be considered a *self-inflicted* balance of payments problem. The U.S. and U.K. central bankers did not fall prey to such easy optimism,[5] but crucial policy decisions are taken by finance ministers rather than by central bankers.

---

[5]See, for example, Paul Volcker's (1978) Fred Hirsch Memorial Address at Warwick University in November 1978 and Gordon Richardson's (1979) Henry Thornton Lecture at the City University of London in June 1979.

To the countries with undervalued currencies in the era of pegged rates—for example, the Federal Republic of Germany—the transition to floating exchange rates also seemed a release from a straitjacket,[6] but none of them embraced benign neglect with the same enthusiasm as the United States or the United Kingdom. Indeed, benign neglect has been an exclusively Anglo-American phenomenon, which has produced disharmony in the Group of 10 and hence has made the Group of 10 countries' behavior much more uncoordinated and unpredictable. This tendency has been especially marked since the rise in oil prices in 1973, to which benign neglect is a wholly inappropriate response. As Governor Richardson (1979, p. 295) has put it: "The imbalances arising from large increases in the oil price are pre-eminently of a kind which it would be inappropriate to attempt to meet by exchange rate movements."

Monetary Targets. One does not need to be a devout monetarist to appreciate the case for monetary targets, as introduced first in the United States and later (in the second half of the 1970s) in the other Group of 10 countries, except for Belgium and Sweden. The main navigational aid to monetary policy under the Bretton Woods system—the official par value of the exchange rate—had disappeared by March 1973 with the transition to floating. The other navigational aid of the 1960s—interest rate targets—had become discredited with the onset of accelerating inflation, which produced an erratic divergence between nominal and real interest rates. If any simple navigational aid was to be found, it had to be a monetary aggregate of one sort or another—for example, money stock more or less widely defined, or monetary base.

But, however strong the case for monetary targets may have seemed at the time they were adopted, experience has served to emphasize their disadvantages rather than their merits. Monetary aggregates have varied so differently as sometimes not to be correlated at all. All have been subject to distortions, owing to disintermediation, changes in methods of payment, etc. None has been markedly successful as a diagnostic device. So monetary targets, far from ensuring consistency and predictability in the official actions of the Group of 10 countries, seem in practice to have made them even more erratic and inscrutable. Sometimes a monetary aggregate is

---

[6]See Otmar Emminger's address to the European-Atlantic Group in London on February 19, 1976.

relied on for diagnostic purposes; sometimes it is displaced by other evidence, such as real interest rates, prices, or unemployment. Sometimes the preferred target variable is switched from one monetary aggregate to another. Sometimes a determined effort is made to achieve the monetary target; sometimes, as with the United Kingdom in 1980, the effort is tacitly abandoned. Sometimes, as noted above in the case of the Federal Republic of Germany and Switzerland, the decision has been taken to direct policy for the time being toward influencing the exchange rate, irrespective of the consequences for the monetary aggregate. Surely the target procedures actually practiced in the Group of 10 countries must bear some of the responsibility for the increased volatility and unpredictability of both exchange rates and interest rates, which have been one facet of the deterioration in the monetary environment in the 1970s.

The Brandt Commission's report (Brandt, 1980, p. 207) said of exchange rates:

> Since the major currencies began to float, the changes of exchange rates have not only been large but also erratic. The significant appreciations of the yen, the Deutschmark and the Swiss franc vis-à-vis the US dollar since 1973 are in keeping with the requirements of balance of payments adjustment. But the wide fluctuations up and down over shorter periods, in spite of official intervention in exchange markets, have served no constructive purpose.

And a U.S. Federal Reserve study commented on interest rates (Truman *et al*, 1981, p. 67):

> ... the high level and the variability of dollar interest rates on world capital markets created difficulties for those developing countries that are major commercial borrowers internationally.

A deflationary bias?

Group of 10 countries whose currencies are at any time becoming weaker (i.e., falling in the market or needing official support) or, alternatively, stronger may well in practice not respond by modifying the stance of their fiscal or monetary policies at all. But where there is a policy reaction, can it be said that it is more likely to occur when a currency is weakening than when it is strengthening?—that is, do the Group of 10 countries operate the adjustment process in a way which, on balance, gives their fiscal and monetary policies a deflationary bias? There is a widespread view that such has been the case, at any rate in the period since the increase in oil prices at the end of 1973. Governor Richardson (1979) was surely subscribing to this view when he stated that, in consequence of the massive increase in oil prices of recent years, "the oil-consuming countries are competing to avoid their share in an overall deficit."

Such a view seems plausible, though evidence to support it is little more than anecdotal. It is not, of course, in doubt that the Group of 10's fiscal and monetary policies have indeed had a deflationary bias since the oil price increase. That is surely clear from the evidence assembled in the *World Economic Outlook* (IMF, 1980, Tables 37 and 40, and 1981, pp. 19–23). What must be decided is how much of this policy realignment was a reaction to the fear of accelerating inflation, and how much (if any) was due to the weakening from time to time of the Group of 10's currencies because of the rise in the real cost of imported oil.

There is a certain amount of anecdotal evidence of a deflationary bias in the National Bank of Belgium's *Report* (1980, p. 11), noting the outflow of capital from European countries with "a large current account deficit," which

> ... led to a scarcity in the supply of funds in these countries, whose interest rates consequently rose in turn. Furthermore, it so happened that in some of the countries in question, particularly the Federal Republic of Germany and Belgium, the rise in prices was moderate; hence real interest rates (that is, the nominal rates deflated by the rise in prices) became very high there, a fact which was hardly consistent with the slackening of economic activity and added to the financial burdens of enterprises. The countries which did not have a balance of payments problem did not concern themselves much with the international repercussions of their domestic monetary policies.

Anecdotal evidence is also quite impressive in the case of the United States and the United Kingdom. The United States abandoned the policy of benign neglect in 1978, when the dollar was weak, and resumed it again in 1981, when the dollar was strong. The United Kingdom tightened fiscal and monetary policies in 1976, in response to the weakening of sterling, but conspicuously failed to relax them in 1980, despite the progressive strengthening of sterling. The German and Swiss authorities, on the other hand, have sometimes seemed to react more symmetrically; they have deliberately allowed their monetary aggregates to overshoot their targets when their currencies were strengthening, while firming up their interest rates (as in 1981) in response to a weakening of their currencies.

There is, however, little to be gained by prolonging this recital of anecdotal evidence. The fact that, as argued above, the policy reactions of the Group of 10 countries are so erratic and unpredictable makes it difficult to identify general tendencies with any degree of confidence.

What *can* be said with confidence is that at no time did the Group of 10 countries seriously attempt to coordinate their policies so as to ensure that the Group of 10 as a whole would accept a fair share (however defined) of the deficit that was the inevitable counterpart, since 1973, of the Organization of Petroleum Exporting Countries' (OPEC) surplus on current account. They almost assumed collective responsibility in this regard at the Bonn summit of 1978, but the initiative quickly faded. When it appeared that the policies actually adopted by the Group of 10 countries put the burden of financing the oil price disequilibrium predominantly on the developing countries, statesmen in the Group of 10 received the news with relief rather than with apprehension, as would have been more appropriate.

ROLE OF THE FUND

The Fund has moved a long way from the "universalism" intended by its founders. The Fund's membership is not homogeneous; in particular, the needs and objectives of the Group of 10 and the developing countries are widely different, and this has to be taken into account by the Fund in its dealings with them.

As for the Fund's activities under Article IV of the Second Amendment, the Group of 10 Fund members have all opted for floating their currencies, either jointly or individually, whereas other Fund members, including the developing countries, have in most cases continued to peg their currencies, though often now to a "basket" rather than to a single Group of 10 currency. The transition from pegging to floating by the Group of 10 countries has in practice reduced the role of the Fund in respect to exchange rates. Although the amended Article IV gives the Fund nominal responsibility for the surveillance of exchange rate arrangements, policies actually followed by the Group of 10 are settled by the countries themselves, either individually or by agreement (as with the European Community's snake and with U.S.-German collaboration on the dollar-deutsche mark rate).

As for the Fund's activities under Article VIII, the Group of 10 countries have long had Article VIII status and rarely seek a waiver of the Fund and GATT rules directed against recourse to restrictions on trade and current payments to deal with balance of payments difficulties. Nor do they impose very drastic restrictions on capital movements. In contrast, most of the developing countries, except those in Latin America and OPEC members, still retain Article XIV status; moreover, they almost all recognize recourse to quantitative restrictions and exchange control as normal and quite acceptable policy instruments for use by countries needing to support their currency in order to maintain it at its pegged value.

Turning now to the Fund's financial transactions with members in balance of payments difficulties, the guidelines for conditionality as applied to drawings by Group of 10 countries are generally accepted as appropriate and inevitable, however harmful they may be to a government's popularity with its electorate. In other words, it is accepted that the treatment for a weak currency means taking deflationary measures; drawings on the Fund are a temporary palliative until these measures begin to work.

A developing country, on the other hand, may not be ready to recognize the appropriateness of deflation as a solution to its balance of payments difficulties. Instead, it may make use of either one or the other of the following arguments to justify a drawing on the Fund, depending on how it diagnoses its balance of payments difficulties:

1. It may argue, "Our earnings from our main export product have collapsed this year, owing to our bad harvest or a world glut or whatever, so we need temporary help until next season's crop is harvested or until prices recover." The Fund is competent to respond to such an approach, especially by virtue of its compensatory financing and buffer stock financing facilities, which have been increasingly used in recent years, as may be seen in Table 1.

2. Or, a developing country's authorities may say, "Our balance of payments is weak and will not cure itself automatically. What we need is long-term financing for, say, an irrigation scheme or a cement plant, thereby permitting a permanent saving of imports or expansion of exports." A developing country seeking external finance on such grounds is almost always seeking *project* financing. To such a country, the division of labor between the Fund and the World Bank seems artificial. Its need for financing arises from its balance of payments difficulties, suggesting an approach

Table 1
USE OF FUND RESOURCES UNDER COMPENSATORY FINANCING AND BUFFER STOCK FACILITIES[1]
(million SDRs)

	1973	1974	1975	1976	1977	1978	1979	1980	1981
Compensatory financing	206	212	18	828	1,753	322	465	863	784
Buffer stock financing	5	—	—	5	—	—	48	26	—

Source: IMF, *Annual Report of the Executive Board for the Financial Year Ended April 30, 1977*, p. 51, and *1981*, p. 82.
[1]In financial year ended April 30.

to the Fund, but the financing it seeks is for projects, suggesting an approach to the World Bank. The Fund has recently become aware of this problem and is trying to adapt its lending procedures accordingly, so the strictures of the Brandt Commission's report (Brandt, 1980, pp. 215–16) are out of date,[7] but it is salutary to be reminded how devastating they were:

> In practice the Fund seems to assume that any country that needs to borrow conditional liquidity must have been incompetent or careless at running its affairs and is therefore likely to benefit from some guidance from a disinterested party. But many borrowing countries do not accept this assumption.
>
> The credit conditions of the IMF thus normally presume that balance of payments problems are a result of too much domestic demand and can be solved by balancing the budget, curbing the money supply, cutting subsidies and setting a realistic exchange rate. Sometimes these measures are appropriate and have been effective. But in many cases these measures reduce domestic consumption without improving investment: productive capacity sometimes falls even more sharply than consumption. This is because many developing countries with deficits have a shortage of food or of basic consumer goods or cannot readily shift resources in line with their new needs. Indeed, the Fund's insistence on drastic measures, often within the time framework of only one year, has tended to impose unnecessary and unacceptable political burdens on the poorest, on occasion leading to "IMF riots" and even the downfall of governments.

The Fund has now responded to the plight of the developing countries—so greatly aggravated by the second sharp rise in oil prices in 1979—by seeking to adapt its lending policies to their present circumstances. As Mr. de Larosière (1981 a, p. 35), Managing Director of the Fund, put it, in an address in Switzerland in February 1981:

> In our response to the explosion in the scale of deficits experienced by our members and to their duration, we have adapted our lending policies both in regard

---

[7]The Introduction to the Brandt Commission's report is dated December 20, 1979.

to the amounts we are prepared to lend and in regard to the nature of the conditions attached to our lending.

Traditionally, a member using the Fund's ordinary resources used to be able to borrow from us a maximum cumulative amount equal to 100 per cent of its quota in the Fund. As circumstances have changed, we have progressively adopted policies whereby a member may now draw on ordinary resources and on resources borrowed by the Fund up to a cumulative amount of 600 per cent of its quota. In 1980 alone the Fund's new lending commitments under adjustment programs agreed with members reached SDR 7.2 billion, more than double the average level of the three preceding years.

We have also adapted the conditions attached to the loans we make. This has meant a broadening of our policy interests, rather than a weakening of our prescriptions for balance of payments adjustment. With our emphasis on bridging temporary balance of payments problems, we have traditionally stressed policies concerning budget positions, monetary policy, and exchange rate policy in our conditions. We still do so. But in present circumstances we have recognized that to rectify a balance of payments position may also require structural changes in the economy and that these may take longer than the one to three years normally set as the length of our programs. Thus, while we continue to stress the importance of appropriate demand management, we now systematically emphasize the development of the productive base of the economy and we contemplate that countries may, therefore, need our financing for longer periods. This new approach is responsive to the circumstances of today, but it continues to stress the basic need for countries to live in accord with their incomes. I might say that this emphasis on structural change is making it even more important than heretofore that we collaborate closely with the World Bank. This is not because we are duplicating the role of that institution, but because we need to be assured that the policies we advocate will be compatible with appropriate investment programs to alleviate the structural deficiencies which are often at the root of members' balance of payments problems.

The Fund's more generous lending to the developing countries is already showing up in the figures of Fund transactions, as set out in Table 2.

Table 2
NEW LOAN COMMITMENTS TO DEVELOPING COUNTRIES AND OTHER USE OF FUND RESOURCES
(billion SDRs)

	1973	1974	1975	1976	1977	1978	1979	1980
1a. New loan commitments under stand-by and extended arrangements in period[1]	0.4	0.4	0.4	0.9	1.4	1.8	2.2	7.2
1b. Purchases, other than under 1a	0.2	1.1	2.1	2.9	0.3	0.6	0.7	1.0
2. Trust Fund loans disbursed	—	—	—	—	0.2	0.7	0.5	1.3

Source: IMF Survey, Vol. 10 (April 20, 1981), p. 114.
[1]Includes supplementary financing where applicable.

To be in a position to honor its more generous lending commitments to the developing countries, the Fund has sought additional resources:

> If we are to lend more for longer periods, we have to have more to lend. The traditional source of our funds has been through quota subscriptions of our members. Last year we completed a 50 per cent increase in our quotas. But that will not suffice to cover our members' needs in the period ahead.... Under our General Arrangements to Borrow with the Group of 10 industrial countries, we continue to have a line of credit to finance borrowings by any one of them. But use of this network of borrowing agreements is limited to this grouping of countries, while the supplementary financing facility, which it was decided to establish in 1977, is on the point of being fully committed. We thus have to enter into new borrowing arrangements now.... We are making plans to obtain lines of credit amounting in total to SDR 6 or 7 billion this year. (de Larosière, 1981 a, p. 35)

> A major element of the Fund's borrowing program was put in place on May 7, when we signed an agreement with the Saudi Arabian Monetary Agency by which the Fund will be able to borrow up to SDR 4 billion a year in each of the next two years, with the possibility of additional amounts in the third year. In addition to the agreement with Saudi Arabia, we are currently discussing medium-term loans with a number of other countries whose balance of payments is strong. (de Larosière, 1981 b, p. 152)

On May 13, 1981 it was reported[8] that the central banks of 13 industrial countries had told the Fund that they were willing to lend it SDR 1.1 billion ($1.3 billion), including about half of that amount through the BIS.

Unfortunately, the flow of the Fund's financing to the developing countries in past years and as projected for the future is small in relation to the enormous borrowing needs of the non-oil developing countries, as evidenced by the rate of their annual borrowing since the first rise in oil prices in 1973. This may be seen from Table 3, which compares the total net external borrowing of the non-oil developing countries from all sources with their use of Fund credit and short-term borrowing by their monetary authorities from other monetary authorities.

A substantial proportion of the total external borrowings shown in Table 3 has been from market sources, especially from the large banks. Here the difficulty is that many of the banks now have so much developing country debt outstanding that they are increasingly reluctant to commit themselves to further lending to developing countries.

---

[8]International Monetary Fund press release No. 81/38, issued May 13, 1981; reproduced in *IMF Survey*, Vol. 10 (May 18, 1981), p. 149.

Table 3

NET EXTERNAL BORROWING BY NON-OIL DEVELOPING COUNTRIES

(billion U.S. dollars)

	1973	1974	1975	1976	1977	1978	1979	1980
Total	10.8	26.2	32.8	34.3	26.6	37.4	47.8	63.5
Long-term borrowing from private sector financial institutions	9.0	12.3	13.2	16.1	17.6	23.0	32.1	24.2
Short-term use of Fund and central bank credit	—	1.5	2.3	3.7	−0.6	−0.5	0.2	3.0

Source: IMF, World Economic Outlook, 1981, p. 129.

On these issues Rimmer de Vries (1980, p. 13), of the Morgan Guaranty Trust Company, has written as follows:

> Increased IMF lending to developing countries represents a significant de-parture from past lending practices of the Fund. The industrial countries tradi-tionally have been the principal "users" of the IMF resources, accounting for about two thirds of all drawings since 1947. It has not been until the past year or so that the developing countries have become the principal users of Fund resources.
>
> While conditionality must remain a central element of IMF lending in order to promote balance-of-payments adjustment, it is important that the policy recom-mendations attached to, and the size of, the various IMF facilities be adapted to ensure prompter and greater usage of the Fund's resources by the member coun-tries. Recent decisions to increase the access of member countries to the Fund's resources and to lengthen the terms of IMF programs under the Extended Facility are steps in the right direction. But, it is also essential for the Fund's staff to become more actively involved in advising countries on an ongoing basis, rather than only at the time in which standby arrangements are negotiated, if Fund relations with a number of countries are to be improved. Maintaining a much larger IMF staff permanently in the various locales undoubtedly would help in this regard.
>
> Increased concentration of the IMF on the problems and funding of the devel-oping countries would bring it much closer to the World Bank. The traditional separation of responsibilities between the Fund and the Bank along program ver-sus project finance lines could become blurred as the Fund places greater emphasis on structural or supply-side factors and the provision of longer-term assistance to these countries. Closer ties between the international financial institutions may represent a realistic response to one of the most pressing problems of the decade—the economic development and financing of the LDCs.

The changing role of the Fund, as de Vries points out, raises the question of whether its present Articles of Agreement and its pro-cedures under these Articles are appropriate to the financial prob-lems of the 1980s. He says, "Its charter was formulated to tackle an entirely different set of problems from those facing the world today and in the future."

One limitation of the Fund's charter is that, although it permits the Fund to borrow, its Articles are not entirely appropriate to a borrowing institution (such as the BIS or the World Bank). One problem relates to the security the Fund can legally offer an investor from whom it borrows—an especially important issue if Fund paper is to be held by private sector investors, as it may have to be in the future. Another problem is that what it borrows and what it lends have to be matched fairly closely in time as well as in amount. This situation makes it difficult for the Fund to borrow large sums outright; instead, it must negotiate with the lender a drawing right to be called on as and when opportunities arise to lend, which may not be very convenient from the lender's point of view.

POSITION OF THE NON-OIL DEVELOPING COUNTRIES

The non-oil developing countries have in recent years been attempting to develop in an economic environment markedly less favorable than in the 1960s. The deterioration cannot in fairness be ascribed mainly to the evolution of the monetary arrangements operated by the Group of 10. It may, however, more fairly be said that the basic problems facing the non-oil developing countries have not been appreciably alleviated—and, indeed, have often been significantly aggravated—by the way the Group of 10 has been operating the international monetary system.

Apart from the evils of the "new protectionism," which are outside the scope of this paper, the underlying causes of the non-oil developing countries' problems may perhaps best be seen as recession, inflation, and the OPEC surplus, whose unfavorable consequences in each case include, inter alia, the unhelpful Group of 10 policy reactions described in this paper.

Recession

The business recession in the Group of 10 countries, as monitored by figures of output and employment, has been disastrous for the non-oil developing countries, whose export markets are overwhelmingly in the Group of 10 economy. The weakness of these markets, combined with a determination by the developing countries to push ahead with their economic development regardless, has aggravated the non-oil developing countries' deficit on current account in 1974 and subsequently. The current account of these countries, like that of other oil importers has, or course, suffered severely from the higher price of imported oil, as seen in Table 4, but the reason that the counterpart of the OPEC surplus has manifested itself so much in deficits run by developing countries, rather than by Group of 10 and other industrial countries, is surely that the latter have been so deeply in recession. The recession in the Group of 10 countries must in the first place be attributed to the oil price rise, whose consequences may be likened to an excise duty, the proceeds of which are saved rather than spent. But the Group of 10 countries have been ready to let the resulting recession run its course—and, indeed, to aggregate it by deflationary fiscal and monetary policies—on account of their mounting anxiety about the pace of inflation.

Table 4
NON-OIL DEVELOPING COUNTRIES: DEFICITS ON CURRENT ACCOUNT
(billion U.S. dollars)

	1973	1974	1975	1978	1979	1980	1981
Oil trade balance	−4.8	−15.1	−14.9	−20.2	−30.2	−44.6	−47.2
Non-oil trade balance	−5.7	−17.3	−25.5	−11.2	−14.9	−16.8	−25.0

Source: IMF, World Economic Outlook, 1981, p. 122.

Inflation

The widespread speeding up of inflation, combined with the erratic variability of its pace in different years and different countries, undoubtedly lies at the root of the degeneration of the international monetary environment in the 1970s, compared with the 1960s. This inflation, as already noted, imparted a deflationary bias to the fiscal and monetary policies of the Group of 10 countries; it also precipitated both their transition to floating exchange rates and their conversion to targeting on monetary aggregates, thereby aggravating the instability and unpredictability of both exchange rates and interest rates.

The OPEC surplus

The counterpart to the OPEC current surplus has been shared unequally between the industrial and the non-OPEC developing countries, with the result that the burden of deficit financing has been excessively imposed on the developing countries, even though their creditworthiness (and hence their ability to finance large deficits) is markedly inferior to that of the Group of 10 and other industrial countries. Whether the Group of 10 countries have set their fiscal and monetary policies deliberately to avoid their share in an overall deficit, as well as to fight inflation, cannot be conclusively established because the evidence is mainly anecdotal; but, in any case, the Group of 10's actions (to whatever cause they are attributed) have been anything but helpful to the non-oil developing countries.

The Group of 10's attitude to the non-oil developing countries' financing problems has been equally unhelpful. The financing of the non-oil developing countries' deficits resulting from the first rise in oil prices was managed mainly through private sector channels, especially by the large banks. The authorities of the Group of 10 countries simply watched this happen, unheedful of the longer-term implications, the seriousness of which is by now all too apparent. And when the precariousness of these arrangements was highlighted by the second round of oil price increases in 1979, the reaction of the Group of 10, as instanced at the Venice summit in 1980, was to dismiss the problem by remitting it to the Fund, regardless of the fact that the Fund was wholly inexperienced in dealing with a problem of this kind and was constrained by a charter and established procedures that scarcely fitted it for the task.

The present plight and gloomy prospects of the non-oil developing countries are well summarized in the initial paragraph of the official communiqué issued after the twenty-fourth meeting of the Group of 24 (1980) on September 27, 1980:

> The Ministers discussed the international economic situation and the adverse implications for developing countries of the further deceleration in the growth rate of industrial countries, persistence of high inflationary pressures, and the continuing underutilization of resources. They noted with grave concern the widening of the deficits on current account of non-oil developing countries from $56 billion in 1979 to $76 billion in 1980. The prospects for 1981 indicate a further deterioration to $80 billion. The main factors accounting for this deterioration are worsening terms of trade, the weak growth in exports to developed countries induced by slow growth rates, the rising wave of trade protectionism in industrial countries, and higher nominal interest rates. The financing of these deficits is becoming increasingly difficult ...

This passage represents a sober assessment of the unfavorable environment in which the non-oil developing countries have to live in 1981 and which as yet shows no sign of improvement. It is an environment which (insofar as it is under any control) is largely controlled by the decisions of the Group of 10 countries; at any rate, there is not very much that the non-oil developing countries can do to improve it.

ROLE OF THE GROUP OF 24

What the Group of 24 seeks to achieve in the interests of the non-oil developing countries, in respect of international monetary arrangements, mainly derives from two preoccupations that have been mentioned above:

1. The instability of their export earnings from the sale of primary products.
2. The transfer of real resources to the developing countries in order to relieve poverty and promote development.

In regard to the first point, the Group of 24 ministers (1980, p. 300), meeting on September 27, 1980,

> noted that the recent liberalizations of the compensatory financing facility have increased the amount of purchases a member can make. However, they requested the IMF to consider further liberalization, including full compensation of the shortfall and longer repayment terms in certain circumstances, taking into account deteriorations in the terms of trade and tying repayments to increases in real exports, and to keep under constant review developments in the area of the stabilization of export earnings, with a view to further improving the benefits to members drawing under the compensatory financing facility. Ministers also urged all concerned to make every effort to bring about the early establishment of a global stabilization scheme on export earnings of developing countries.

In regard to the second point, the Group of 24 ministers made their usual plea for "a substantial increase in the transfer of real resources." But in pursuing this aim by seeking appropriate modifications to the international monetary system, the Group of 24 encounters the strongly held conviction in the Group of 10 that it is not the role of the international monetary system to facilitate transfers of real resources. That function is rather the role of development financing in its various forms, and it is best to have a one-to-one matching of policy instrument and objective. Hence, the dialogue between the Group of 24 and the Group of 10 often takes the form of skirmishes at the border between monetary arrangements proper and development financing. In particular:

1. *The issuance of SDRs.* Here the Group of 10 has sought (successfully so far) to limit the issuance of SDRs to the assessed need for reserve assets—and reserve assets are in the Group of 10's view needed solely to finance temporary "swings" in a country's balance of payments rather than to facilitate a long-term

transfer of real resources. Hence, the Group of 10 opposes any version of the "link" between SDRs and development financing.

2. *Gold.* The Group of 24 has sought ways in which some of the capital gain from the revaluation of monetary gold might be siphoned off for the benefit of the developing countries. Their only success so far has been the sale by auction of one sixth of the Fund's gold holdings, the proceeds of which (in excess of SDR 35 an ounce) have been earmarked for the benefit of the developing member countries of the Fund.

3. *Drawings on the Fund.* Here, as mentioned earlier, the original interpretation of the Fund's charter, limiting the use of Fund drawings to the financing of temporary swings in a member's balance of payments, has now been modified so that the Fund may transgress (albeit to only a limited extent) into project financing.

But such border skirmishes, even when the Group of 24 eventually has its way, serve to moderate only slightly the inhospitable environment in which the non-oil developing countries are presently operating. There is no negotiable change to the international monetary system in the foreseeable future that would facilitate an appreciably greater transfer of real resources from the industrial countries to the developing countries. Indeed, with the possible contraction of the recycling transactions of the private sector banks, the more likely change is in the contrary direction, despite the Fund's manifest readiness to participate much more actively in financial recycling.

REFERENCES

Bank for International Settlements (BIS), *Forty-Seventh Annual Report* (Basle, June 13, 1977).

Brandt, Willy, *North-South: A Programme for Survival*, Report of the Independent Commission on International Development Issues under the Chairmanship of Willy Brandt (London, 1980).

de Larosière, J. (1981 a), "Policies Concerning Surveillance, Adjustment, and Liquidity Control Stressed in de Larosière Speech," Address by the Managing Director of the Fund to the European Management Forum's 1981 Symposium at Davos, Switzerland, February 3, 1981 in *IMF Survey*, Vol. 10 (February 9, 1981), pp. 34–36.

———— (1981 b), " 'Grim' World Economic Situation Presents Major Policy Challenges," Address by the Managing Director of the Fund to the Commonwealth Club of California at San Francisco, May 8, 1981 in *IMF Survey*, Vol. 10 (May 18, 1981), pp. 149–52.

de Vries, Rimmer, "International Economic Issues and Priorities," paper presented to the Congressional Economic Conference at Washington, December 10, 1980. Reprinted in *World Financial Markets* (December 1980), pp. 1–13.

Gardner, Richard N., *Sterling-Dollar Diplomacy in Current Perspective: The Origins and Prospects of Our International Economic Order* (New York, Columbia University Press, new, expanded edition with revised introduction, 1980).

Group of 24 communiqué, *IMF Survey*, Vol. 9 (October 13, 1980), pp. 299–302.

International Monetary Fund, *Articles of Agreement*, original (Washington, December 27, 1945).

———, *Articles of Agreement*, Second Amendment (Washington, April 1, 1978).

———, *World Economic Outlook: A Survey by the Staff of the International Monetary Fund* (Washington, May 1980).

———, *World Economic Outlook: A Survey by the Staff of the International Monetary Fund*, IMF Occasional Paper No. 4 (Washington, June 1981).

Lipschitz, Leslie, and V. Sundararajan, "Pegging to a Currency Basket in a World of Floating Rates," *Finance and Development*, Vol. 17 (June 1980), pp. 25–28.

National Bank of Belgium, *Report* (Brussels, 1980).

Organization for Economic Cooperation and Development, *The Balance of Payments Adjustment Process*, a report by Working Party No. 3, Economic Policy Committee (Paris, August 1966).

Richardson, Gordon, "The Prospects for an International Monetary System," the Henry Thornton Lecture given by the Governor of the Bank of England at the City University, London, June 14, 1979. Reprinted in *Bank of England Quarterly Bulletin* (London, September 1979), pp. 290–97.

Truman, Edwin, *et al*, "The New Federal Reserve Operating Procedure: An External Perspective," in Board of Governors of the Federal Reserve System, *New Monetary Control Procedures: Federal Reserve Staff Study*, Vol. 2 (Washington, 1981).

Williamson, John H., *The Failure of the World Monetary Reform, 1971–74* (New York University Press, 1977).

Developing Country Interests in Proposals for International Monetary Reform

GRAHAM BIRD

The Second Amendment to the Articles of Agreement of the International Monetary Fund embodies a number of objectives for the future course of international monetary reform.[1] In terms of international liquidity, these include fostering the special drawing right (SDR) as the principal reserve asset in the international monetary system, thereby implying a diminution in the roles of reserve currencies, in particular the dollar, and gold. In terms of adjustment, the Second Amendment reflects a willingness of Fund member countries to accept a greater degree of exchange rate flexibility than was incorporated under the Bretton Woods system. To the extent that such reforms improve the efficiency of the international financial system and encourage the growth of trade and output, they are in the interests of all participants. At this highly aggregated level there may be little reason to distinguish between industrial and developing countries. However, while there may be a net gain from such reform, it is legitimate to ask about the distribution of the constituent gains and losses.

As efficiency issues alone do not always represent the entire picture, it is valid to take equity factors into account. The Fund's Committee of Twenty (Committee on Reform of the International Monetary System and Related Issues), for instance, advocated "the promotion of the net flow of real resources to developing countries"

---

[1]For a description of the Second Amendment, see Gold (1978).

as a "main feature" of international monetary reform. This paper examines a number of proposals for reforming the international monetary system that have been made, particularly following the publication of the Committee of Twenty's report (IMF, 1974) and notes specifically how their adoption would be likely to affect developing countries.

Some of the proposals examined have been put forward with the prime intention of assisting developing countries; others have had rather different motivations. For the most part, attention is focused on proposals that have been formally considered within the Fund, such as the link, the substitution account, and gold demonetization. To a rather lesser extent, attention is focused on the credit-granting arrangements of the Fund itself, and some mention is made of proposals put forward in other forums, such as the plan to introduce a commodity-backed international reserve asset, discussed at the Arusha Conference, as well as proposals that lie outside the auspices of the Fund, such as the plan to establish an exclusively "Southern" currency.

It should be stated at the outset that the phrase "developing country interests" is somewhat inappropriate in the title of this paper, implying, as it does, a homogeneity of interests that does not always, or even often, exist. In this paper the term "developing countries" is for the most part defined to exclude oil exporting developing countries.

DEVELOPING COUNTRIES AS A SPECIAL CASE

Taking a broad historical perspective, there is a growing feeling among members of the international community that developing countries encounter international financial problems that differ either in kind or in degree from those encountered by industrial countries. In recognition of this, a number of financing facilities have been introduced by the Fund, primarily to help developing countries.[2] The Committee of Twenty took the view that developing countries required and warranted special treatment, and subsequently the Development Committee (formally the Joint Ministerial

---

[2]The list includes the compensatory financing facility in 1963, the buffer stock financing facility in 1969, and the extended Fund facility in 1974. A Trust Fund and various subsidy accounts have also been established to assist poor countries.

Committee of the Fund and World Bank on the Transfer of Real Resources to Developing Countries) has been charged with examining ways to encourage an additional flow of resources to developing countries.

The argument that developing countries are a special case is based on a number of points. Fundamentally, these relate either to the vulnerability of developing countries to balance of payments shocks or to their ability to cope with disequilibria and the adjustment costs involved.[3] The supposed balance of payments vulnerability rests heavily on the claim that export receipts of developing countries are relatively unstable. The factual basis for this claim is not clear-cut, and differences exist both between countries and over time, but perhaps on balance the available evidence tends to support it.[4] Certainly, following the oil price rise of 1973, the balance of payments of most developing countries was adversely affected by an increase in import prices and a reduced growth in export demand. The ability of developing countries to cope with the related deficits depends on their access to financing and on their capacity to correct their balance of payments. Again, in this context there are marked differences between countries that, by convention, are grouped together. For countries entering the post-1973 period with relatively large reserve holdings or those regarded as being creditworthy by international commercial banks, financing has offered a practical as well as theoretical short-term alternative. Whether it is also a long-term alternative depends on how productively the resources are used. However, evidence on the distribution of commercial bank lending to developing countries clearly shows that few developing countries have been able to gain access to commercial credit. Furthermore, as far as noncommercial borrowing is concerned, the less creditworthy countries have, until recently, been unable or unwilling to draw large amounts from the Fund (Bird, 1981 a). Thus, for a number of developing countries—in particular, the low-income countries—the financing option has in effect not been available. They have therefore been forced to adjust.

The method of adjustment adopted has frequently been to contract import volume,[5] and this, in turn, has had a deleterious effect

---

[3] There is a third argument maintaining that the terms of trade of developing countries are subject to secular decline and that this creates long-term balance of payments difficulties for them.

[4] For a review of the evidence, see Bird (1978).

[5] Empirical evidence for this is presented in Dell and Lawrence (1980).

on the growth of per capita gross national product (GNP). Adjustment through export expansion—a course followed by relatively few developing countries—is made more difficult by the low levels of demand and increasing protectionism in industrial countries. Furthermore, to the extent that more developing countries attempt to adjust in this manner, it tends to become a less feasible alternative.

For a number of reasons, developing countries feel that postwar international monetary arrangements have discriminated against them: first, in terms of the distribution of the adjustment burden, which puts greater pressure on deficit countries than on surplus countries to adjust, especially deficit countries that have limited scope for financing; and second, in terms of the distribution of the seigniorage associated with the creation of international reserves, which has not gone to them but to richer countries.

An important component of the new international economic order desired by the South is that changes in the international monetary system be designed to direct a larger share of the benefits of its operation to developing countries. Whether this simultaneously implies a real sacrifice for industrial countries depends on whether the reforms improve the monetary system's overall efficiency. The importance of distinguishing clearly between efficiency and equity reaffirms itself throughout the discussion below.

THE SDR LINK

Nowhere is this distinction more apparent than in the debate over the link, the establishment of which has for more than a decade formed the centerpiece of developing country objectives with respect to international monetary reform. The general arguments both in favor of the link and against it are well documented in the literature.[6] Rather than presenting an overview of these, therefore, this section addresses itself to a more limited number of questions that are nevertheless both fundamental and topical in the light of recent changes in the SDR—especially the introduction of a market-equivalent rate of interest. These are:

1. What factors determine the benefits to developing countries from a link?

---

[6]See, for example, Bird (1978), Cline (1976), Haan (1971), Maynard and Bird (1975), Park (1973), and Williamson (1976 a).

2. Is there a case for having a market-equivalent rate of interest on SDRs?
3. Does the existence of such an interest rate rule out the possibility that developing countries will gain from a link?
4. What form of link will developing countries favor, and is this form likely to prove attractive to industrial countries?

Before moving on to these questions, however, a number of more general points may be made briefly. First, the link is a device intended to provide additional aid, redistributing the world's wealth in favor of developing countries. Second, the method by which the link attempts to obtain this result is by allocating all or part of the seigniorage associated with the creation of international reserves to developing countries—though the total quantity of reserves created should be based on the needs of the system for international liquidity. Third, there may be incidental, but probably relatively insignificant, benefits for industrial countries in terms of an increase in exports, output, and employment; not only will world wealth be redistributed but it may also increase. Fourth, although the claim that the link will be inflationary is theoretically correct, especially in conditions of world full employment, all quantitative studies agree that the size of this effect is likely to be small, even for surplus countries (Cline, 1976). Fifth, the link raises political as well as economic issues, as it poses questions relating to the democratic control of aid flows; many versions take the associated aid outside the control of individual governments and put it under the control of the Fund and other international financial agencies.

Advocacy of the link clearly depends primarily on equity considerations. The argument may be expressed as follows: under international financial systems, profits are to be made from reserve creation, arising from the fact that the value of reserves exceeds their costs of production. Under a gold standard, the profits go to gold producers, and possibly gold holders, while under a foreign exchange system they go to reserve currency countries. By comparison with a system based on gold, a system based on foreign exchange involves an additional social saving because of the lower cost of producing paper currency, but at the same time the seigniorage enjoyed by producers is reduced, inasmuch as there are costs associated with being the world's banker and inasmuch as interest is paid on externally held liabilities. However, seigniorage will remain positive as long as the marginal productivity of the real resources acquired by reserve currency countries exceeds the sum of these costs. A gold-exchange system is, therefore, not neutral in terms of the transfer of real resources; these flow from the rest of the world to gold-producing and gold-holding countries and to reserve currency countries. These arguments have led to the identification of the United States as the major beneficiary of the postwar international financial system. At the same time, both the strength and the weakness of the various link proposals are that the unrequited real resource flow would be directed away from the United States and toward developing countries. The strength lies in the equity of such a proposal. The weakness lies in the fact that the United States is likely to resist such a change. But what would be the resource flows implied by a link? An answer to this question may be provided by returning to the first question posed above.

Benefits to developing countries from a link

The total benefits to developing countries from a link depend, first, on the number of SDRs allocated to them, and second, on the benefits per SDR. From a user's point of view, the benefits vary positively with the social marginal productivity of real resources and inversely with the social discount rate, the interest rate on SDR net use, and the size of any reconstitution requirements. The benefits to users exceed the grant element associated with SDRs to the extent that the excess of the rate of return to real resources over the rate of discount exceeds the commercial interest rate. For countries holding 100 per cent of their cumulative SDR allocation, the benefit from an allocation of SDRs is essentially the liquidity yield on them. For countries making a net acquisition of SDRs while holding a given portfolio of foreign exchange, the marginal liquidity yield is reduced by the real resource cost of earning the additional SDRs. While a high rate of interest on SDRs favors countries acquiring them, a low rate of interest favors net users. Only a handful of developing countries have held their entire cumulative allocation of SDRs, and even fewer have actually acquired them. The vast majority have been net users and for this reason have benefited in the past from the relatively low rate of interest on SDRs.

While there are a number of difficulties involved in imputing real resource flows from data on net use and acquisition, attempts to estimate the effect of the unlinked SDR scheme on real resource transfers strongly suggest that the initial flow of real resources has been toward developing countries, implying that an "informal link" has operated.[7] Since the potential permanent real resource inflow available to net users of SDRs rises as the reconstitution requirement diminishes and falls as the rate of interest on SDRs rises, it might be expected that developing countries have a somewhat ambivalent view on recent changes in regard to the SDR that have lowered the reconstitution requirement from 30 per cent to 15 per cent and then to zero and at the same time raised the interest rate from 60 per cent of the combined market rate to 80 per cent and, from May 1981, to 100 per cent. In fact, in terms of short-run potential real resource inflows, developing countries have probably gained more from the abrogation of the reconstitution requirement than they have lost from the interest rate increase. However, in the medium to long term, this situation will be reversed.[8]

The benefits to developing countries from SDRs, however, are considerably greater than figures on resource flows suggest, since such flows fail to take into account either the marginal productivity of the resources received, which may be particularly high in the case of developmental imports, or the fact that significant benefits are derived from holding SDRs, as well as from spending them.[9] Furthermore, developing countries may have benefited indirectly from SDR allocations to industrial countries through induced policy changes in the recipient countries, which may have resulted in an increased capacity for developing countries both to earn foreign exchange by exporting to industrial countries and to acquire it through increased investment in and aid to developing countries by industrial countries.

While the introduction of a formal link would increase the direct benefits to developing countries, it would reduce or remove this indirect benefit.[10] The problem here is one of quantification. Certainly, the indirect benefit to developing countries has not been immediately apparent following recent allocations of SDRs.

---

[7]For an explanation and alternative estimations of this, see Helleiner (1974) and Bird (1976). It has also been shown, however, that, after a period of time and as soon as the interest due on previous link allocations exceeds the volume of the new allocations, the real resource flow becomes negative (Isard and Truman, 1974).

[8]Assessment of such changes by developing countries will therefore depend significantly on the discount rate.

[9]For an attempt to take these factors into account, see Bird (1979 a).

[10]However, to the extent that the link serves to raise national income in industrial countries and thereby developing countries' exports, there might be an additional secondary benefit to developing countries.

Also difficult to quantify is the extent to which conventional aid is likely to be seen by donors as being independent of the link. If aid donors regard the link as a substitute for other forms of aid, developing countries may lose overall from its introduction. Certainly if, as seems likely, the distribution of linked aid is different from that of conventional aid, the pattern of overall aid disbursement will change as a result of introducing the link and the change may well be regressive. However, the quantity of aid is not the whole story; a link may still be advantageous from the viewpoint of developing countries, even if it leads to a small net reduction in overall aid, if at the same time it raises the quality of aid in terms of raising the grant element, reducing the level of conditionality, and relaxing the associated tying arrangements. Because the increase in the rate of interest clearly emerges as having reduced the benefit of SDRs to developing country users, an important question is whether this increase was necessary and whether it was in their interests in other ways.

The case for a market-equivalent interest rate

From the viewpoint of the efficiency of the international monetary system, there is a strong case for SDRs to carry a market-equivalent interest rate. This stems from the theory of the optimum quantity of money. Applied to SDRs, the argument runs as follows.[11] The optimum stock of SDRs is reached when their marginal benefit in the form of the liquidity yield equals their marginal cost of production. As the latter is almost zero, SDRs should be created up to a point where the marginal liquidity yield is also almost zero. The international community will benefit from having such an optimum stock of SDRs in terms of the balance of payments strategies permitted, which will involve more financing, a slower rate of adjustment, and a lower welfare cost in terms of lost output and unemployment. To encourage this optimum stock of SDRs to be held over the long run, however, the opportunity cost of holding SDRs needs to be reduced to practically zero. This reduction may be achieved by paying a rate of interest equivalent to the rate of return on other assets. Even though the "basket" method of SDR valuation makes the capital value of SDRs more stable than that of the individual

---

[11]For a more rigorous presentation of the argument, see Clark (1972), Grubel (1973), and Johnson (1970).

currencies comprising the basket, central banks will find SDRs an unattractive asset if the rate of interest they carry is significantly below that available on convertible currencies.

The motivation for raising the interest rate on SDRs has clearly been to encourage their acceptance as the principal reserve asset in the international financial system. Developing countries have therefore found themselves in an awkward dilemma. To make the link an effective and significant source of aid, they want SDRs to be the principal source of reserve creation. To ensure this role, SDRs need to carry a commercial interest rate. But a commercial interest rate seems to lower the grant element on SDRs to zero and means that the seigniorage goes to holders of SDRs in proportion to their holdings, rather than to net users.

Some antagonists have, in any case, criticized the objective of nonneutrality as embodied in the link. Indeed, as originally established, the SDR was intended to be neutral with respect to resource transfers. To this end, SDRs are allocated on the basis of Fund quotas that are assumed to reflect countries' long-run demand for reserves to hold. The real resource flows that have actually taken place were, therefore, not an intentional part of the SDR scheme. Moving over to a "market" method (Grubel, 1972) of allocating seigniorage will reduce the size of the informal link, and the majority of the developing countries will lose.

Support for neutrality is based on two arguments: first, that the existing distribution of resources throughout the world is acceptable, or indeed optimal (largely a normative issue); second, that it is inappropriate to induce real resource transfers through international monetary reform. This argument is valid only to the extent that the inclusion of a link in SDR allocation imposes costs in terms of efficiency. Raising the interest rate to a commercial level would seem to defend the SDR's integrity, while by encouraging recipients to hold their allocations it would seem to nullify any inflationary repercussions. So where does this leave the developing countries?

If it is accepted that efficiency dictates a commercial interest rate, the question immediately arises as to whether this is completely inconsistent with any form of SDR link.

The link and market interest rates

Although a competitive SDR interest rate certainly reduces the benefits of the link to net users, it is invalid to conclude as a result

that these benefits fall to zero. First, most of the developing countries that are able to raise commercial credit must pay a rate above
the combined market rate used for calculating the rate of interest on
SDRs (in percentage terms, as much as 15 per cent higher). Furthermore, the rate on SDRs represents a weighted average of rates
across countries, and these may be subject to considerable disparity. To a certain extent, then, the grant element on SDRs depends on the currency in which commercial borrowing would otherwise have been undertaken.[12] These two factors combine to suggest
that SDRs may continue to incorporate a significant grant element
for developing countries, even with a so-called market-equivalent
interest rate.

Second, some developing countries find it impossible to borrow
even at commercial interest rates; these countries face an availability constraint. The allocation of SDRs to them, even at a commercial interest rate, will help to overcome this. Indeed, to the
extent that capital market imperfections prevent resources from
moving to where their marginal productivity is highest (in developing countries?), the link serves to raise international economic efficiency by encouraging world output to rise.

Third, from a theoretical point of view, it is the interest rate on
the marginal acquisition of SDRs that needs to be at a commercial
level. In terms of efficiency, there is no reason why the rate paid by
developing country users should not be subsidized, thereby raising
the grant element. The problem here is the practical one of how the
subsidy would be financed. In principle, financing could be arranged
by transfer of SDRs from industrial countries to developing countries, with the former retaining the interest obligations, or by allocation of additional SDRs to developing countries in perpetuity, or
by a charge imposed by the Special Drawing Rights Department of
the Fund at a lower rate for developing countries on their net use
than the rate paid to countries acquiring SDRs.[13]

Finally, aside from the interest rate on them, SDRs are a form of
unconditional credit; they involve no fixed repayment schedule and
require no statement of need by users. Developing countries, wary

---

[12]Care has to be exercised here, however, since to an extent the interest rate dis-
persion reflects the likelihood and expected direction of exchange rate variation in a
particular currency.
[13]However, this would still leave the problem of dealing with a deficit in the Special
Drawing Rights Department of the Fund.

of borrowing from the Fund because of the conditionality associated with some types of Fund drawings and viewing commercial borrowing as also involving a form of conditionality, may find SDRs very attractive. Furthermore, since net users only have to pay interest and do not have to repay capital, in the short run payments on SDR net use therefore tend to be lower than they would be for an equivalent commercial loan.[14] On the other hand, developing countries are concerned that an increasing interest rate on SDRs brings with it an increase in general Fund charges. There is also the possibility that a higher rate may induce a greater reluctance on the part of surplus countries to adjust by spending reserves. In each of these cases, a higher interest rate on SDRs imposes costs on developing countries.

Different links and developing country preferences

Although it is usually described as "the link," numerous proposals for a link share the basic idea of raising the proportion of any given SDR allocation to developing countries. One set of proposals involves an "inorganic link," through which developed countries would make voluntary contributions in the form of currencies or SDRs to development agencies or developing countries at the time of each SDR allocation. Some versions of this inorganic link imply that contributions could only be spent in the contributing country. The only difference between an inorganic link and conventional aid is that such a link would be related to the receipt of SDRs. Not surprisingly, then, developing countries may regard any form of inorganic link as inferior to an organic version. The only reason they might support its introduction is that they see it as better than nothing and as standing more chance of being accepted and implemented because it requires no change in the Fund's Articles of Agreement. An inorganic link might be a stepping-stone toward an organic link, which involves a formal connection between the creation of SDRs and the provision of development financing and which requires amendments to the Articles of Agreement.

There are a number of variants of the organic link, including

  (a) an increase in the proportion of SDRs allocated directly to developing countries,

---

[14]Other forms of lending to developing countries may involve grace periods that duplicate this SDR effect.

(b) a direct allocation of SDRs to development agencies, and

(c) an agreed contribution of SDRs to development agencies or
developing countries by industrial countries.

Version (a) could be based on existing Fund quotas, or it could
involve a change in the distribution of quotas in favor of developing
countries that would also raise their access to Fund resources in
general and their voting rights, or it could involve severing the
connection between the distribution of SDRs and Fund quotas. It
can be argued that quotas do not provide an appropriate basis on
which to distribute linked SDRs. After all, as noted earlier, quotas
are supposed to reflect countries' demand for reserves to *hold*. A
principal objective of the link is, however, that SDRs should be
spent by developing country recipients. It might be more appropriate, therefore, to distribute SDRs on the basis of per capita income,
reflecting the link's aim of redistributing wealth. Furthermore, the
distribution formula could be amended to take more account of balance of payments instability and the costs of adjustment. On both of
these criteria, a larger proportion of SDRs would go to developing
countries.[15]

Under version (b), development agencies could either exchange
the SDRs allocated to them for currencies to be used to finance
loans to developing countries or transfer the SDRs to the accounts
of countries supplying developmental goods, allowing these recipients to pay exporters in domestic currency. From the point of view
of developing countries, a drawback of this version, compared with
version (a), is that the additional financing might be tied to projects
or might be conditional on the acceptance of specified macroeconomic policy objectives in such a way that the quality of the aid is
reduced. The development agencies that were involved could also,
therefore, exert an important influence over the attitudes of developing countries toward version (b) (Helleiner, 1974). For similar
reasons, developing countries might be expected to disfavor the
intermediation of industrial countries that would be involved in version (c). Clearly, the only reason why any developing country is
likely to favor some form of intermediation, as opposed to direct
country allocation, is if it stands to receive more SDRs as a result.
Since, for any given allocation of SDRs, more for some developing
countries means less for others, it is clear that the precise form of

---

[15]For empirical verification, see Hawkins and Rangarajan (1970).

link is a potentially contentious issue among developing countries.[16] While they are likely to show a uniform preference for an organic and untied version of the link, beyond that their interests may be expected to diverge.

More recently, two further types of link that have been proposed and discussed within the Fund would integrate the link with the activities of the Fund. Version (d) would involve SDRs being used to provide the financing for some form of subsidy account. Under this version, SDRs could either be directly allocated to such an account, or contributions could be made by initial recipients voluntarily or according to a prearranged formula. The account would then redirect the SDRs at its command to developing countries or only to low-income countries either as grants (in which case contributors would themselves have to retain the obligations associated with the SDRs contributed) or as a line of interest-bearing credit (in which case the developing countries receiving the SDRs would be asked to meet the related interest obligations). In this latter case, there would be no "subsidy" as such, although developing countries would still receive more SDRs than they would under a distribution based on quotas. In many ways this version differs little from versions (b) and (c). One significant difference, however, is that, as proposed, the SDRs would be used by developing countries to help meet Fund charges. In this way version (d) of the link is, to an extent, tied to Fund conditionality and may therefore be less attractive to developing countries, though clearly the idea of subsidized interest rates would appeal to them.

Under version (e), SDRs would either be directly allocated or contributed to a special account, which would use them to support stabilization programs approved by the Fund. In effect, developing countries agreeing on a program with the Fund would gain access to more resources than was previously the case. The SDRs could be used either to expand drawings under existing tranches and facilities or to finance a new Fund lending facility. In one sense, developing countries might find such a scheme attractive, since they would receive more financing for accepting a program to which they had

---

[16]As Williamson (1976 a) reports, during the course of the Committee of Twenty's discussions developing countries were able to come up with a common position, which involved SDRs being allocated on the basis of quotas that were weighted in their favor. The weighting factor for the least developed countries would be higher than for other developing countries.

already agreed in order to secure a Fund stand-by arrangement or extended facility drawing. Version (e) would therefore provide an extra incentive for developing countries to turn to the Fund. However, there is little doubt that they would prefer a scheme of direct and unconditional allocation to one that involves the intermediation of the Fund, as the appropriateness of the Fund's conditionality for developing countries is in some debate. Given the market-equivalent interest rate on SDRs, creditworthy developing countries might be expected to prefer to borrow from the Eurocurrency market because such borrowing is to some extent independent of Fund conditionality.[17] Version (e) would become more attractive to developing countries if the SDRs allocated to them by the special account did not have to be repaid and if the interest rate on their use of the SDRs was subsidized by, for instance, contributors retaining all or part of the related obligations.

On balance, even with a market-equivalent interest rate on SDRs, there still seems to be considerable scope for introducing a link that would be of significant advantage to developing countries—and perhaps, in particular, to low-income countries that find it less easy to obtain financing from private capital markets. However, one way in which developing countries might make a link more palatable to industrial countries is to point out the contribution it could make to solving the problem of recycling. If recycling is at a suboptimal level, the world economy as a whole pays the cost in terms of lost output and employment. A link will be of much greater benefit to developing countries, however, if the SDR's relative importance in the international financial system can be increased.

PROPOSED SUBSTITUTION ACCOUNT

The long-term objective of a substitution account is usually presented as that of improving the structural operation of the international monetary system by replacing reserve currencies, and perhaps also gold, with SDRs. In this way, the account would make a contribution toward establishing the SDR as the principal inter-

---

[17]The relationship between the Fund and the commercial banks is complex. In a significant number of cases, the availability of private financing rests on the conclusion of a Fund stand-by arrangement by the borrower. For further analysis of the relationship between the official and private sectors in international lending, see Bird (1981 a and 1981 b).

national reserve asset and would not only help in bringing the quantity of international reserves under more central and purposeful control but would also help in eradicating instabilities generated by central banks that switch the composition of their reserves.

From this definition it might be anticipated that developing countries would be strongly in favor of such an account, since they would benefit both from increased exchange rate stability and from the possibility of adapting an SDR system in order to include a link. Clearly, the establishment of a link will be of little benefit to developing countries unless the creation of SDRs occurs at frequent intervals and in substantial amounts. From the viewpoint of the developing countries, what is needed is a system in which the incremental demand for reserves is met by an additional supply of SDRs. The link and the proposed substitution account therefore seem to be complementary. While a link establishes a structural connection between the creation of SDRs and the provision of financial flows to developing countries, a substitution account attempts to ensure some structural connection between reserve growth and SDR creation. Both of these connections are needed if reserve growth is to lead to more financing for developing countries.[18]

It is not surprising, then, that the reservations of developing countries during recent discussions about the establishment of a substitution account have related primarily to the *specifics* of the actual account proposed rather than to the general principle of substitution.

Criticisms of a substitution account by developing countries have related to the following factors:[19]

(a) its effect on the SDR;
(b) its effect on the process of international adjustment and the distribution of the adjustment burden;
(c) its effect on exchange rate instability and the management of global liquidity;
(d) its effect on developing countries as holders of reserves; and
(e) its financial arrangements.

---

[18]To guarantee this, other sources of reserve growth would have to be checked.
[19]For a fuller presentation of these criticisms, see Kadam (1979).

Effect on the SDR

The concern of developing countries in this context has two dimensions: first, that the issuance by a substitution account of a viable and high-yielding SDR-denominated asset may damage the prospects that the SDR will become the international monetary system's principal reserve asset; and second, that the existence of a competitive rate of interest on assets issued by the account will raise the rate of interest on SDRs and thereby the charges on the use of Fund resources in general. Indeed, this second concern has been presented as perhaps the major deterrent to the support of a substitution account by the developing countries (UNCTAD, 1972). However, given the recent increase in the rate of interest on SDRs, this is no longer a valid objection. Attention of developing countries should perhaps now be more appropriately focused on ways in which an SDR system based on competitive interest rates may be used or adapted to direct financial flows to them and on ways in which the concessionary element of such flows may be raised for the low-income countries. One method would involve charging reserve centers a higher rate of interest on the account's holdings of their currency than is paid to depositors, using the differential for development financing.[20]

Effect on international adjustment

In principle, a substitution account provides an opportunity for encouraging reserve currency countries to adjust their balance of payments. This may be achieved by requiring such countries, particularly the United States, to amortize the account's holdings of their currencies over time by buying back previously issued liabilities with SDRs that have been either allocated to them or earned through the net exportation of real resources. Amortization was a constituent element of versions of the substitution account discussed by the Committee of Twenty, but it was abandoned in later

---

[20]Bird (1981 c) provides a fuller description of this scheme and others, as well as calculations of the financial flows that might be generated by them. Proposals by the Brazilian and Iranian representatives during the Committee of Twenty meetings involved onlending to developing countries by the substitution account of the currencies deposited with it. The Brazilian scheme further incorporated the idea that currency loans should be used only to finance imports from the issuers of those currencies, thus neutralizing the effects that an untied scheme might have on reserve growth and inflation.

versions, which as a result were seen by developing countries as having the prime objective of supporting the U.S. dollar. As noted earlier, it is a central part of the criticism by developing countries of the postwar international financial system that there have been asymmetrical pressures on countries to adjust, with the nonreserve currency deficit countries carrying a relatively large proportion of the burden.

Amortization of reserve currencies also provides an opportunity to introduce a version of the link that does not rely on net additions to international reserves (Maynard, 1972) or that permits the additional financial flow to developing countries to exceed any overall increase in the quantity of international reserves—something that would be impossible under the more conventional versions of the link. This opportunity results from the fact that amortization implies a fall in the quantity of international reserves, as dollars held outside the United States, where they are counted as reserves, are returned to the United States, where they are not so counted. Indeed, without this compensating increase in linked SDRs, developing countries as a group could easily lose from the world deflationary impact of balance of payments correction in the United States. Individually, developing countries might still lose, even with a compensating link, if the distribution formula for SDRs differs from the pattern of U.S. imports among developing countries. From the point of view of the world demand for their exports, developing countries might therefore be expected to prefer redistribution of the adjustment burden to take the form of expansionary policies in surplus countries rather than deflationary policies in the United States. In view of this, it is only by moving toward an asset settlement system based on SDRs, and away from a liability system that relies on deficits in the United States for additional reserves, that developing countries will be able to gain a larger share of the benefits from reserve creation. Furthermore, developing countries see the gold-exchange system as imparting an inflationary bias to the world economy because the creation of reserves is uncontrolled.

Effect on exchange rate stability and global liquidity management

The concern of developing countries is that a substitution account will do little to help stabilize exchange rates through a reduction in the incidence of currency switching, since it will convert only the relatively involatile currency holdings of central banks, and not the more volatile privately held balances.

With regard to the management of global liquidity, it has been argued (Kadam, 1979) that the account will create reserves simply as a reflex to the reserves already created by individual national authorities and will do nothing to induce the more democratic control of reserve creation from which developing countries stand a chance of benefiting. In a narrow sense this is true but, as implied earlier, the consolidation of reserve currencies that a substitution account would involve may be seen as a first step toward an SDR system based on asset settlement and could therefore eventually lead to the better management of global liquidity.

Developing countries as holders of reserves

Concern has been expressed that developing countries could lose from the introduction of a substitution account in their role as holders of reserves. This could be brought about if a market in SDR-denominated assets failed to develop, if such assets had a low degree of usefulness, if they carried a low rate of interest relative to that available in the Eurocurrency market, where a number of developing countries have placed reserves, or if the possible sterilization of reserves forced developing countries to turn to the Eurocurrency market for funds at a time when it was both difficult and expensive to borrow from that market. The conclusion is that developing countries might prefer to hold their reserves in the form of dollars rather than in SDR-denominated assets.[21]

Of course, if participation in the account were to be voluntary, there would be no reason for developing countries to convert dollars into SDRs unless they considered this to be to their own advantage. On the other hand, voluntary participation may be less effective for bringing about a move toward establishing the SDR as the principal reserve asset, and developing countries may thus benefit from a higher degree of compulsion. With a compulsory substitution account, developing countries would simply have to regard the loss of freedom with respect to reserve management as a price they have to pay. The question, then, is not so much a matter of whether there

---

[21]It may be noted that SDRs could be converted into foreign exchange when this is needed for balance of payments purposes. In general, there is a strong case for basing a substitution account on SDRs.

are costs but rather whether these exceed the benefits. For the majority of developing countries this is unlikely to be the case, although it may well be, at least initially, for those richer developing countries with significant reserve holdings and Eurocurrency deposits that would be by-passed as recipients of SDRs in some versions of the link. To argue that developing countries as a group benefit more from the free operation of the Eurocurrency market and from a largely unmanaged international financial system[22] seems to ignore the position of a large number of them, in particular the low-income countries, that have few dealings with the private market. Again, however, it seems that developing countries will not have an unambiguous view.

Financial arrangements of the account

Although the prime purpose of a substitution account is to change the composition of reserves, its financial arrangements could also exert an influence over the total quantity of reserves—and this could be significant for developing countries. Assuming, for example, that currencies deposited with the account are to be invested in the issuing country and that interest is to be paid to the account in the same currency, and assuming further that interest is to be paid on SDRs issued by the account in the form of SDRs, the total quantity of reserves would rise at a rate equivalent to the interest on the SDRs, expressed as a fraction of total reserves. If, on the other hand, interest on the account's holdings of currencies is to be paid in SDRs, this would reduce the total quantity of reserves, compared with a system where interest is paid in the issuer's own currency. Whether total reserves would actually fall would depend on the rate of interest paid to the account by reserve centers, compared with that paid by the account to recipients of SDRs. A profit for the account implies a reduction in total reserves; a loss implies an increase in total reserves; and breaking even implies no change in total reserves.

A more specific concern of developing countries in the discussions about a substitution account in early 1980 was over the proposal that the Fund's gold should be used to provide backing for it and to guarantee its financial viability. Developing countries, not surpris-

---

[22]See, for example, Lal (1980).

ingly, viewed this suggestion as being inconsistent with the whole concept of the Trust Fund and saw it as implying a "reverse link." In conjunction with their view that the version of the account then being discussed made the United States the principal beneficiary, the use of the Fund's gold to support the account rather than to provide concessional assistance for the poorer developing countries was particularly unacceptable.

Since the general objectives of a substitution account, as presented at the beginning of this section, are to the advantage of developing countries and since the account could be organized so as to be of direct benefit to developing countries in terms of generating additional financial inflows, it is not in their interests to resist all attempts to introduce such an account but to argue for a version of the account that directs at least a share of the direct benefits to them.

GOLD

The mechanics of a substitution account could, in principle, be applied equally well to gold as to reserve currencies. Furthermore, substitution of gold would also be consistent with objectives of the Second Amendment to the Fund's Articles to reduce the role of monetary gold and enhance the role of the SDR. The implications for the total quantity of reserves would depend initially on the SDR price paid for gold deposits relative to the price at which gold is valued for calculating reserves. Assuming that reserve gold is valued at its market price, the activities of a gold substitution account would only reduce total reserves and thereby create the opportunity for additional SDR allocations if a price below the market value is paid for gold deposits. The acquisition and holding of gold by the Fund would, however, be inconsistent with the declared objective of reducing the monetary role of gold. In the longer run, therefore, the account's stock of gold would have to be disposed of by gradually selling it for industrial and artistic use. Profits accruing to the account could then, in principle and at least in part, be directed toward developing countries, with depositing countries also perhaps receiving a secondary payment.[23]

---

[23]See Bird (1981 c) for a fuller discussion.

A central problem with all reforms that try to use the operation of
the international monetary system for the benefit of developing
countries is that changes that are technically feasible may not be
acceptable in practice to industrial countries, whose compliance under existing institutional arrangements is necessary for their activation. The potential conflict between what is equitable and what is
acceptable is highlighted by what has happened with respect to gold
during the 1970s. Events in this sphere of international finance have
also clearly shown how the stated intentions of the Fund and the
aspirations of its developing member countries may be frustrated in
what are largely unforeseen ways. Since the Jamaican Accord of
1976, a stated objective of international monetary reform has been
to reduce the monetary role of gold—an objective that developing
countries have seen as in their own interests. In an attempt to help
realize this objective, the Fund abandoned the official price of gold
and undertook to dispose of a third of its gold stock. It was agreed
that 25 million ounces of gold would be sold back to Fund members
in proportion to their quotas at a price of SDR 35 an ounce and that
a further 25 million ounces would be sold at a series of public auc-
tions over a period of four years, with the profits going to a Trust
Fund that would make disbursements on concessional terms to eligible developing countries, essentially the poorer developing countries. Thus, developing countries scored an apparently significant
advance, inasmuch as an element of international monetary reform
became structurally related to the provision of additional financial
assistance to developing countries. There is no doubt that the Trust
Fund has provided eligible countries with both an absolutely and
relatively important source of low-conditionality financing. However, neither can there be doubt that developing countries have
actually lost as a result of the abandonment of the official gold price
and the dramatic increase in the market price of gold that this
change probably facilitated. Furthermore, to the extent that concern over the future stability and form of the international monetary
system has caused the demand for gold and therefore its price to
rise, the failure to restore confidence in the system and to find
credible solutions to international financial problems has acted
against the interests of developing countries. Inasmuch as the instabilities of the 1970s are a reflection of the rise in the price of oil,
non-oil developing countries have been affected by this phenomenon
twice over.

The general move toward revaluing reserve gold at its market price has meant that countries have experienced an increase in their reserves in proportion to their gold holdings. Such revaluation has generated both a wealth effect, in the form of potential resource transfers, and a liquidity effect. Concentrating initially on the wealth effect, the prime beneficiaries have been the gold-holding and gold-producing countries. It has been estimated that 90 per cent of reserve asset gold is held by industrial countries, with five of them holding more gold individually than all the non-oil developing countries together. It has also been estimated that the net gain for industrial countries from gold revaluation during the 1970s was well in excess of $400 billion, compared with under $30 billion for non-oil developing countries.[24]

The inequitable distribution of the gains from the sale of gold by the Fund is further emphasized if they are calculated on a per capita basis and if allowance is made for the fact that a large proportion of the gold that developing countries hold as a group is held by India and Afghanistan.

The liquidity effect of the revaluation of gold has been to prevent any *de facto* demonetization of gold. To the contrary, with gold valued at its market price, it reasserts itself as the principal reserve asset and as the major source of reserve growth during the 1970s. Far from there being a move toward the greater control of reserves as envisaged in the Second Amendment of the Fund's Articles, the aggregate value of reserves depends to a very significant degree on the vagaries of the gold price, which at best is likely to be only loosely related to the requirements of the system for international liquidity. Some insight into the significance of these changes for developing countries may be gained by calculating how much more the reserves of developing countries would have risen if the aggregate reserve growth during the 1970s had been brought about through the creation of SDRs. The answer seems to be about $100 billion. Reserve growth through gold revaluation, as opposed to SDR creation, is clearly to the relative advantage of industrial countries (and, in particular, the major gold holders among them) and to the relative disadvantage of developing countries.

---

[24]Strong empirical support for the argument that developing countries have been relatively disadvantaged by the revaluation of gold is presented by Brodsky and Sampson (1980).

The neutrality of reserve growth, so much a theme of the case against the link, has not been achieved in recent years, and the potential resource transfer has been in favor of the wealthiest industrial countries. Developing countries may therefore express legitimate interest in proposals designed to redirect this potential resource transfer. Technically there are a number of ways for achieving this. One, as outlined above, would be through a gold substitution account. A second would be to impose some form of tax on the windfall profits of gold holders—as global fiscal policy may in principle be a more appropriate instrument for achieving a redistribution of wealth than international monetary policy. However, neither of these proposals seems to meet the necessary condition of acceptability to industrial countries. Of greater relevance, therefore, might be the proposal to use the remaining stock of gold held by the Fund to provide financing for developing countries.[25] This general notion itself incorporates a number of possibilities, and developing countries may disagree among themselves over the most appropriate arrangements by which the transfer would be achieved.

The financing could, for example, be used to enable the Fund to expand its activities or to widen them by introducing new lending facilities or by changing the conditions under which resources are lent. Alternatively, it could be used to subsidize interest payments or to provide some kind of guarantee fund to support commercial lending to developing countries. Each of these uses implies that the financing would be related to Fund conditionality, and thus these uses might not be favored by potential recipients. As regards the provision of subsidies, the views of individual developing countries would no doubt depend on whether they would be eligible for them or not. Low-income countries might prefer this variant, compared with a guarantee fund that they might feel would not be of principal benefit to them unless the guarantees were to be offered only on their commercial borrowing. At the same time, countries that had previously had access to private financing without a guarantee might also be apprehensive about the effects that a guarantee system would have on their relative creditworthiness.

The financing could, of course, be channeled directly and unconditionally to developing countries according to some distribution

---

[25]Such an arrangement has been advocated by a number of authors. See, for example, de Silva (1979), Bird (1979 b), Brandt (1980), and Brodsky and Sampson (1980).

formula. Again, the views of individual developing countries would depend heavily on the formula adopted—whether, for example, it was related to Fund quotas or to some other measure of need. Another option would be to distribute the financing through international development agencies, such as the World Bank or regional development banks, or through a new world development fund. Again, the attitudes of individual countries would depend on their potential access to such institutions. Countries that preferred program aid rather than project aid or that did not feel able to meet commercial interest rates might, for example, be opposed to distribution through the World Bank.

However, there is another problem. If the Fund sold its stock of gold, a further appreciation in the price of gold could again confer greater benefits on the purchasers of gold—almost certainly the industrial countries—than on the developing countries. This implies either that some form of international capital gains tax would be needed or that the Fund should use its stock of gold only as collateral for raising loans from private capital markets. In this case the low-income and less creditworthy countries may feel that they would be excluded from the additional commercial financing that would result. Furthermore, to the extent that loans also involved Fund-type conditionality, recipients might feel that they had had the worst of both worlds.

FUND CONDITIONALITY[26]

Many of the proposals discussed in this paper would involve an extension of the activities of the Fund, although reforms of the Fund could also be undertaken independently. To the extent that the reforms provide the Fund with additional resources to lend to developing countries, one criticism of the Fund will be tempered—namely, that the quantity of finance received does not warrant the degree of Fund influence that is exerted. However, attitudes of developing countries toward such reform will depend significantly on two factors: first, their view as to the appropriateness of Fund conditionality, and second, the availability of alternative reforms.

---

[26]This section is brief because the subject matter is the principal concern of an Overseas Development Institute project that is examining the relationship between the Fund and economic management in developing countries. It would, therefore, be unwise to prejudge the results of this study.

The debate over conditionality is multifaceted (Bird, 1981 a), but an important element is that while the Articles of Agreement of the Fund constrain it to take an essentially short-term view of balance of payments correction and to advocate policies accordingly, developing countries view their balance of payments difficulties in a long-term developmental context. While a diagnosis of over-expansionary demand policies as the principal cause of balance of payments problems may be accurate in many instances, it need not always be the case. If it is not, although restrictionary financial policies may improve the short-term balance of payments, the more fundamental and perhaps externally generated problems are largely concealed and left uncured. An initial response to this analysis of the problems of developing countries is to advocate an expansion in the relative availability of low-conditionality finance, a movement away from a short-term demand-side approach toward a medium to long term supply-side approach, and a change in access and repayment criteria. In respect to the latter, for example, access to the compensatory financing facility would be made to depend on externally generated adverse movements in the terms of trade as a whole, rather than only on those caused by a shortfall in export receipts, and on the relating of repayments to the Fund to some aspect of the balance of payments.[27]

However, such proposals are not without problems, and some of them could offer developing countries fewer benefits than expected. The relaxation of conditionality could, for example, have an adverse effect on private financial flows to developing countries. Given the skewed distribution of these flows, a limited number of developing countries could carry the cost of lower conditionality, and new borrowers might not be able to gain access to private financing.

Furthermore, with less strict conditionality, the Fund might find it more difficult to borrow directly from capital markets if the need arises or to persuade industrial countries to increase Fund resources in other ways, such as by raising quotas. To the extent that lower conditionality also implies a relaxation in the Fund's general surveillance of economic policy in industrial as well as in developing countries, it could also have an adverse effect on the interests of developing countries. If, instead of relaxing conditionality, the pro-

---

[27]Numerous proposals of this type have been made. One example of the advocacy of such reforms may be found in Dell and Lawrence (1980).

posal is to change its form, the question becomes: What should this new form be? One possibility would be to move away from the quantitative precision implied by setting targets that may be particularly difficult to attain in a developing country environment[28] and to move toward a form of conditionality based on general policy measures. Developing countries may, however, find the systematic involvement of the Fund in precise policy formulation even more unappealing than they do the setting of performance criteria. In any case, there is the difficult problem of finding suitable criteria for monitoring the success of policy orientation.

Even a move toward a supply-side approach may not be in the interests of developing countries if this does not simultaneously herald a move away from conventional demand-side factors. The result could be an increase in the overall extent of conditionality.[29] Apart from anything else, there is legitimate debate over what constitutes supply-side factors. Do these not include devaluation, exchange and trade controls, and interest rate policy? Furthermore, there may be inconsistencies between supply-side factors, such as improving infrastructure, and demand-side factors, such as keeping government expenditure and credit creation under control. It is clear that a movement toward supply management is highly unlikely to eradicate all areas of disagreement and conflict between the Fund and developing countries. It may even have the opposite effect.

The argument here is not necessarily that some relaxation in Fund conditionality is not in the interests of developing countries, but rather that the issues are more complex than is often implied. Furthermore, the impression should not be given that developing countries have no influence over their own interests with respect to conditionality. First, as the Fund maintains, the imposition of strict conditions may reflect a late request to the Fund for assistance. While the Fund may help to break the vicious circle between strict conditionality and late requests by relaxing conditionality, developing countries may also help significantly in advance by turning to the Fund before their economic problems reach crisis proportions, when there is little alternative to a strict stabilization program.

---

[28]For a review of some of the problems, see Sharpley (1981) and Sutton (1981).

[29]For a discussion of the apparent move by the Fund toward supply-side considerations, see Bird (1981 a), but for a discussion of the problems in making this move effective, see Killick (1981), who examines the history of Kenya's negotiations with the Fund in the context of an extended facility drawing.

Furthermore, it is not sufficient for developing countries merely to argue that Fund conditionality is inappropriate; what is needed is an articulation of the available alternatives. The evidence drawn from developing countries that have rejected Fund-type stabilization programs in favor of alternative strategies is far from uniformly optimistic.[30] Where it turns out that the Fund does actually know best what targets are most appropriate, developing countries may damage their own interests by ignoring the Fund's advice. In these circumstances, less strict conditionality may permit developing countries to postpone necessary adjustment and thereby cause their basic economic situation to deteriorate more than necessary. In this sense, strict conditionality may be in the interests of developing countries. Given the problem of demarcating between the twin considerations of development and the balance of payments, there is the further question of whether the Fund is the most appropriate body to help deal with the economic difficulties faced by developing countries, and in particular the low-income countries. Rather than trying to change the Fund in such a way as to make it more of a development-financing institution, there may be a case for establishing a new institution, such as the world development fund proposed by the Brandt Commission that would have the defined purpose of filling the medium-term, program-financing gap that exists between the Fund and the World Bank and would perhaps give developing countries the degree of institutional control and influence that they feel is lacking in the Fund.

A brief consideration of proposals that have been put forward in rather more exclusive forums (such as the Arusha Conference), or that involve reforms within developing countries, is undertaken in the next two sections.

A COMMODITY-BACKED INTERNATIONAL CURRENCY

Providing commodity backing for an international currency is an idea of surprising resilience. Recent support for such a scheme has come from a background paper for the Arusha Conference on the International Monetary System and the New International Order.[31] Significantly, there is no direct mention of the scheme in the Confer-

---

[30]See Sutton (1981) for a review of the evidence.

[31]Rweyemamu (1980). For further and earlier discussion of an international commodity reserve currency, see Keynes (1942), Graham (1944), Friedman (1951), Hart, Kaldor, and Tinbergen (1964), Grubel (1965), Hart (1966 and 1976), and Kaldor (1976).

ence's final statement, the so-called Arusha Initiative, in which it is simply stated that "decisions need to be taken to make the [SDR] the principal reserve asset in international payments and to ensure that the role of national currencies in international settlements is effectively reduced. For that purpose the SDR should be made more attractive." However, in order to "acquire the attributes of an international currency," the background paper maintains that the SDR needs "solid backing, redeemability and more automatic forms of issue limitation." To this end, it suggests that SDRs be issued against the deposit of warehouse receipts for commodities constituting one or more commodity units. A commodity unit would be made up of a basket of basic storable commodities, of which the relative amounts would reflect their relative importance in international trade. The value of SDRs would be defined in terms of the commodity unit, and a world central bank would fix the buying and selling prices for the commodity units, denominated in SDRs, with a margin of, say, 5 per cent between them. In addition to the backed issue of SDRs, there would be an additional fiduciary issue of SDRs linked to development financing.

The principal benefits from the introduction of a commodity-backed currency involve its supposed ability to "address the three problems that are hindering the viability and proper functioning of the international economy: inadequate growth of output and employment, persistent rise in prices, and instability of primary exports." Further analysis suggests, however, that a commodity-backed SDR is neither necessary nor sufficient to ensure the realization of these goals.[32]

With respect to primary product price instability, although the price of the bundle of commodities would tend to be stabilized, this would not necessarily be the case for all the individual commodities comprising the composite unit. Indeed, in circumstances where not all primary product prices move in the same direction, as might be the case if price instabilities are primarily caused by supply-side changes or if the increasing prices of some commodities in the bundle have to be counterbalanced by offsetting falls in the prices of other commodities in order to stabilize the price of the bundle, then the scheme could raise the price instability for individual commodities. Furthermore, even if prices were to be stabilized, it does

---

[32]This is a conclusion reached by Sengupta and Stewart (1981), on whose analysis this section draws heavily.

not follow that export earnings would also always be stabilized. Again, while the price of the bundle would be stabilized in terms of new SDRs, this does not automatically mean that the purchasing power of primary producers would be stabilized in terms of manufactured goods, since the domestic currency price of manufactures might rise or the exchange rate between new SDRs and the national currencies of producers of manufactured goods might depreciate.

Flexibility in exchange rates between national currencies and the new SDR could also disrupt the scheme's potentially advantageous effects on world inflation. Furthermore, in this connection the scheme would at the outset only provide backing for a proportion of international money and would not, therefore, exert precise control over international credit creation because other components would remain uncontrolled. Indeed, the Arusha proposal does not suggest tying the fiduciary issue of SDRs to commodities in any way.

As for the effects on world output and employment, the principal benefit of a commodity-backed SDR would appear to be its automatic countercyclical impact on the world's supply of international reserves. However, even this may be overstated. First, considerable slippage may result from the inconstancy in the quantities of other reserve assets. Second, the automaticity could operate in a perverse fashion; the effect of a major increase in the price of oil, for example (assuming that oil is included in the composite unit), would be to reduce the quantity of SDRs in what would tend to be an already deflationary environment.

In view of the uncertainties of the benefits from a commodity-backed SDR and the certain and significant storage, administrative, and negotiating costs,[33] there seems to be a strong case for developing countries to pursue a policy that puts emphasis on modifying the existing unbacked SDR. In principle, such modifications could equally well achieve the greater central control of international liquidity and the pattern of resource transfers advocated by commodity-backing supporters. If industrial countries are not prepared to accept changes in the existing SDR scheme that would direct more resources to developing countries as a group, they seem unlikely to support a scheme that would do this automatically. Furthermore, actions have already been taken to make the SDR a more

---

[33]For an estimation of these, see Grubel (1965), Hart (1976), Colebrook (1977), and Sengupta and Stewart (1981).

attractive reserve asset, and it is yet to be established that commodity backing is needed to accomplish this.

If the prime purpose of a commodity-backed SDR is to stabilize primary product prices, there are arguments for supporting a system of individual commodity buffer stocks in preference to a commodity-backed currency which, at best, would only have an incidental effect on price stability. Buffer stocks are subject to a range of well-recognized theoretical and practical difficulties. Not least among these is the problem of financing. Perhaps a more rewarding approach for developing countries would therefore be to investigate the possibility of using unbacked SDRs to finance commodity stabilization schemes. In prospect, such an arrangement would offer the possibility not only of stabilizing primary product prices but also of increasing the relative importance of SDRs in the international financial system and of providing some degree of monetary stabilization.[34]

The participants at Arusha were therefore probably wise to resist the temptation of making the introduction of a new commodity-backed SDR a specific part of their program for reform, since it seems to have little chance of success and will not be in the interests of developing countries.

The foregoing analysis suggests that there may be some justification for the feeling among developing countries that they have been disadvantaged by the operation of the postwar international monetary system. The proposals discussed in this paper envisage reforms largely within existing institutional arrangements. An alternative course of action is for developing countries to make their own arrangements.

FINANCIAL ARRANGEMENTS AMONG DEVELOPING COUNTRIES[35]

Various financial arrangements among developing countries could involve reserve pooling, clearance or payments unions, or even the establishment of an exclusively "Southern" currency. Such plans involve an attempt to make more efficient use of scarce hard cur-

---

[34]See Bird (1978) for further discussion.
[35]The case for these has been most cogently argued by Stewart and Stewart (1980) and Sengupta and Stewart (1981).

rencies and to promote more trade among developing countries
through the provision of additional credit. Although in many ways
exclusive financial arrangements of this type may be appealing to
developing countries frustrated by the lack of progress in their
negotiations with the North and by the slow growth of export markets in developed countries, they are subject to numerous practical
(though not necessarily insuperable) problems. Not least among
these is how to deal with persistent creditors and debtors. Furthermore, such schemes may be of rather more appeal to some developing countries than to others, depending on the pattern of their
trading relationships. Inasmuch as the expenditure of one developing country is effectively tied to the output of other developing
countries, schemes of this nature seem to represent a second-best
solution for developing countries as a group by comparison with an
equivalent allocation of SDRs.

SOME REMAINING ISSUES

This paper has taken as its prime focus a number of specific
proposals for international monetary reform and examined them in
terms of their impact on developing countries. It has been noted
throughout, however, that the interests of developing countries may
be far from uniform. A significant number of middle-income and
higher-income developing countries have apparently suffered little
from the breakdown of the international monetary system and the
associated move to the marketplace. They have been able to attract
commercial credit and to maintain growth and development. These
countries may have relatively little motivation for reform, and they
are concerned that any move back toward a more centrally organized set of international financial arrangements will confer few
benefits on them and may indeed be to their absolute disadvantage.
From the point of view of their own self-interest, they may be wary
of reforms involving the intermediation of international financial
and development institutions, guarantees, and the like. These interests are largely shared by oil exporting developing countries that
have found it convenient to place their unspent revenues on the
Eurocurrency market.

It is the remaining developing countries that have a vested interest in restoring the greater degree of central control that would
come, in particular, from the establishment of the SDR as the prin-

cipal reserve asset and from the related reforms. The strategic importance of the Eurocurrency market in recycling has worked against their interests in two ways. Not only have they been deemed uncreditworthy by commercial banks and have therefore been unable to gain access to private finance, but also an impression has been created in some influential circles that financing problems of developing countries may be left to the market, which provides an automatic and responsive mechanism as well as the necessary discipline and pressure for adjustment. The private market has been seen as a preferable substitute for official intervention, and as a result the perceived need for international financial reform has been reduced.

Ignored so far in this paper has been the question of exchange rate flexibility—not because it is an unimportant issue but because it has been defined to lie outside the paper's terms of reference, inasmuch as there is no structured proposal to discuss. Developing countries, in general, have been rather skeptical about floating rates because of a number of areas of concern, including increased uncertainty and the inadequacy of forward cover, the implications for commodity price stability and the relative prices of developing country imports and exports, and the implications for reserve and debt management. Of more direct relevance in the context of this paper is the fact that floating exchange rates represent a move away from a centrally managed financial system and, in principle, reduce the need for additional reserve assets. In practice, of course, the period of generalized floating has been accompanied by a rapid growth in aggregate international reserves and by new issues of SDRs. Some evidence suggests that the concern of developing countries that their interests are damaged by the move to generalized floating may be overstated[36]—not least because a system of fixed exchange rates, which superficially appears to eliminate a number of problems, may be against their interests if it requires for its maintenance extensive resort to import and exchange controls in industrial countries.

The negotiating strategy for developing countries as far as international monetary reform is concerned involves two dimensions.

---

[36]Cline (1976) and Williamson (1976 b). For reviews of the position of developing countries in a world of floating exchange rates, see Bird (1978), Stewart (1980), and Helleiner (1980).

The first is to agree and to maintain agreement among themselves on a package of proposals. In fact, they have shown considerable skill at doing this. The second is to identify proposals that are not only to their overall advantage but also that industrial countries may be persuaded to accept. An additional problem is that industrial countries will not necessarily have an unambiguous view, as has been illustrated by negotiations over the link. Industrial countries may, however, be expected to become generally more receptive to proposals of the kind discussed in this paper if and when their preoccupation shifts away from inflation and toward unemployment.

Finally, to return to a point made earlier, there is a mutuality of interests between developing and industrial countries in having a well-functioning international financial system that encourages the growth of world trade and output. Indeed, perhaps more than other countries, developing countries lose from international instability and recession. Thus, it could be rather narrow-minded of developing countries to resist all reforms that do not appear to maximize their own direct benefits. However, this is also a reason why developing countries are likely to remain in a relatively weak bargaining position.

REFERENCES

Bird, Graham, "The Informal Link Between SDR Allocation and Aid: A Note," *Journal of Development Studies*, Vol. 12 (April 1976), pp. 268–73.

_____, *The International Monetary System and the Less Developed Countries* (London, 1978).

_____ (1979 a), "The Benefits of Special Drawing Rights for Less Developed Countries," *World Development*, Vol. 7 (March 1979), pp. 281–90.

_____ (1979 b), "An Integrated Programme for Finance and Aid," *The Banker* (September 1979), pp. 87–93.

_____ (1981 a), "The IMF and the Developing Countries: Evolving Relations, Use of Resources and the Debate over Conditionality," Overseas Development Institute Working Paper, No. 2 (London, March 1981).

_____ (1981 b), "Financing Balance of Payments Deficits in Developing Countries: The Roles of Official and Private Sectors and the Scope for Cooperation Between Them," *Third World Quarterly* (July 1981), pp. 473–88.

_____ (1981 c), "Reserve Currency Consolidation, Gold Policy, and Financial Flows to Developing Countries: Mechanisms for an Aid-Augmented Substitution Account," *World Development*, Vol. 9 (July 1981), pp. 609–619.

Brandt, Willy, *et al*, *North-South: A Programme for Survival* (London, 1980).

Brodsky, David A., and Gary P. Sampson, "Gold, Special Drawing Rights and Developing Countries," *Trade and Development*, No. 2 (Autumn 1980), pp. 49–68.

Clark, Peter B., "Interest Payments and the Rate of Return on International Fiat Currency," *Weltwirtschaftliches Archiv*, Vol. 108 (1972), pp. 537–64.

Cline, William R., *International Monetary Reform and the Developing Countries*, Brookings Institution (Washington, 1976).

Colebrook, Jay, "The Cost of Storing Primary Commodities," *Journal of World Trade Law*, Vol. 11 (1977), pp. 369–77.

Dell, Sidney S., and Roger Lawrence, *The Balance of Payments Adjustment Process in Developing Countries* (New York, 1980).

de Silva, L., "Gold, the International Monetary Fund and the Third World," International Foundation for Development Alternatives, Dossier No. 5 (Lyons, March 1979).

Friedman, M., "Commodity Reserve Currency," *Journal of Political Economy*, Vol. 59 (June 1951), pp. 203–32.

Gold, Joseph, *The Second Amendment of the Fund's Articles of Agreement*, IMF Pamphlet Series, No. 25 (Washington, 1978).

Graham, Benjamin, "World Commodities and World Currency" (New York, First Edition, 1944).

Grubel, Herbert G., "The Case Against an International Commodity Reserve Currency," *Oxford Economic Papers*, Vol. 17 (March 1965), pp. 130–35.

_____, "Basic Methods for Distributing Special Drawing Rights and the Problem of International Aid," *Journal of Finance*, Vol. 27 (December 1972), pp. 1009–1022.

_____, "Interest Payments and the Efficiency of the International Monetary System," *Economic Notes*, Monte dei Paschi di Siena, Vol. 2 (September–December 1973), pp. 63–81.

Haan, Roelf L., *Special Drawing Rights and Development* (Leiden, 1971).

Hart, Albert G., "The Case For and Against International Commodity Reserve Currency," *Oxford Economic Papers*, Vol. 18 (July 1966), pp. 237–41.

_____, Nicholas Kaldor, and Jan Tinbergen, "The Case for an International Commodity Reserve Currency," in *Proceedings of the UN Conference on Trade and Development*, Vol. 3 (New York, United Nations, 1964).

_____, "The Case as of 1976 for International Commodity-Reserve Currency," *Weltwirtschaftliches Archiv*, Vol. 112 (1976), pp. 1–32.

Hawkins, Robert G., and C. Rangarajan, "On the Distribution of New International Reserves," *Journal of Finance*, Vol. 25 (September 1970), pp. 881–91.

Helleiner, G. K., "The Less Developed Countries and the International Monetary System," *Journal of Development Studies*, Vol. 10 (April–July 1974), pp. 347–73.

_____, "The Impact of the Exchange Rate System on the Developing Countries," UNDP/UNCTAD Project INT/75/015, UN Doc. UNCTAD/MFD/TA/13 (September 1980).

International Monetary Fund, *International Monetary Reform: Documents of the Committee of Twenty* (Washington, 1974).

Isard, Peter, and Edwin M. Truman, "SDRs, Interest and the Aid Link: Further Analysis," *Quarterly Review*, Banca Nazionale del Lavoro, Vol. 27 (March 1974), pp. 88–93.

Johnson, Harry G., *Efficiency in Domestic and International Money Supply* (Guildford, 1970).

Kadam, V. B., "Implications for Developing Countries of Current Proposals for a Substitution Account," UNDP/UNCTAD Project INT/75/015, UN Doc. UNCTAD/MFD/TA/1 (1979).

Kaldor, Nicholas, "Inflation and Recession in the World Economy," *Economic Journal*, Vol. 86 (December 1976), pp. 703–14.

Keynes, John Maynard, "The International Control of Raw Materials," memorandum to U.K. Treasury, April 14, 1942. Reprinted in *Journal of International Economics*, Vol. 4 (August 1974), pp. 299–315.

Killick, Tony, "The IMF and Economic Management in Kenya," Overseas Development Institute Working Paper, No. 4 (London, July 1981).

Lal, Deepak, *A Liberal International Economic Order: The International Monetary System and Economic Development*, Essays in International Finance, No. 139, Princeton University (October 1980).

Maynard, Geoffrey W., "Special Drawing Rights and Development Aid," Overseas Development Council Occasional Paper, No. 6 (Washington, September 1972).

———, and Graham Bird, "International Monetary Issues and the Developing Countries: A Survey," *World Development*, Vol. 3 (September 1975), pp. 609–31.

Park, Y. S., *The Link Between Special Drawing Rights and Development Finance*, Essays in International Finance, No. 100, Princeton University (September 1973).

Rweyemamu, Justinian F., "Restructuring the International Monetary System," *Development Dialogue* (1980: 2), pp. 75–91.

Sengupta, Arjun, and Frances Stewart, *Framework for International Financial Cooperation*, A Report for the Centre for Research on the New International Economic Order, mimeographed, 1981.

Sharpley, Jennifer, "The Potential of Domestic Stabilization Measures in Developing Countries," DERAP Working Paper, A 198, Development Research and Action Programme, Chr. Michelsen Institute (Bergen, March 1981).

Stewart, M .J., "Floating Exchange Rates in the 1970s, and Their Impact on the World Economy," Commonwealth Secretariat, FMM (80) 9 (August 1980).

Stewart, Frances, and Michael Stewart, "A New Currency for Trade Among Developing Countries," *Trade and Development*, No. 2 (Autumn 1980), pp. 69–82.

Sutton, Mary, "The Costs and Benefits of Stabilization: Some Latin American Experiences," Overseas Development Institute Working Paper, No. 3 (London, May 1981).

United Nations Conference on Trade and Development, "The Consolidation of Currency Balances and Developing Countries," in *Money, Finance and Development: Papers on International Monetary Reform* (New York, United Nations, 1972).

Williamson, John, (1976 a), "SDRs: The Link," paper originally presented at the Massachusetts Institute of Technology Conference on the New International Economic Order in May 1976. Reprinted in *The New International Economic Order: The North-South Debate*, ed. by Jagdish N. Bhagwati (MIT Press, 1977).

——— (1976 b), "Generalized Floating and the Reserve Needs of Developing Countries," in *The International Monetary System and the Developing Nations*, ed. by Danny M. Leipziger, Bureau for Program and Policy Coordination, U.S. Agency for International Development (Washington, 1976).